D1711534

GOETHE'S *FAUST*

75. Jeffrey L. Sammons. SIX ESSAYS ON THE YOUNG GERMAN NOVEL. 1972. 2nd ed. 1975. Pp. xiv, 187. Cloth $8.00.
76. Donald H. Crosby and George C. Schoolfield, eds. STUDIES IN THE GERMAN DRAMA. A *FESTSCHRIFT* IN HONOR OF WALTER SILZ. 1974. Pp. xxvi, 255. Cloth $10.75.
77. J. W. Thomas. TANNHÄUSER: POET AND LEGEND. With Texts and Translations of his Works. 1974. Pp. x, 202. Cloth $10.75.
78. Olga Marx and Ernst Morwitz, trans. THE WORKS OF STEFAN GEORGE. 1974. 2nd rev. and enl. ed. Pp. xxviii, 431. Cloth $12.90.
79. Siegfried Mews and Herbert Knust, eds. ESSAYS ON BRECHT: THEATER AND POLITICS. 1974. Pp. xiv, 241. Cloth $11.95.
80. Donald G. Daviau and George J. Buelow. THE *ARIADNE AUF NAXOS* OF HUGO VON HOFMANNSTHAL AND RICHARD STRAUSS. Pp. x, 274. Cloth $12.95.
81. Elaine E. Boney. RAINER MARIA RILKE: *DUINESIAN ELEGIES*. German Text with English Translation and Commentary. 1975. Pp. xii, 153. Cloth $10.75.
82. Jane K. Brown. GOETHE'S CYCLICAL NARRATIVES: *DIE UNTERHALTUNGEN DEUTSCHER AUSGEWANDERTEN* AND *WILHELM MEISTERS WANDERJAHRE*. 1975. Pp. x, 144. Cloth $10.25.
83. Flora Kimmich. SONNETS OF CATHARINA VON GREIFFENBERG: METHODS OF COMPOSITION. 1975. Pp. x, 132. Cloth $11.50.
84. Herbert W. Reichert. FRIEDRICH NIETZSCHE'S IMPACT ON MODERN GERMAN LITERATURE. FIVE ESSAYS. 1975. Pp. xxii, 129. Cloth $9.90.
85. James C. O'Flaherty, Timothy F. Sellner, Robert M. Helm, eds. STUDIES IN NIETZSCHE AND THE CLASSICAL TRADITION. 1976. Pp. xviii, 278. Cloth $14.95.
86. Alan P. Cottrell. GOETHE'S *FAUST*. SEVEN ESSAYS. 1976. Pp. xvi, 143. Cloth $10.95.

For other volumes in the "Studies" see pages 141 ff.

Send orders to: (U.S. and Canada)
The University of North Carolina Press, P.O. Box 2288
Chapel Hill, N.C. 27514
(All other countries) Feffer and Simons, Inc., 31 Union Square, New York, N.Y. 10003

NUMBER EIGHTY-SIX

UNIVERSITY
OF NORTH CAROLINA
STUDIES IN
THE GERMANIC LANGUAGES
AND LITERATURES

Goethe's *Faust*
Seven Essays

by
Alan P. Cottrell

With a Preface by Ernst Behler

CHAPEL HILL
THE UNIVERSITY OF NORTH CAROLINA PRESS
1976

Library of Congress Cataloging in Publication Data

Cottrell, Alan P. 1935–
Goethe's Faust: seven essays.

(University of North Carolina studies in the Germanic languages and literatures; no. 86).
Bibliography, pp. 135–140.
1. Goethe, Johann Wolfgang von, 1749–1832. Faust—Addresses, essays, lectures. I. Title. II. Series: North Carolina. University. Studies in the Germanic languages and literatures; no. 86.

PT1925.C58 832'.6 75-46540
ISBN 0-8078-8086-8

Manufactured in the U.S.A.

For Fred R. Amrine
in gratitude

Das höchste Erlebnis auf der Erde ist eben doch der Mensch. Man segnet die Erde um eines einzigen Menschen willen, den man erlebt hat. Man erfährt durch ihn eine "Menschenweihe," wie man sie vorher gar nicht ahnte.

—Friedrich Rittelmeyer

Contents

Preface

Although these seven essays are devoted to Goethe's *Faust* and each finds its starting-point in specific themes in the work, one could term Alan Cottrell's book a monograph on *Faust* only by considerably narrowing the intent of his analyses. To be sure, the attraction of these investigations derives to a great extent from the manner in which they unfold inner relationships between the two parts of the drama according to Goethe's concepts of prefiguration, analogy, polarity, metamorphosis, and intensification ("Steigerung"). The unity of the work thus becomes clearly evident; the often neglected second part regains its position of equality next to the first, and the reader perceives an underlying coherence which joins the initial "Zueignung" to the very last lines of the drama.

Again and again these investigations focus with almost microscopic precision on individual aspects of *Faust:* in these passages the linguistic "body" of the poem is brought clearly into view and we are made to realize how in his highly conscious choice of syllables, consonants, and vowels Goethe was able to portray the metamorphoses of life in words, or how he could shape, within the structure of a line, the macrocosmic order of which that very line speaks. In other passages Goethe's view of living, active nature, as revealed to him in plant life, or his vision of light and color, emerges through the interpretation of a single stanza, even a word.

This constant variation of perspective leads to important discoveries for *Faust* scholarship. The technique sometimes is applied to single episodes which suddenly reveal essential structural and thematic significance, or to momentous questions such as those of poetic imagination and genius, which *Faust* shares with works of the Romantic Movement in Europe and America. Of special interest is Alan Cottrell's treatment of the themes of redemption and grace, his solution of the controversial problem of Goethe's Christianity and Hellenism. This leads him to a number of astounding thoughts which represent a decisive step forward in the interpretation of *Faust*.

Such observations, however, do not reveal the genuine character of this book. The author's thought process consists in a constant widening of scope, until from each particular topic of investigation and from ever new aspects of *Faust*, Goethe emerges in his full intellectual stature. This is not achieved solely in the traditional manner of consulting Goethe's other writings for a better understanding of *Faust*. To be sure, Alan Cottrell takes seriously the maxim that

Goethe's work is of one piece and that each aspect of his poetry, dramas, novels, his scientific writings, as well as his correspondence and recorded conversations illuminates each other facet of his work. The author substantiates the dynamic unity of Goethe's opus and demonstrates equal intimacy with the poetic, scientific, and theoretical writings. Yet Goethe's intellectual stance must be understood in a much more fundamental sense. It is his central spiritual impulse which is not only elaborated here through seven different approaches, but is also raised as a profound challenge to our time. In short, *Faust* is projected into the cultural context of the modern world. Goethe's mode of thinking is applied to the spiritual problems of our age, not to provide definitive answers, but as a stimulus to further creative thought.

What is this spiritual impulse, this Goethean mode of thinking? Alan Cottrell finds it in a particular attitude of mind which forms the unified basis underlying both Goethe's artistic imagination and his scientific method. Both sides of Goethe's work derive from one common root, namely, a visual reasoning ("anschauende Urteilskraft"), a creative contemplation which apprehends images and forms in their material embodiment and penetrates the spiritual realities of nature through a precise insight into the interrelatedness of spirit and matter. Goethe the poet and Goethe the scientist are united in Goethe the thinker. The most fascinating parts of these investigations are without doubt those which reveal the importance for *Faust* of Goethe's scientific writings and, conversely, find in *Faust* unexpected illumination of his scientific investigations. Goethe's art appears as a poetic transformation of his scientific vision, and his science reveals the same insight into the metamorphoses of living nature which directs his poetic imagination.

These insights are important to Goethe scholarship. Yet the author does not content himself with mere theoretical understanding. He holds that we have yet to discover this perhaps most crucial aspect of Goethe's work for ourselves, and that we should look to Goethe as a source of inspiration for solutions to present scientific and social problems, a source which we have perhaps overlooked in our critical and aesthetic preoccupation with Goethe. He contends that Goethe's intellectual stance and the epistemology and method implicit in it are capable of opening as yet largely unexplored avenues of thought which lead to invaluable new understanding.

Goethe's challenge to the thinking of our age relates especially to the morality of science. Just as Goethe saw in the life of nature a continual evolution of forms, so too did he see human knowledge as capable of ever higher levels of development. Goethe tasks the scientist with grave responsibilities. A moral discipline is demanded of him which would lead to the development of new organs of apprehension and understanding enabling him to transcend our mechanistic view of nature and penetrate into spiritual realities which could lead to the elevation of life itself.

At this point, however, Alan Cottrell's essays will best speak for themselves, since such thoughts on Goethe's humanism are the substance of his book. One last word, however, may be permitted concerning his approach to Goethe. He emphasizes that Goethe's mode of thinking is alive and never ceases to generate new insight. This fundamental thesis is not only developed but is also applied as a critical method in this book. For it is precisely Goethe's epistemology and the method of "zarte Empirie" which informs each of these studies and which permits Alan Cottrell to detect the great in the small, the general in the particular, and to reveal in every instance of his interpretation the great unity underlying Goethe's world view.

University of Washington
Seattle, Washington

Ernst Behler

Acknowledgments

I should like to thank the editor of *The German Quarterly* for permission to reprint from volume 45 (1972), 4–19, the study "Chalice and Skull: A Goethean Answer to Faust's Cognitional Dilemma." I should also like to thank the editor of the *Modern Language Quarterly* for permission to use the study "Zoilo-Thersites: Another 'sehr ernster Scherz' in Goethe's *Faust II*," which appeared originally in volume 29 (1968), 29–41, of that journal.

In addition I wish to express my thanks to the following publishers for permission to reprint passages from the articles and books listed below:

Ernst Cassirer, *Rousseau, Kant, Goethe*. Trans. from the German by James Guttman, *et al.* Princeton, N. J., Princeton University Press, 1945, © 1973. Reprinted by permission of Princeton University Press.

Noam Chomsky, "The Case against B. F. Skinner," *The New York Review of Books*, 17, no. 11, 1971. Reprinted with permission from *The New York Review of Books*. Copyright © 1971 Nyrev Inc.

T. S. Eliot, *On Poetry and Poets*. London, Faber and Faber Ltd., 1957. Reprinted by permission of Faber & Faber Ltd. and by permission of Farrar, Straus & Giroux, Inc., New York.

Wilhelm Emrich, *Die Symbolik von Faust II*. Third edition, Frankfurt am Main & Bonn, Athenäum Verlag, 1964. Reprinted by permission of Akademische Verlagsgesellschaft Athenaion.

Richard Friedenthal, *Goethe—sein Leben und seine Zeit*. München, R. Piper & Co. Verlag, 1963. Reprinted by permission of R. Piper & Co. Verlag.

Ronald Gray, *Goethe the Alchemist*. Cambridge, Cambridge University Press, 1952. Reprinted by permission of Cambridge University Press.

Werner Heisenberg, *Wandlungen in den Grundlagen der Naturwissenschaft*. Tenth edition, Stuttgart, S. Hirzel Verlag, 1973. Reprinted by permission of S. Hirzel Verlag Stuttgart.

Walter Heitler, "Die Naturwissenschaft Goethes. Eine Gegenüberstellung Goethescher und modern-exakter Naturwissenschaft," *Der Berliner Germanistentag 1968*, ed. Karl Heinz Borck & Rudolf Henss. Heidelberg, C. Winter, 1970. Reprinted by permission of Carl Winter Universitätsverlag. The article also was published in Walter Heitler, *Naturphilosophische Streifzüge*, Braunschweig, Vieweg, 1970. Reprinted by permission of Friedrich Vieweg & Sohn Verlagsgesellschaft mbH.

Jacques Lusseyran, *And There Was Light*, translated by Elizabeth R. Cameron. Boston and Toronto, Little, Brown and Company, 1963. Reprinted as follows: From *And There Was Light* by Jacques Lusseyran, by permission of Little, Brown and Co. English translation Copyright © 1963 by Little, Brown and Co. Copyright © 1963 by Jacques Lusseyran. Reprinted also by permission of William Heinemann Ltd. Publishers, London.

John Middleton Murry, *Heaven and Earth*. London, Jonathan Cape, Ltd., 1938. Reprinted by permission of The Society of Authors, 84 Drayton Gardens, London.

Friedrich Rittelmeyer, *Menschen untereinander Menschen füreinander*. Stuttgart, Verlag Urachhaus Stuttgart, 1959. Reprinted by permission of Verlag Urachhaus Stuttgart.

Paul Roubiczek, *Existentialism, For and Against*. Cambridge, Cambridge University Press, 1964. Reprinted by permission of Cambridge University Press.

B. F. Skinner, "A Lecture on 'Having' a Poem," *Cumulative Record. A Selection of Papers*. Third edition, New York, Appleton-Century Crofts, 1972. Reprinted by permission of Prentice-Hall, Inc., as follows: B. F. Skinner, *Cumulative Record*, 3rd ed. © 1972, pp. 350–54. Reprinted by permission of Prentice-Hall, Inc., Englewood Cliffs, New Jersey. The article was also published in the *Saturday Review*, 55, no. 29, 15 July 1972, pp. 32–35. © 1972 *Saturday Review Inc.* Reprinted courtesy of *Saturday Review*.

Rudolf Steiner, *Geisteswissenschaftliche Erläuterungen zu Goethes Faust*. Third edition, Dornach, Verlag der Rudolf Steiner-Nachlaßverwaltung, 1967. Reprinted by permission of Rudolf Steiner-Nachlaßverwaltung.

F. J. Stopp, "Ottilie and 'das innere Licht.' " *German Studies Presented to Walter Horace Bruford*. London, George G. Harrap & Co. Ltd., 1962. Reprinted by permission of George G. Harrap & Co. Ltd.

Humphry Trevelyan, "The Significance of Goethe's Science," *The Goethe Year*, London, Maxson & Co. Ltd., 1949. Reprinted by permission of Pergamon Press Ltd., Oxford.

Karl Viëtor, *Goethe. Dichtung, Wissenschaft, Weltbild*. Bern & München, Francke Verlag, 1949. Reprinted by permission of Francke Verlag.

Leslie A. White, *The Science of Culture*. New York, Noonday, Farrar, Straus & Giroux, © 1949, third printing, 1971. Reprinted by permission of Farrar, Straus & Giroux, Inc.

Elizabeth M. Wilkinson & Leonard A. Willoughby, "The Blind Man and the Poet." *German Studies Presented to Walter Horace Bruford*. London, George G. Harrap & Co. Ltd., 1962. Reprinted by permission of George G. Harrap & Co. Ltd.

Michael Wilson, "Goethe's Farbenlehre," *The Goethe Year*. London, Maxson & Co. Ltd., 1949. Reprinted by permission of Pergamon Press Ltd., Oxford.

List of Abbreviations

SD	Stage Direction (in *Faust*)
DVLG	Deutsche Vierteljahrsschrift für Literaturwissenschaft und Geistesgeschichte
ÉG	Études Germaniques
GQ	The German Quarterly
JDSG	Jahrbuch der Deutschen Schillergesellschaft
MLN	Modern Language Notes
MLR	Modern Language Review
PEGS	Publications of the English Goethe Society
PMLA	Publications of the Modern Language Association of America

Introduction

When the aged Goethe sealed up the "sehr ernste Scherze" of *Faust*, Part II, and wrote that he could not yet share them with his friends, he demonstrated a strikingly astute appreciation of the trends which would mold the intellectual life of the decades to come. He knew that his efforts would be poorly rewarded ("schlecht belohnt"),[1] especially by those who later felt themselves called upon to enlighten the public concerning *Faust* from the vantage point of positivistic science. The correctness of Goethe's prognosis was perhaps most strikingly illustrated when fifty years later, in the full flower of the mechanistic Weltanschauung, no less a figure than Emil Du Bois-Reymond delivered his famous "Rektoratsrede" at the Friedrich-Wilhelms-Universität in Berlin under the title "Goethe und kein Ende." It is symptomatic of the times that on such an august occasion the speaker felt fully justified in delivering himself of the following words of wisdom: "Wir sind an die Fabel des Faust so gewöhnt, dass es uns ausnehmend schwer fällt, sie mit frischem Blick zu betrachten. Gelingt dies, so erstaunt man über deren tiefe psychologische Unwahrheit."[2] The seemingly unassailable epistemology underlying Du Bois-Reymond's position is of course completely closed to any understanding of the spiritual striving which moves Faust to seek ". . . was die Welt/ Im Innersten zusammenhält" (382–83). Ten years earlier Du Bois-Reymond had set forth his intellectual position that there are certain absolute limits set to human cognition. The lecture "Über die Grenzen des Naturerkennens," delivered on 14 August 1872 before a congress of German scientists and physicians in Leipzig, culminates in the statement:

> Gegenüber den Räthseln der Körperwelt ist der Naturforscher längst gewöhnt, mit männlicher Entsagung sein "*Ignoramus*" auszusprechen. Im Rückblick auf die durchlaufene siegreiche Bahn trägt ihn dabei das stille Bewusstsein, dass, wo er jetzt nicht weiss, er wenigstens unter Umständen wissen könnte, und dereinst vielleicht wissen wird. Gegenüber dem Räthsel aber, was Materie und Kraft seien, und wie sie zu denken vermögen, muss er ein für allemal zu dem viel schwerer abzugebenden Wahrspruch sich entschliessen: "*Ignorabimus*."[3]

[1] Letter to Wilhelm von Humboldt, 17 March 1832. *Goethes Briefe*, HA (Hamburger Ausgabe) IV, 481.

[2] Emil Du Bois-Reymond, *Goethe und kein Ende*. Rede bei Antritt des Rectorats der koenigl. Friedrich-Wilhelms-Universität zu Berlin, am 15. October [sic] 1882 (Leipzig, 1883), p. 15.

[3] Emil Du Bois-Reymond, *Über die Grenzen des Naturerkennens, Die sieben Welträthsel*. Zwei Vorträge (Leipzig, 1884), p. 46.

The full splendor of philistinism which blinds Du Bois-Reymond to even an elementary awareness of Goethe's purpose unfolds before us in the following pronouncement from "Goethe und kein Ende":

> Wie prosaisch es klinge, es ist nicht minder wahr, dass Faust, statt an Hof zu gehen, ungedecktes Papiergeld auszugeben, und zu den Müttern in die vierte Dimension zu steigen, besser gethan hätte, Gretchen zu heirathen, sein Kind ehrlich zu machen und Elektrisirmaschine und Luftpumpe zu erfinden; wofür wir ihm denn an Stelle des Magdeburger Bürgermeisters gebührenden Dank wissen würden.[4]

Goethe would doubtless have enjoyed the amusing rejoinder which this inanity elicited a year later from Alfred Freiherr von Berger in a little volume published as a rebuttal: "Was aber Elektrisirmaschine und Luftpumpe betrifft, so frage ich Herrn *Du Bois-Reymond*, woher er denn wisse, dass Faust sie nicht erfunden habe."[5] The main point is of course that not everyone who feels moved to indict Goethe's world view is capable of comprehending it. Berger puts his finger on this very point when he says: "Man hat bei Besprechung dessen, was Faust als Denker erlebt, sein Denken immer zu sehr nach Analogie des geistigen Geschehens beurtheilt, wie es sich vielleicht, von Leidenschaften unbeirrt, in dem Haupte eines *Kant*, eines *Gauss*, eines—*Du Bois-Reymond* abspielt."[6] Faust is a passionate thinker who fully accepts the moral implications of the assertion that man's thinking can never attain to the truth which informs nature: "Und sehe, daß wir nichts wissen können!/ Das will mir schier das Herz verbrennen" (364–65). Du Bois-Reymond, on the other hand, remains cheerfully unaffected by the implications of his own world view: "Faust denkt nicht so, wie Herr *Du Bois-Reymond* denkt, und das *ignorabimus* des Letzteren ist also auch etwas Anderes, als die innerliche Katastrophe, welche in Faust der Erkenntniss des *ignorabimus* entspricht."[7] There were prominent figures in the nineteenth century such as Herman Grimm, Carlyle and above all Emerson who understood and honored Goethe, yet their voices were not easily heard through the clamor of triumphant materialism.

Goethe was right. In this atmosphere *Faust* was not understood. Goethe had long since seen through the superficialities, meretricious enticements and awesome dangers which attend upon materialistic thinking. And he had given poetic expression to this insight in countless passages in *Faust*—indeed, even programmatically in the persons of Wagner and above all, Mephistopheles. Goethe had long since anticipated and transcended the world view of a Du Bois-Reymond, yet that world view was on the march and was not interested in what Goethe had

[4] *Op. cit.*, p. 23.

[5] Alfred Freiherr von Berger, *Goethes Faust und die Grenzen des Naturerkennens*. Wider "Goethe und kein Ende" von Emil Du Bois-Reymond (Wien, 1883), p. 37.

[6] *Ibid.*, p. 12.

[7] *Ibid.*, p. 14.

to say. Goethe's message was not mechanical but organic and developmental, and like the plant seed needed time to germinate. In our own age the atmosphere is very different. The best scientists and humanists are questioning the dogmatic assumptions of the nineteenth century. A climate of increasingly open-minded and sincere inquiry into the nature of man and his world has also favored a searching reexamination of *Faust* and of Goethe's thinking in general. In striking contrast to the second half of the nineteenth century we find a host of penetrating and sensitive critical views of *Faust*, including those of Hertz, Weinhandl, Spranger, Viëtor, Stöcklein, Emrich and Diener, to name only a few.

In the seven essays contained in this volume I should like to offer a fresh look at a number of themes in *Faust*. It is perhaps helpful to state at the outset what these essays are *not*. They do not undertake to deal with the entire *Faust* drama nor to present a comprehensive new reading of it. Nor do they proceed from one theme and develop it with reference to the poem as a whole. They are rather a collection of essays which work out seven different themes quite independently of one another. The reader will find, however, that the essays share one or all of three major elements in common. The first is methodological. In many instances I have tried to develop a theme through very close textual analysis, often down into the syntax and the vowel/consonant structures. For *Faust* is not philosophy but high *poetry* and it is rewarding to trace the embodiment of Goethe's vision in the language, the poetic diction, the "Sprachleib." At the same time, however, I have sought to relate the themes and images to the larger context of the drama as well as to others of Goethe's works.

Secondly, I have sought to relate significant questions raised in *Faust* to the cultural situation of our own times. *Faust* above all other poems depicts the struggles of modern western man for spiritual autonomy and self-determination. It is therefore in many respects still a vital comment on the predicament of man today, although it was completed nearly a century and a half ago. In his later years Goethe was much concerned with the advent of technology and its ethical implications. One need only think of his interest in a Panama canal and the looming industrialism which finds germinal expression in the "factories" of the *Wanderjahre*. Goethe prided himself on the fact that his world view was capable of application to ever changing conditions. This suggests that it is in keeping with his intentions that we continue to ask ourselves how his insights speak to the problems of our own age. One must of course take care to remember that Goethe wrote in the cultural context of the late eighteenth and early nineteenth centuries, and not to distort his intent. One must, however, also develop an eye for the germinal aspects of Goethe's poetry and thought—those aspects which could not be fully understood in his own times and which contain growth forces for the future. In Goethe's lifetime there were those who, like Napoleon, were blissfully unaware of anything later than *Werther*. *Iphigenie*, when it first appeared, certainly did not reap unqualified appreciation. Each generation discovers a new side of Goethe's work.

The *Divan* was very late in receiving due attention. *Faust II* has finally begun to be widely known as a serious poetic achievement only in our own times, and the natural scientific studies are still largely ignored.

This brings us to the third element which a large number of these essays share in common: I have undertaken to relate many themes and images to the thinking underlying Goethe's natural scientific works. In the entire corpus of Goethe's writings these are probably the most difficult to comprehend, and will surely be the last significant segment of his life's work to be fully understood. Yet Goethe's work is of one piece and we shall not appreciate the depths of his poetical works until we read them out of a deep understanding of his science. In contrast to the poetry Goethe's science is perhaps somewhat unfamiliar. By way of introduction, therefore, let us survey briefly the problem of the reception of this science in the nineteenth and twentieth centuries.

Goethe's science was controversial at its inception and has remained so to this day. There have been those who spoke appreciatively of Goethe as the father of plant morphology, yet few understood the non-Kantian epistemological mode which informs it.[8] The *Farbenlehre*, which Goethe himself considered his greatest achievement, is still the object of controversy or, worse, the victim of indifference. There are many who have assumed this science to be irrelevant or even, in the words of Du Bois-Reymond on the *Farbenlehre*, "die todtgeborene Spielerei eines autodidaktischen Dilettanten."[9] This mechanistic and uncomprehending attitude toward the epistemology underlying Goethe's science comes to expression in 1918 in Ostwald's remark: "Statt: Wär' nicht das Auge sonnenhaft, wie könnten wir das Licht erblicken, kann man mit gleichem Rechte fragen: wär' nicht das Auge tintenhaft, wie könnten wir die Schrift erblicken, oder irgendeinen anderen Satz von gleicher 'Tiefe.' "[10] Yet occasionally quite another note is struck, as in the case of T. S. Eliot, who late in his life completely revised his view of Goethe's science. In reference to Ernst Lehrs' *Man or Matter* Eliot writes:

> What Dr. Lehrs did for me was to suggest that Goethe's scientific views somehow fitted with his imaginative work, that the same insight was struggling for expression in both, and that it is not reasonable to dismiss as utter nonsense in the field of scientific enquiry, what we accept as inspired wisdom in poetry . . . I will say that in consequence of what Dr. Lehrs has written about Goethe's science, I think I understand parts of *Faust*, such as the opening scene of Part II, better than before; and now I believe that Part II is a greater work than Part I—the contrary of what I had always been told by those more learned than myself.[11]

[8] Cf. the Appendix.

[9] *Goethe und kein Ende*, p. 29.

[10] Wilhelm Ostwald, *Goethe, Schopenhauer und die Farbenlehre* (Leipzig, 1918), p. 8.

[11] T. S. Eliot, "Goethe as the Sage," An address delivered at Hamburg University on the occasion of the award of the Hanseatic Goethe Prize for 1954, in May, 1955. *On Poetry and Poets* (London, 1957), p. 215.

The attitude of Du Bois-Reymond is echoed in our own day by Richard Friedenthal, who announces: "Goethes *Farbenlehre* steht aber außerhalb des Ganges der Wissenschaft. Sie ist eine Goethe-Lehre. Sie ist autochthon und autokratisch konzipiert. Man kann sich ihr nur als Gläubiger und Jünger anschließen oder sie biographisch als einen Zug seines Wesens zu begreifen suchen."[12] Yet the eminent and subtle critic Middleton Murry writes of Goethe's science in an altogether different way: "It was a science which was preparatory to a renewal of the religious consciousness; not a science which foolishly plumed itself on having abolished religion. And above all, it was genetic and dynamic both in its investigation of Nature, and in its effect upon the man who practised it."[13] And on the subject of the controversial *Farbenlehre* Murry writes:

> It is not in the least to be deplored that his poetical genius became diffused over investigations that were not poetical; it is not even to be regarded as an aberration that he considered his *Farbenlehre* of more importance than any other of his works. He was not quite so deluded as he is supposed to have been. He was asserting a truth in his rejection of the Newtonian theory of light—the truth of the incommensurability of the immediately apprehended phenomenon—which science has been ever since in danger of neglecting.
>
> This attitude of Goethe's is so far from being outmoded that it belongs still to the future.[14]

Nevertheless, a quarter of a century later Friedenthal has launched a full-scale indictment of Goethe's *Farbenlehre*, and he assures us that no physicist has been "converted" to it: "Niemand hat nach seiner Lehre gemalt, wie er das im stillen hoffte, kein Färbermeister hat sie benutzt, wie er das anregte, und kein Physiker hat sich bekehrt, wie Goethe ebenfalls von der Zukunft erhoffte."[15] The word "bekehrt" suggests that for the physicist only rejection or discipleship, not a dispassionate evaluation of Goethe's *Farbenlehre*, is possible. Yet twenty-two years before the appearance of Friedenthal's Goethe biography the world famous physicist Werner Heisenberg had delivered a lecture in which he discusses the subject in a very much more balanced way than does Friedenthal, and in which he makes the following statement on the question of Newton vs. Goethe: "Die beiden Theorien stehen an verschiedenen Stellen in jenem großen Gebäude der Wissenschaft. Sicher kann die Anerkennung der modernen Physik den Naturforscher nicht hindern, auch den Goetheschen Weg der Naturbetrachtung zu gehen und weiter zu verfolgen."[16] And in 1968, five years after Friedenthal's

[12] Richard Friedenthal, *Goethe—sein Leben und seine Zeit* (München, 1963), p. 367.

[13] John Middleton Murry, *Heaven and Earth* (London, 1938), p. 220.

[14] *Ibid.*, p. 231.

[15] Friedenthal, *Goethe—sein Leben und seine Zeit*, p. 535.

[16] Werner Heisenberg, "Die Goethesche und die Newtonsche Farbenlehre im Lichte der modernen Physik," (lecture delivered in Budapest on 5 May 1941) published in *Wandlungen in den Grundlagen der Naturwissenschaft* (10th ed., Stuttgart, 1973), p. 75. For a lucid analysis of serious shortcomings of the

indictment which is an echo of Du Bois-Reymond's declaration "Goethes Farbenlehre ist längst gerichtet,"[17] another renowned and highly reputable physicist, Walter Heitler, makes a very strong plea for Goethean science. He urges us not only to take it seriously but to develop it further. He discusses the methods of modern physics and states, entirely in keeping with Goethe's view, "Die Physik im üblichen Sinn lehrt also streng genommen nichts über Farben."[18] Moreover, Heitler states that the science of colors *must* be *non*-Newtonian ("Eine Wissenschaft von den Farben muß *anders* aussehen als die Newtonsche Physik"[19]), and as though in direct reply to Friedenthal's pronouncement "Goethes *Farbenlehre* steht aber außerhalb des Ganges der Wissenschaft" Heitler states that our whole concept of science is itself lopsided and that Goethe's work is after all thoroughly scientific:

> Wir sind heute so geblendet von den Erfolgen der Wissenschaft in Galileischer Richtung, daß wir oft nichts anderes mehr als "wissenschaftlich" anerkennen. Nur das Quantitative, Materielle, Mechanistische gilt als Wissenschaft. Deshalb liegt gerade für uns und heute die grundlegende Bedeutung Goethescher Wissenschaft darin, gezeigt zu haben, daß saubere Wissenschaft im reinen Bereich der Gestalten wie der Qualitäten ebenso möglich ist wie in der Galileischen Richtung.[20]

Heitler's view is a vindication by a twentieth-century physicist of the position taken by Rudolf Steiner, editor of Goethe's natural scientific writings for Kürschner's *Deutsche National-Literatur* and the Weimarer Ausgabe. Steiner was a man of profound genius whose Goethe studies remain controversial because they undertake to uncover the epistemology *implicit* in Goethe's work. In his subsequent anthroposophical work Steiner builds in part on Goethe's science, but in his commentaries on the natural scientific works he does not *distort* Goethe, as he is often unfairly accused of doing. Steiner's knowledge of Goethe is encompassing and exact, and the case he makes for Goethean science recommends itself not the least by a precision and inward mobility of concept formation every bit the equal of Goethe's own.

We see, then, that the controversy which came to expression in the 1880's in the polar opposite views articulated by Du Bois-Reymond and Rudolf Steiner is by no means resolved but has been variously restated in our own times. It is interesting that there are an increasing number of voices in the culture, including thoroughly competent physicists, who suggest that Goethe's science may be the next, and perhaps most significant, of various aspects of the poet's work to be

optics of Goethe's *Farbenlehre* in view of modern physics cf. George Wells, "Goethe's Scientific Method and Aims in the Light of His Studies in Physical Optics," *PEGS*, 38 (1968), 69–113.

[17] *Goethe und kein Ende*, p. 25.

[18] Walter Heitler, "Die Naturwissenschaft Goethes, Eine Gegenüberstellung Goethescher und modern-exakter Naturwissenschaft," *Der Berliner Germanistentag 1968* (Heidelberg, 1970), p. 14.

[19] *Ibid.*, p. 15.

[20] *Ibid.*, p. 19.

"discovered" long after his death. If this be the case, we shall find ourselves involved in one of the most difficult and fascinating discussions which have resulted from the ongoing efforts of generations to come to grips with Goethe's genius. I am of the opinion that despite the shortcomings of Goethe's science its underlying epistemology and methodology are sound and capable of the further development which Steiner and Heitler hope to see. I also feel that Goethe's science is centrally important to his world view and to his art. Indeed, the more deeply and clearly we come to understand Goethe's science the more richly and precisely shall we understand *Faust*.[21]

The larger number of the present seven essays reflect this concern for Goethe's scientific thought. An attempt has been made to bring that thought to bear on various specific aspects of the poem. This may take place on several levels. First, one may discuss images, such as the colors "Purpur und Grün" or the figure of Proteus, which harbor specific thoughts in the scientific writings.[22]

Secondly, one may find that in certain subtle ways Goethe's scientific epistemology and method are also at work in *Faust*. The botanical law of metamorphosis, for instance, orders the flow and transformation of themes, of images

[21] One must point to the many invaluable contributions which have already been made in this direction by such scholars as Hertz, A. Wachsmuth, Diener, Weinhandl, Hiebel, etc. Every serious *Faust* critic knows that such themes as the "farbiger Abglanz," the Mothers and Homunculus cannot possibly be discussed fully without specific reference to the natural scientific studies. This stream of *Faust* criticism, to which I am deeply indebted, is one which will expand as our understanding of the scientific works increases.

[22] The extent of Goethe's direct use of such images was not always recognized. Thus in Friedrich Theodor Vischer's malicious but very amusing satire *Faust. Der Tragödie Dritter Theil*, published under the pseudonym "Deutobold Symbolizetti Allegoriowitsch Mystifizinsky" one of the "Mothers," who are sitting over coffee with Mephistopheles, exclaims:

> O Armer! Seht, er schämt sich! Purpurröthe
> Kämpft mit dem Schwefelgelb, ein rein Orange
> Entsteht aus der chromatischen Melange!
> O, sieh dieß Schauspiel an, verklärter Göthe!
> Sieh hin, wie er vor Aerger nun erblaut,
> Wie Blau mit Gelb als Grünes sich erschaut,
> Wie Grün mit Roth als Wechselsupplement
> Sich hebt und mehrt, gesteigert strahlt und brennt!
> Wir möchten gern dieß Farbenphänomen
> Im zweiten Theil des Faust verwendet seh'n,
> Man findet dort so viel Geologie,
> Der Farbenlehre nur gedenkst du nie!

—Deutobold Symbolizetti Allegoriowitsch Mystifizinsky, *Faust. Der Tragödie Dritter Theil* (Tübingen, 1886), p. 50. Today the situation is not quite so gloomy, as Andreas Wachsmuth has demonstrated in his excellent study "Goethes Farbenlehre und ihre Bedeutung für seine Dichtung und Weltanschauung," *Goethe*, 21 (Weimar, 1959), pp. 70–93. Cf. also Peter Schmidt, *Goethes Farbensymbolik* (Berlin, 1965).

in the work and ultimately even of the vowels and consonants in given lines.

Finally, Goethe's scientific studies offer insights into a number of larger questions as to the nature and destiny of the human being as these are reflected in *Faust*. These are profound questions which confront western man today: is man capable of developing conscious insight into the spiritual laws of nature and the human soul, insight for which Faust yearns, or is he condemned to remain a prisoner of mechanistic science, "eating dust" for Mephistopheles? Is man a being of innate spiritual worth and capable of unfolding what is called "genius" or is he, as in the Skinnerian view, a creature completely determined and "beyond freedom and dignity"? Is the world of "Bergschluchten" a trite metaphor or a profound testament to Goethe's view of the laws of man's higher nature, of his "entelechy"? Can the thoughts which Goethe evolves in the *Farbenlehre* and in his numerous comments on the unfolding of higher organs of understanding cast light upon the image of man's evolving presented in that and other scenes?

These are thoughts which run through the seven essays contained in this volume. The studies make no claim to completeness. I offer them as a step toward a fuller understanding of Goethe's poem. My hope is that they will stimulate the reader's thought in new directions. If they convey even a little of the quiet joy which I derived from Goethe's work while writing them I shall consider the undertaking well worthwhile. The greatest joy lies perhaps in the discovery that one may return to Goethe's works again and again through the years and one finds that they are perennially new and continue to reveal secrets one had not suspected were there. Goethe's writings are the creations of a great soul in a constant process of generation and growth. Like the work of any great genius they will always contain more than we can fathom and they challenge us to grow and develop with them for as long as we are able. Such is the price of their understanding. Goethe tells us as much himself:

> Ein Mann, der länger gelebt, ist verschiedene Epochen durchgegangen; er stimmt vielleicht nicht immer mit sich selbst überein; er trägt manches vor, davon wir das eine für wahr, das andre für falsch ansprechen möchten: alles dieses darzustellen, zu sondern, zu bejahen, zu verneinen, ist eine unendliche Arbeit, die nur dem gelingen kann, der sich ihr ganz widmet und ihr sein Leben aufopfern mag.[23]

[23] *Geschichte der Farbenlehre*. Einleitung. Erich Trunz, ed., *Goethes Werke*, Hamburger Ausgabe (Hamburg, 1960–62), XIV, 9.

I

Chalice and Skull
A Goethean Answer to Faust's Cognitional Dilemma

In that portion of the scene "Nacht" (606–807) which appeared in 1808 in *Faust: Der Tragödie erster Teil*, the aged Faust has reached the nadir of his striving. In his despair at having been rejected by the Earth Spirit he sits in the night before Easter Sunday and contemplates suicide. The riddle of Faust's existence as here portrayed is also the dilemma of modern western man, who is unable to resolve the dualities of mind and body, subject and object, spirit and matter. Faust has reached the point at which he is ready to destroy his earthly body in the hope of breaking through the barrier which separates him from the spiritual world. In this sense one can say that Mephisto has already gained access to Faust and, as the spirit of negation, is infecting his consciousness in the hope that the prophecy of the "Prolog im Himmel," "Staub soll er fressen" (334) may be fulfilled. Indeed, Faust already views himself in this role: "Dem Wurme gleich' ich, der den Staub durchwühlt" (653), and this despite the fact that Mephisto as a character does not appear until several scenes later (1322).

In order to effect the suicide Faust determines to drink poison which he has prepared in a vial (690). Curiously, however, Goethe does not merely let him drink the contents of the vial, but introduces a crystal goblet, or cup ("kristallne reine Schale," 720) from which Faust intends to drink the poison. Presumably the vial would have sufficed, and one wonders why the cup is introduced. Faust handles the vial with reverence (691). Were it merely necessary to show Faust drinking the poison, all mention of the "Schale" (720–31) would have been superfluous. Having expressed Faust's hopes for uniting with the spiritual world (696–719) Goethe could have continued, with an entirely smooth transition, at line 732 ("Hier ist ein Saft . . ."). He did not, however. He inserted the image of the crystal chalice (720–31) and one must ask what this image adds to the conception of the scene.

Just as the alchemical devices and books which adorn Faust's study are a link to the past, so also is the cup a possession which has served in the family on festive occasions, a tradition which adds an elevated note to the present scene: "Du glänztest bei der Väter Freudenfeste" (723). The tradition dictated that the drinker proposing a toast "explain" in rhyme some of the figures which decorate the cup.

Goethe twice uses the word "zugebracht," linking the cup's function at the ancestral banquets ("Wenn einer dich dem andern zugebracht," 725) with that in the present scene ("Der letzte Trunk sei nun, mit ganzer Seele,/ Als festlich hoher Gruß, dem Morgen zugebracht!" 735–36). Just at this moment of the highly festive toast which is to reduce Faust to dust, the music announcing the Easter message of Christ's Resurrection releases the childhood memories which dissolve Faust's ego-centeredness and prevent the suicide. The symbol of the cup therefore does for Goethe what the vial could not have done. It enables him to heighten the symbolism of the death-draught to the level of a sacramental act. This event is of enormous poetic power, for it is an anti-sacramental deed to be committed at the Easter season, when the image of the cup is at once associated with that of the Cup of the Last Supper (note the wording: "der letzte Trunk"). Esoteric traditions (in which Goethe took a keen interest) also relate the image of the Cup to the attainment of spiritual maturity (Grail) or, as pointed out by Alice Raphael, to spiritual baptism.[1]

Of central pertinence to our further elaboration of the significance of the chalice is another image in this scene. Amongst the "Urväter-Hausrat" (408) which adorns Faust's study is the skull which represents a continual reminder of mortality (664–67). As a quintessential distillation of matter, in which the spirit once dwelled, the skull is a symbol of the whole dilemma in which Faust finds himself. In the present context the skull's symbolic function is that of the traditional Baroque *memento mori* with a conscious allusion to *Hamlet*. The skull mocks Faust ("Was grinsest du mir, . . . ," 664) as a reminder of his inability to find spirit in matter, and he therefore projects his own dilemma back into the person who once inhabited the skull (664–67).

On a deeper level the skull's metaphorical function is determined by the context of the scene itself. The time is the dawn of Easter, the festival commemorating the triumph of spirit over matter following the events of Golgotha, the "place of the skull." These religious overtones are clearly of central significance for the poet. Their significance is deepened by the fact that these intimations are inaccessible to Faust. To be meaningful to him they would have to be accessible through the only path which he, the representative of a dawning modern scientific mode of cognition, could accept: knowledge. In the absence of this *knowledge* of the spirit Faust remains desperate, and the *memento mori* gains access to his consciousness in the most destructive way—inducing the drive to self-murder. Faust is prepared to partake of a very Mephistophelean anti-sacrament, in lifting the chalice full of poison to the rising sun of Easter morning. Faust's tragic illusion (or rationalization) is that he views self-destruction as a legitimate means to attain

[1] Cf. the discussion of the goblet in *Faust II*, Act I, when Faust returns from the realm of the Mothers: Alice Raphael, *Goethe and the Philosophers' Stone* (London, 1965), pp. 148, 221. For further discussion of this imagery cf. Wilkinson and Willoughby, *Goethe: Poet and Thinker* (New York, 1962), pp. 127–32.

access to higher worlds. He attempts to break through the confines of matter, as they are symbolized most vividly in the skull. In this way he hopes that while his spiritual forces withdraw from the earthly world ("Des Geistes Flutstrom ebbet nach und nach," 698) they will be led forth into the world of pure spirit, which is symbolized in two profound metaphors—the *ocean* ("Meer," 699; "Spiegelflut," 700) and the *sun* ("Feuerwagen," 702) of Easter morning.

The entire deed turns on the destruction or redemption of the spiritual kernel of man—his "I." The word "ich" occurs repeatedly in the "Nacht" scene. In the conjuration of the Earth Spirit it is asserted with all the violence of self-doubt: "Ich bin's, bin Faust, bin deinesgleichen!" (500) and yet is doomed to disillusionment: "Ich Ebenbild der Gottheit!/ Und nicht einmal dir!" (516–17). The word "ich" occurs six times between lines 690 and 701, and it is emphasized in line 734: "Den ich bereitet, den ich wähle." In this way Goethe underscores Faust's belief that he is acting freely when he commits self-murder in order to attain bliss. This profoundly ironic possibility finds further expression in the recurrence here of the word *Flut* (733), this time a poisonous "braune Flut" *within* the "Höhle" of the goblet. The image is here rendered doubly profound, for the goblet, into which Faust pours the poison, assumes an added metaphorical association with the human body. The word "Höhle" also appears in another context as just such a metaphor when Faust, leaning on Baroque tradition, refers to his body as a "Trauerhöhle" (1589). Significantly, he does so at just that other desperate moment of world- and self-negation, the great curse (1583–1606).

The human body, which man may freely mold into a vessel for spiritual maturity,[2] is also open to abuse. In despair or illusion man may negate his spiritual origin and allow the power of negation access to his inner life by his own free choice ("Den ich bereitet, den ich wähle," 734). Then the "Spiegelflut" (700) of spirit which he hopes to attain is perverted into the poisonous "braune Flut" of destruction. And how could it be otherwise? The imagery is thoroughly consistent. The "braune Flut" is a liquid robbed of its purity—rendered destructive through admixture with the element of matter; in Mephisto's terminology, with dust ("Staub"). This is on a deeper level a grotesque distortion of the image of the Christian sacrament, for the wine is itself water which has undergone an admixture with elements of matter. This latter process, however, takes place through the creative power of growth in the living, weaving realm of the Earth Spirit, through the grapevine, and attains fulfillment through the forces of the sunlight.

Once we have established the function of the image of the cup in the larger context sketched above and have seen how Goethe, in using it, was able to deepen the entire metaphoric context of the scene, we must ask what meaning is added through the reference to the traditional custom of explaining the cup's engraved

[2] Cf. the esoteric traditions discussed by Alice Raphael, *Goethe and the Philosophers' Stone*.

(or raised) pictures while proposing a toast. Faust is reminded here, as well as by the Easter music a few lines later, of his youth ("manche Jugendnacht," 729). The image itself recalls to mind Keats's "Ode on a Grecian Urn" and Mörike's "Auf eine Lampe." The latter also is decorated with figures which challenge the beholder to attempt to resolve their message.[3] The central point here is the *mental activity* called forth by the contemplation of the object. The lamp, and the cup, are the products of the activity of a creative artist. A conscious, creative spirit has in each case molded matter according to his design and has imbued it with form. The images, or forms, then rest permanently in their material embodiment and challenge the beholder to enter imaginatively into their laws and discover their secrets. Similarly, the physician's skull stands before the gaze of Faust as the supreme rune—the form of which he is unable to decipher. It is a vivid reminder of "man's state," and it remains a riddle for him. Faust recalls only the fact that at one time these forms were the outer encasement of a living mind. Faust then holds in his hands the crystal goblet, but he stands alone, isolated in his doubt and despair. He thus forgoes the activity of explaining its figures in rhyme ("sie reimweis zu erklären," 727). The very fact that Faust is alone, with no one to whom to pass the cup, is itself symbolic of his titanic spiritual isolation from the society of men.

Faust, in his extremity, is pulled back from the edge of the abyss by the sound of the Easter music. Recollections of childhood and the healing charm of music, which Goethe knew so well,[4] imbue Faust with a new desire to live. In a sense he is himself reborn as the chorus fills the air with the message of the Resurrection. He cannot believe this message in any orthodox sense ("Die Botschaft hör' ich wohl, allein mir fehlt der Glaube," 765). Neither could Goethe. This is, however, not the point. The point is that a process takes place within Faust which amounts to a reanimation of his being. The spirit of negation releases its grip and new life quickens within. Because he had attained considerable distance from the struggles reflected in *Werther* and the *Urfaust*, Goethe was able to formulate the present scene with great objectivity. This passage, which appeared in 1808, represents the work of the poet who decades earlier had overcome the Wertherian-Faustian demand for immediate access to the absolute at all costs. Goethe had meanwhile set about the painstaking work of forging a method of investigation which might allow nature to reveal her secrets to him in the clarity of thinking. His botanical studies had come to fruition on the journey to Italy, where Goethe, who himself felt "reborn,"[5] was at last able to discover the ideal *Urpflanze*, the spiritual

[3] Such an image raises innumerable questions concerning the nature of art. Cf. the exchange between Emil Staiger and Martin Heidegger in Emil Staiger, *Die Kunst der Interpretation* (Zürich, 1955), pp. 9–49.

[4] Cf. in the later "Trilogie der Leidenschaft" the third poem, "Aussöhnung" (1823), HA I, 385–86.

[5] ". . . ich zähle einen zweiten Geburtstag, eine wahre Wiedergeburt, von dem Tage, da ich Rom betrat." *Italienische Reise*, 3 December 1786, HA XI, 147.

archetype which he saw weaving before him in the material world of the plant kingdom. The same investigative method, employing what he called "anschauende Urteilskraft," Goethe further applied to the metamorphosis of animal forms and thus also in the realm of zoology learned to read the language of the creative spirit in the natural world.

In the sphere of esthetics also, Goethe found himself "reborn" in Italy. Standing before the works of classical art he recognized in them a free further development, by man, of the same organic laws which inform the world of nature. Goethe, in short, had begun so to school his thinking, that he could apply it to the phenomena of nature and of art and in so doing participate in and thus also *know* their hidden spiritual laws. Goethe was thus able to gain distance from the scene "Nacht," and in completing it he could give vivid form to a dilemma through which he himself had passed and which he had overcome.

In September of 1826, nearly two decades after the appearance of the expanded "Nacht" scene, the seventy-seven year old Goethe composed a poem which in a particularly beautiful way illuminates the imagery of the passages we have been discussing. This is the poem commonly called "Schillers Reliquien" ("Im ernsten Beinhaus war's, wo ich beschaute").[6] Here we see Goethe himself in the contemplation of a skull.[7]

The poem begins with a macabre *memento mori* reminiscent of the "Nacht" scene, as the poet describes his encounter with the dismembered skeletons in the mausoleum. Goethe is not overwhelmed by the sight, however, and does not lose himself in Faustian brooding. He explains that he is an adept who is able to read the language of organic forms: "Doch mir Adepten war die Schrift geschrieben,/ Die heil'gen Sinn nicht jedem offenbarte" (15–16). Equipped with a trained eye and living, mobile thoughts, he feels free and even warm in the cold, narrow room, "Als ob ein Lebensquell dem Tod entspränge" (21). It is easy to

[6] HA I, 366–67.

[7] Much painstaking research has attempted to ascertain whether or not the skull in question, which Goethe took to be Schiller's and even had removed to his house for quiet contemplation, really *was* the skull of his friend. This question of the skull's authenticity will not concern us here, for it merely dwells on the outer circumstances of the occasion, whereas it is the message of the poem itself which should interest us. Cf. particularly Karl Viëtor, "Goethes Gedicht auf Schillers Schädel," *PMLA*, 59 (1944), 1156–72; also Wolfgang Martens, "Goethes Gedicht 'Bei Betrachtung von Schillers Schädel,' " *JDSG*, 12 (1968), 275–95. For related references cf. the listing of E. Trunz, HA I, 570.

Goethe was himself aware of the danger inherent in evaluating works of art with the tools of external historical or scientific analysis. Cf. the remarks reported by Eckermann under the date of 27 December 1826: "Da wollen sie wissen welche Stadt am Rhein bei meinem Hermann und Dorothea gemeint sei!—Als ob es nicht besser wäre, sich jede beliebige zu denken!—Man will Wahrheit, man will Wirklichkeit und verdirbt dadurch die Poesie." In view of this comment from the same year (1826) in which the poem was written it becomes clear that Goethe consciously *avoids* reference to Schiller's name, not out of sentimentality or squeamishness but in order to preserve the atmosphere of timelessness in which he would have it read. Cf. Ernst Beutler, ed., *Goethe, Gespräche mit Eckermann*, Artemis Ausgabe (Zürich, 1949), p. 195.

read past such a line as this without registering the full impact of its message: Goethe feels as though a source of life were springing forth from death. How could one possibly express more precisely, without employing traditional theological language, the Easter mood of Resurrection?

In contrast to the traditional Baroque imagery of the first half of the poem the second half conjures forth a mood of solemn awe and festive reverence. Indeed, the poem's very structure serves to reinforce the contrast of these two moods. The poem consists of thirty-four lines, in terza rima. The exact middle of the poem thus falls between lines seventeen and eighteen, which are of considerable interest: "Als ich inmitten solcher starren Menge/ Unschätzbar herrlich ein Gebild gewahrte." The verb "gewahrte" identifies the act of *seeing* which introduces the contemplations of the remainder of the poem, while the preceding line describes the location of the skull amongst the "starre Menge," the jumble of bones described in the first half of the poem. This contrast of dead bones vs. the act of perceiving life in their midst then echoes once again in the following two lines, this time internalized and expressed in terms of emotion: "Daß in des Raumes Moderkält' und Enge/ Ich frei und wärmefühlend mich erquickte" (19–20). The transition from death experience to the awareness of new life, described in terms of the act of perception at the heart of the poem (17–18), thus is heightened as it dawns in the realm of feeling (19–20) and through a final *Steigerung* rises to the level of thinking, as the poet summarizes his new insight in the line alluded to above: "Als ob ein Lebensquell dem Tod entspränge" (21).

Equipped with the eye of the adept the poet reads in the skull's forms the "secret" ("geheimnisvoll" l. 22; "geheim" l. 26) message imprinted in them by the world of spirit. Indeed, so powerful is the experience that the poet breaks through the realm of everyday consciousness and awakens by the "ocean" of creative forces which have molded the skull: "Ein Blick, der mich an jenes Meer entrückte,/ Das flutend strömt gesteigerte Gestalten" (24–25). The word "Meer" recalls to mind the imagery which welled up in Faust's soul as he prepared to drink the poison in order to achieve union with the spiritual cosmos:

> Des Geistes Flutstrom ebbet nach und nach.
> Ins hohe Meer werd' ich hinausgewiesen,
> Die Spiegelflut erglänzt zu meinen Füßen,
> Zu neuen Ufern lockt ein neuer Tag.
> (698–701)

That which Faust had longed to experience, the realm of spiritual creativity, the "ewiges Meer" of the Earth Spirit (505), the mature Goethe now describes in the tranquility of reverent contemplation. In the skull which he holds in his hands he perceives the vessel formed by the creative forces of nature as the earthly home of the entelechy of his friend. It is interesting to note that this poem provides an illustration of a statement which Faust makes before grasping the vial of poison:

"Was du ererbt von deinen Vätern hast,/ Erwirb es, um es zu besitzen" (682–83). One of the items which Faust has—literally—inherited from his physician-father is the skull which leers at him and whose secrets remain closed to his spirit. Goethe, however, earns ("erwirbt") a conscious understanding of the Schiller skull's secrets through the mode of his contemplation.

We spoke above of the natural scientific method which Goethe developed and practiced and which enabled him to penetrate to the spiritual forces at work within nature. In his botanical writings Goethe describes the leaf of the plant as the basic form which, in continual rhythmical expansion and contraction, metamorphoses itself into all the organs of the plant. This leaf-form he characterizes as "der wahre Proteus."[8] We will recall that it is the figure of Proteus who constantly changes form and finally, in the shape of a dolphin, carries Homunculus out into the ocean in the fairytale world of the festival at the end of the "klassische Walpurgisnacht," saying "Komm *geistig* mit in feuchte Weite" (8327; italics mine). Once again it is the image of the sea which Goethe employs as that element which, as a life-giving medium, is in constant flow as a cradle of form. I mention this passage here because it illustrates the inner consistency of Goethe's creative imagination within both the poetic and the scientific works.[9]

No sooner has Faust expressed his desire to set forth into the oceans of spirit in the passage quoted above (698–701) than he recalls the fact that the morning is near and the sun about to rise:

> Ein Feuerwagen schwebt auf leichten Schwingen
> An mich heran! Ich fühle mich bereit,
> Auf neuer Bahn den Äther zu durchdringen,
> Zu neuen Sphären reiner Tätigkeit.
>
> (702–5)

Yet he is unable to find a path which will open the way to such experiences and he therefore pours the poison, the "braune Flut," into the crystal goblet, and prepares to toast the dawn through suicide.

In an uncanny parallel to this scene, the poet of "Schillers Reliquien,"

[8] *Italienische Reise*, 17 May 1787, HA, XI, 375.

[9] Such an image as the ocean is of course capable of the most varied metaphorical use. Thus Goethe employs it quite differently in the final act of *Faust II* as a symbol for the threatening, elementary power of nature, as well as of the surging passions within man. Faust's palace and parks are surrounded by dikes designed to restrain these forces. Stöcklein characterizes this use of the symbol in connection with the entelechy which either controls and forms the elements (including elemental emotions) or is controlled by them: "Zusammenfassendes Symbol dafür: Das Hinausschieben des Ufers gegen das andringende Element!" Cf. Paul Stöcklein, *Wege zum späten Goethe* (Hamburg, 1960), pp. 103–4. Cf. also Emrich's characterization of Faust's struggle with the elements as "... im Grunde ein metaphysischer Kampf auf Leben und Tod zwischen Fausts formbildender seelischer Kraft, der 'unsterblichen Entelechie,' die Goethe hier mythisch als 'inneres Licht' bezeichnet, und dem widerlich-sinnlosen 'Streit' der Elemente ..." Wilhelm Emrich, *Die Symbolik von Faust II* (Frankfurt a. M., 1964), p. 398.

enraptured by the vision of the sea of creative forms, at once is cognizant of their message: "Geheim Gefäß! Orakelsprüche spendend,/ Wie bin ich wert, dich in der Hand zu halten." This "vessel" ("Gefäß") he too lifts up as in a "toast" to the sunlight:

> Dich höchsten Schatz aus Moder fromm entwendend
> Und in die freie Luft zu freiem Sinnen,
> Zum Sonnenlicht andächtig hin mich wendend.
> (28–30)

Here, too, the theme of free will is of central importance. Yet the contrast is striking: in the place of the tragic-ironic blindness of the suicidal Faust ("ein Saft . . . Den ich bereitet, den ich wähle," 732–34) we find the poet lifting his vessel to the sun in selfless reverence ("fromm," "andächtig") and therefore also in true spiritual freedom ("Und in die freie Luft zu freiem Sinnen"). In "Schillers Reliquien," as we pointed out above, it is the *mood* of Resurrection which informs the poem ("Als ob ein Lebensquell dem Tod entspränge"). It is therefore utterly appropriate that the poet's act of lifting the "vessel" ("Geheim Gefäß") of the skull out of the darkness and into the light of the sun should prompt him to formulate the final four lines of the poem. For these lines are neither traditional (as the Baroque imagery) nor hymnic (as the preceding ones), but contemplative in the most characteristic sense of the "weltanschauliche Gedichte" of the poet's old age. In them Goethe in a very real sense breaks through to a new dimension within the poem itself:

> Was kann der Mensch im Leben mehr gewinnen,
> Als daß sich Gott-Natur ihm offenbare?
> Wie sie das Feste läßt zu Geist verrinnen,
> Wie sie das Geisterzeugte fest bewahre.

In contrast to the description of private experiences as this is presented in the rest of the poem, these concluding words sum up in deceptively simple language the quintessence of Goethe's view of the scientist's task. "Gott-Natur" is that living world of Nature which Faust so desperately seeks to understand and which Goethe himself was able to enter, if only to a limited degree, cognitionally. In this sense these lines represent the conceptual articulation of that awareness which announced itself in the immediate sensation of rebirth expressed in the line "Als ob ein Lebensquell dem Tod entspränge." It is a mood of Easter, which—with no theological or Biblical allusions whatsoever—informs the mode of thinking Goethe sought to practice in his scientific studies, and which finds expression in the imagery employed in the poetry we have been discussing. Goethe could not accept religion as it was represented by the churches of his day. But for him both science and art, properly conceived, contain *within* them the true being of religion:

Wer Wissenschaft und Kunst besitzt,
Hat auch Religion;
Wer jene beiden nicht besitzt,
Der habe Religion.[10]

The poem on Schiller's skull, with its celebration of man's ability to penetrate the secrets of the "Gott-Natur," is cast in a form of unusual power, the terza rima. This form is of course celebrated as that of the *Divine Comedy* of Dante. It is particularly well suited to the subject matter of "Schillers Reliquien" in that the poet may employ it to allude formally to the living, weaving forces of spirit in the flow of forms in nature, of which the poem speaks. The rhyme scheme aba bcb cdc, with its forward-moving pattern and lilting feminine rhyme-words expresses beautifully the intricate "wechselnd Weben" of the world of nature, as it is described by the Earth Spirit (506). The living transformation of imagery is further enhanced formally by the fact that the syntactical structure breaks through the three-line metrical units. The poem is crowned with one "extra" line at the end. This additional line brings the flow of the stanzas to a halt just as the poet celebrates—not the release of matter into spirit (33), but the incorporation of spirit into the permanency of matter: "Wie sie das Geisterzeugte fest bewahre" (34), in this case the involution of the entelechy into the vessel of the skull. Thus this reflection on the permanency of spirit's incorporation in the form of matter is greatly strengthened by the poet's handling of the form of his poem.

There is only one other instance in the entire corpus of Goethe's poetry where he employs the terza rima. While the passage contains no reference to the image of the cup, this highly unusual coincidence of the use of the exalted verse form invites, indeed demands comparison. The passage is of a sublimity equal to that of "Schillers Reliquien" and is related to that poem not only formally but also through the image of the sun. It is the monologue which Faust speaks at the end of "Anmutige Gegend" as he awakens from slumber to a new life: "Des Lebens Pulse schlagen frisch lebendig . . ." (4679–4727). The parallels between this monologue and the two passages we have been discussing are striking. Once again the sun forms the frame of reference for the striving of man. Just as in the "Nacht" scene Faust had hoped to break through to the "ether" of pure spirituality as the sun ("Feuerwagen," 702) neared: ". . . Ich fühle mich bereit,/ Auf neuer Bahn den Äther zu durchdringen," so now we see the rejuvenated Faust awakening to the same approach of the sun heralded by the "etheric dawn": "Des Lebens Pulse schlagen frisch lebendig,/ Ätherische Dämmerung milde zu begrüßen." Just as Faust, saved from suicide by the Easter chorus, returns to his tasks on earth, the abode of the Earth Spirit ("Die Träne quillt, die Erde hat mich wieder!" 784), so now does the earth speak to him of his new tasks: "Du, Erde, . . . Beginnest schon,

[10] HA I, 367.

mit Lust mich zu umgeben" (4681–83), and urges him to strive for the highest existence (4685). The sun gradually appears, Faust is blinded by the "Flammenübermaß" (4708) and finds the proper human environment in the reflected light of the rainbow in the oft-cited passage "Am farbigen Abglanz haben wir das Leben." Here he once again encounters the "Gott-Natur" of "Schillers Reliquien," the "wechselnd Weben" of which the Earth Spirit speaks. This realm of inwardly active nature reveals to Faust, in the limitations of earthly reflection, the spiritual creativity which appears in its quintessential form in the light of the sun.

In the monologue in "Anmutige Gegend" the weavings of the spirit in the world of nature, i.e. the workings of the Earth Spirit, again find onomatopoetic expression in the profusion of dental fricatives (*s*, *sch*), while the alliteration of *w* and *b* in line 4722 reinforces the principle of "Dauer im Wechsel" in the image of the rainbow:

> Von Sturz zu Sturzen wälzt er jetzt in tausend,
> Dann abertausend Strömen sich ergießend,
> Hoch in die Lüfte Schaum an Schäume sausend.
> Allein wie herrlich, diesem Sturm ersprießend,
> Wölbt sich des bunten Bogens Wechseldauer,[11]
> (4718–22)

This monologue in terza rima is in a sense an expansion of the celebration of the "Gott-Natur" presented in the terza rima on Schiller's skull. That poem's rhetorical question, "Was kann der Mensch im Leben mehr gewinnen,/ Als daß sich Gott-Natur ihm offenbare?"—a question posed as the poet lifts the skull up to the sunlight—again finds an answer in the recognition of the workings of the absolute in the realm of nature. This time, however, the answer comes through the world of color, rather than of contour: "Am farbigen Abglanz haben wir das Leben."

Interesting variations on the theme of the chalice are provided by two other occurrences of the image of the cup in *Faust I* which are illuminated by the foregoing discussion. One is the rejuvenation scene in the "Hexenküche," the other Margarete's song "Es war ein König in Thule."

The scene "Hexenküche" antedates the section of the "Nacht" scene we have been discussing, as it was completed in Italy and published in 1790 in *Faust, ein Fragment*. The context of the scenes is similar in that here, too, the drinking of a powerful potion is to effect Faust's rejuvenation. This time, however, Mephisto's role is not that of the invisible spirit of negation poisoning Faust's desire for enlightenment with thoughts of self-destruction. Mephisto is now visibly present on stage, and the atmosphere is comic-grotesque. Mephisto here seeks to facilitate

[11] For a detailed discussion of the formal elements of Faust's monologue cf. Kurt May, *Faust II. Teil, In der Sprachform gedeutet* (München, 1962), pp. 26–36.

Faust's physical reanimation—a vivid distortion of Faust's earlier attempt to achieve initiation into spiritual consciousness. In both scenes Goethe refers to the liquid to be drunk as a *Saft*. In the "Hexenküche" Mephisto recommends the witch's potion with the words: "Ein gutes Glas von dem bekannten Saft!" (2519), whereas Faust had described the poison in his chalice as ". . . ein Saft, der eilig trunken macht" (732). The atmosphere of distorted sacramental action surrounds both scenes. Faust's suicide attempt, because of its conscious intent to destroy life, is a veritable *anti-sacrament*, from which he is saved by the intervention of circumstances in the form of the Easter music. The imbibing of the potion in the "Hexenküche," because it provides mere physical, rather than spiritual, renewal, is in essence a *pseudo-sacrament*.

Margarete's poem "Es war ein König in Thule" dates from approximately 1774 and is therefore the earliest of all the passages under consideration. Here the image of the cup serves in the narrower function as love-token and symbol of eternal fidelity. The golden goblet is so precious that the poet refers to it as the "heiliger Becher" (2777), reminiscent of the words used to describe Schiller's skull: "Geheim Gefäß, Orakelsprüche spendend" (26). We here once again find the image of the ocean ("Meer" 2774; "Flut" 2778; "Und sinken tief ins Meer" 2780).[12] On a deeper level within the context of this poem the cup is a metaphor for the human body, a precious vessel which at death is returned to the "ocean" and is engulfed by the spiritual all. The imagery of the "König in Thule" speaks of the overcoming of death through the sacrifice of oneself into a larger love. In this case, however, the process occurs entirely in the sphere of feeling and does not present a challenge in the cognitional realm. As such it is appropriate that this particular vision should well up in Margarete's soul.

The discussion of Goethe's employment of the image of the cup has led us into a number of widely varied examples. However, they are all drawn from one corpus of poetry and hence illuminate one another once the interrelated imagery is identified. Each instance involving this image has certain salient features in common with the other occurrences. The reason for the fascination exerted by the image of the chalice lies in its enormous potential as a metaphor. As matter given form by the mind of the creative artist it serves as a simile for the human body, created by the artistic "Gott-Natur" to be a vessel for the indwelling of the spirit, the entelechy. In this sense it becomes an archetypal image for the interpenetration of spirit and matter, of "Geist" and "Stoff." To "read" the forms wrought into it,—to learn to *understand* the interrelationship of these two realms—this is the challenge to the modern scientific consciousness as Goethe viewed it.

[12] Ernst Beutler refers to this ocean as "das Meer als das heilige Grab einer heiligen Liebe." He also sees in the last two lines of stanza two ("Die Augen gingen ihm über/ So oft er trank daraus") a definite allusion to St. John's Gospel. The passage in question (John 2:35–36) describes Christ approaching the grave of Lazarus: "Und Jesu gingen die Augen über. Da sprachen die Juden: 'Siehe, wie hat er ihn so lieb gehabt.' " Ernst Beutler, *Essays um Goethe* (Bremen, 1962), p. 344.

It is this dilemma and a boundless urge to activity, which have driven Faust to the edge of suicide.

In the realm of feeling this was Werther's problem, and that of the young Goethe. On this level it is reflected also in the tortured complaints of the frustrated Faust in the "Nacht" scene of the *Urfaust* (which dates from 1775–76). As Goethe expanded his own cognitional mode through the method he developed in the natural scientific studies, he found access to the very "open secrets" which the aged Faust was unable to grasp. With reference to the image of the vessel, this development is clearly reflected, as we hope to have shown, in the contrasting imagery of the 'anti-sacrament' of the "Nacht" scene and the spiritually alive cognitive process reflected in "Schillers Reliquien." The mature Goethe was able to activate the forces of growth and metamorphosis in the cognitional process itself. In so doing he was able to direct this process to the phenomena of nature and bring the spirit to light in matter. The vessel of his inner being he therefore filled, not with the "braune Flut" of negation and despair, but with the living water of the spirit, "jenes Meer . . . Das flutend strömt gesteigerte Gestalten."

Always, for Goethe, the highest frame of reference for the divine forces weaving through the "Gott-Natur" was the sun. Moreover, the preeminent position which Goethe assigns to the sun within the natural world order corresponds to that which he assigns to Christ within the moral world order. This is documented by the following extract from a conversation with Eckermann shortly before Goethe's death:

> Ich halte die Evangelien alle vier für durchaus echt, denn es ist in ihnen der Abglanz einer Hoheit wirksam, die von der Person Christi ausging und die so göttlicher Art, wie nur auf Erden das Göttliche erschienen ist. Fragt man mich: ob es in meiner Natur sei, ihm anbetende Ehrfurcht zu erweisen? So sage ich: durchaus!—Ich beuge mich vor ihm, als der göttlichen Offenbarung des höchsten Prinzips der Sittlichkeit. —Fragt man mich, ob es in meiner Natur sei, die Sonne zu verehren, so sage ich abermals: durchaus! Denn sie ist gleichfalls eine Offenbarung des Höchsten, und zwar die mächtigste, die uns Erdenkindern wahrzunehmen vergönnt ist. Ich anbete in ihr das Licht und die zeugende Kraft Gottes, wodurch allein wir leben, weben und sind und alle Pflanzen und Tiere mit uns.[13]

This statement illustrates rather vividly the fact that the Christian imagery associated with the Easter theme of death and rebirth was for Goethe of equal importance with the image of the sun, the source of life-giving growth forces in the natural world. The sun occupies this exalted position in "Schillers Reliquien" and also in the monologue in terza rima in "Anmutige Gegend." I have made so bold as to suggest that just as it is the dawning of the Easter morning which accompanies Faust's awakening from the nightmare of contemplated suicide, so also it is a process of rebirth and resurrection, an "inner sun," which Goethe was able

[13] Conversation of 11 March 1832. *Gespräche mit Eckermann*, pp. 770–71.

to activate within his own thinking and which he sought to apply in his study of nature. Such an assertion can of course not be "proven" in an external sense.[14] It can, however, be discovered as one more of Goethe's "open secrets" by a patient examination of the facts. This particular "open secret" happens to be one of the profoundest in Goethe's mature world view, and it is well known that the poet was careful to put forth his deepest convictions in guarded, indeed veiled, form. One must approach such a "secret" again and again, from every side of Goethe's work—the poetry, the dramas, the natural scientific works, the conversations and letters, etc. One then discovers that those "open secrets" which most skillfully elude easy categorization and empirical manipulation are for this very reason those which are the most alive, and the most deeply rooted in Goethe's mind and heart.

[14] It is the purpose of this study, however, to demonstrate the inner consistency and appropriateness of this reading. What is more, there is additional evidence to support this view. In the alchemical writings, with which Goethe was familiar, there is a definite connection between the image of the sun and the being of Christ. Ronald Gray notes that when the color red was observed in the alchemical experiment "the metals had not only been transformed into gold, but the Philosophers' Stone had been created." Ronald Gray, *Goethe the Alchemist* (Cambridge, 1952), p. 18. What is more: "Gold was his aim only in so far as it was the 'highest' metal and the symbol of the Sun" (p. 19). Gray then points to the Christian interpretation: "For the Christian alchemist indeed the Stone was identified with Christ, although the fact was rarely stated" (p. 19). It is likely that Goethe read the materials which deal with this symbolic nexus: "This symbolism could have been known to Goethe either through Georg von Welling or through Gottfried Arnold" (p. 20).

II

"... bald mit Blättern, bald mit Blüten ..." Metamorphoses of Nature and of Man in *Faust*

In the years 1798–99, over a decade after his discovery in Italy of the "Urpflanze"—the ideal plant which offered him the cognitional "key" to the entire plant kingdom[1]—Goethe had begun work on an extended didactic poem on nature. The bold plan was never completed, but a fragment, "Die Metamorphose der Pflanzen,"[2] was finished in June 1798. Here Goethe leads his "Geliebte," Christiane, through the garden and describes in charming and graceful imagery the laws which he had earlier set forth in scientific terms in the *Versuch, die Metamorphose der Pflanzen zu erklären* (1790). Central to these studies is the concept of the leaf as the basic form of the ideal plant, and all other organs—calyx, corolla, stamens etc. as but metamorphoses of this form. One must therefore study the plant in its "becoming" ("werdend"), for it is in one sense a time-organism: "Werdend betrachte sie nun, wie nach und nach sich die Pflanze,/ Stufenweise geführt, bildet zu Blüten und Frucht" (9–10). The leaf-form is a living being—Goethe calls it "der wahre Proteus"[3]—which can now hide, now reveal itself in all the organs of the plant. Goethe dips into the phenomena of the vegetative world with his powerful cognitive forces and follows this Protean being in its endless transformations.

Faust, too, seeks to grasp Nature in its active essence. In contemplation of the "sign of the macrocosm" he exclaims: "Ich schau' in diesen reinen Zügen/ Die wirkende Natur vor meiner Seele liegen" (440–41). It is that hidden spiritual life, the "Wirkenskraft und Samen" (384) which Faust longs to grasp and which Goethe sought to describe in part in his botanical writings.

In the poem "Die Metamorphose der Pflanzen" Goethe draws a striking comparison between the multitude of plant forms and a chorus:

[1] "Die Urpflanze wird das wunderlichste Geschöpf von der Welt, um welches mich die Natur selbst beneiden soll. Mit diesem Modell und dem Schlüssel dazu kann man alsdann noch Pflanzen ins Unendliche erfinden, die konsequent sein müssen, das heißt, die, wenn sie auch nicht existieren, doch existieren könnten und nicht etwa malerische oder dichterische Schatten und Scheine sind, sondern eine innere Wahrheit und Notwendigkeit haben. Dasselbe Gesetz wird sich auf alles übrige Lebendige anwenden lassen." *Italienische Reise*, Neapel, 17 May 1787, HA XI, 324.

[2] HA I, 199–201.

[3] *Italienische Reise*, 17 May 1787, HA XI, 375.

Viele Namen hörest du an, und immer verdränget
Mit barbarischem Klang einer den andern im Ohr.
Alle Gestalten sind ähnlich, und keine gleichet der andern;
Und so deutet das Chor auf ein geheimes Gesetz,
Auf ein heiliges Rätsel . . .

(3–7)

The welter of the plants' unfamiliar names produces merely a cacophony in the beloved's ear. It is different with the plethora of forms, however, for the eye discerns a basic similarity underlying their multiplicity. Therefore the eye which contemplates the myriad forms actively, tracing their inner relatedness, experiences the metamorphoses musically; the visual perceptions are reborn as tone, and the garden sounds inwardly as a chorus which sings of sacred mysteries. The leaves, stalks, blossoms, seeds—the aspect which the plants present the eye in *space*—if perceived in its Protean flux as "wirkende Natur," in *time*, reveals the music of an invisible spirit-chorus. The thought is as bold as it is beautiful. And it casts light on that passage at the end of Part II, Act III of *Faust* in which the chorus of Trojan women who have formed the retinue of Helen choose, after her death, not to return to Hades but rather to translate themselves into elemental spirits of nature:

Zurückgegeben sind wir dem Tageslicht,
Zwar Personen nicht mehr,
Das fühlen, das wissen wir,
Aber zum Hades kehren wir nimmer.
Ewig lebendige Natur
Macht auf uns Geister,
Wir auf sie vollgültigen Anspruch.

(9985–91)

The comparison of these two passages points to the underlying unity of Goethe's world outlook. In the first instance Goethe the morphologist describes the plant metamorphoses step by step and points to a sacred chorus of life which resounds to him from within, and in the second Goethe the poet presents us the reverse process in strangely haunting imagery: the chanting chorus, visible on the stage, gradually slips into the elements of nature which it will help to animate from within. "Die Metamorphose der Pflanzen" is peculiarly well suited to illustrate this unity of outlook, for it expresses Goethean scientific concepts in an artistic form. Moreover, if we take the above discussion as a point of departure, several passages in *Faust II* show striking similarities—in some instances even down to details of Goethe's use of vowels and consonants—with the morphological mode of Goethe the botanist.

For Goethe, nature and art are inwardly related; the artist creates according to the same laws which inform nature. Goethe writes of the Greek artists: "Ich habe die Vermutung daß sie nach eben den Gesetzen verfuhren, nach welchen die

Natur verfährt und denen ich auf der Spur bin."[4] Art, then, is that conscious extension of nature which rests on natural laws but is brought to birth by the activity of the human being. The artist, like Faust, must penetrate to the hidden realm of the Mothers, the womb of creative cosmic laws and life forces, where all is activity: ". . . Gestaltung, Umgestaltung,/ Des ewigen Sinnes ewige Unterhaltung" (6287–88). This is the domain, beyond space and time ("Um sie kein Ort, noch weniger eine Zeit" 6214) in which reside the spiritual archetypes of the phenomenal world ("Des Lebens Bilder, regsam, ohne Leben" 6430). They come into being in the world in two ways: "Die einen faßt des Lebens holder Lauf,/ Die andern sucht der kühne Magier auf" (6435–36). The manuscript provides an alternate reading of the second line: "Die andern sucht getrost der Dichter auf."[5] The intention is clear: the spiritual forms flow into the world on the one hand as the kingdoms of nature and on the other as art. But the difference lies in the fact that works of art come about only when man exercises his naturally-given creative faculties and draws forth from the spirit the inspirations which he can then embody in his artistic creations. These creations are thus a higher nature within nature, a "second nature": ". . . die Kunst wird mir wie eine zweite Natur, die gleich der Minerva aus dem Haupte Jupiters, so aus dem Haupte der größten Menschen geboren worden."[6] The discovery of the artistic creations of antiquity was of overwhelming significance for Goethe for the reason that in them he found an embodiment and further revelation of those very laws which occupied his attention as a natural scientist: "Diese hohen Kunstwerke sind zugleich als die höchsten Naturwerke von Menschen nach wahren und natürlichen Gesetzen hervorgebracht worden. Alles Willkürliche, Eingebildete fällt zusammen, da ist Notwendigkeit, da ist Gott."[7]

In Italy Goethe felt himself reborn. The rebirth encompassed the two sides of his strivings, the scientific and the artistic: the scientific in his discovery, after years of active investigation in the plant kingdom, of the archetypal plant ("Urpflanze"), and the artistic in his encounter with classical art, particularly sculpture. These two sides of Goethe's being are intimately related. The whole thrust of his study of plant metamorphosis is in an intimate sense sculptural. His discoveries in both realms fill him with a religious awe, so that eleven years later, in "Die Metamorphose der Pflanzen," he tells us that the "chorus" of the plants speaks of laws mysterious and sacred (". . . ein geheimes Gesetz,/ . . . ein heiliges Rätsel . . ."). And while still in Rome he exclaims in the face of classical art: "da ist Notwendigkeit, da ist Gott."

Helen, the object of Faust's passionate searchings in Part II, is the grand embodiment of these spiritual laws of nature and art in their highest perfection. In

[4] *Italienische Reise*, Rome, 28 January 1787, HA XI, 167–68.

[5] HA III, 545.

[6] *Italienische Reise*, Rome, 11 August 1787, HA XI, 383–84.

[7] *Italienische Reise*, 6 September 1787, HA XI, 395.

her Faust has his productive encounter with the archetype of beauty. It is just because the mature Goethe came to understand the role played by the laws of nature in the genesis of art that he chose to abandon his original plan to portray Faust's plea for Helen's release before the throne of Persephone and replace it with the tremendous myth of becoming which constitutes a large part of Act II, the "klassische Walpurgisnacht."[8] Goethe plunges into the archaic depths of the mythological past and conjures forth the myriad beings which embody imaginatively the hidden forces of nature and of the human soul. From the ancient, monolithic sphinxes at the beginning of the "klassische Walpurgisnacht" to the graceful train of Grecian Nereids and Dorids in the water-festival at the end, Goethe presents a gradual process of development and refinement which culminates in Helen. When Helen appears on the stage in Act III she is surrounded by the chorus of captive Trojan women who serve as her retinue. They too are beings which contribute to and support her appearance, yet they belong in reality to that realm of "nature spirits" or elemental spirits who, for instance, speak to Goethe as a chorus in the plant world but who have no soul of their own, no "personality" ("Zwar Personen nicht mehr . . ." 9986). Thus the words of their leader, Panthalis, when after Helen's death they balk at returning to Hades: "Wer keinen Namen sich erwarb noch Edles will,/ Gehört den Elementen an; so fahret hin!" (9981–82).

The chorus divides into four groups which may be thought of as representing the four elements: spirits of earth, air, water and fire.[9] The first group become tree spirits, the second mountain spirits and echoes, the third spirits of water and the fourth fiery spirits of the vine. All four groups speak in richly onomatopoetic language. We shall confine ourselves here to an examination of two short passages which illustrate Goethe's ability to portray the delicate metamorphosis of these figures into the elements of nature through the use of language itself.

The first is a passage spoken by the group who will become tree-spirits:

> Wir in dieser tausend Äste Flüsterzittern, Säuselschweben
> Reizen tändelnd, locken leise wurzelauf des Lebens Quellen
> Nach den Zweigen; bald mit Blättern, bald mit Blüten überschwenglich
> Zieren wir die Flatterhaare frei zu luftigem Gedeihn.
>
> (9992–95)

The sense of limitless vegetation in the image "tausend Äste" and the profusion of dental fricatives in the compounds "Flüsterzittern, Säuselschweben" lift the reader out of the grip of gravity and allow him to follow with his musical sense the liquid *l*-sounds which carry the sap on its rise from root through stem to branch: ". . . *l*ocken *l*eise wurze*l*auf des *L*ebens Que*ll*en/ Nach den Zweigen . . ." In the branches the tree spirits bring about the unfolding of leaves and blossoms

[8] Cf. Wilhelm Emrich, *Die Symbolik von Faust II* (Frankfurt a. M., 1964), pp. 242–47.

[9] So, for instance, Trendelenburg. Adolf Trendelenburg, *Zu Goethes Faust* (Berlin and Leipzig, 1919), pp. 128 ff.

as delicate adornment of the whole ("Zieren wir die Flatterhaare . . ."). The subsequent description of the falling fruit completes the image of the vegetative cycle—an artistic miniature "Urpflanze."

Let us now examine closely the words "bald mit Blättern, bald mit Blüten . . ." The German orthography deceives the eye, for the *d* of "bald" is in reality pronounced as a voiceless stop: [balt]. This is of considerable interest here, for we note that with respect to their consonant skeleton both "bald" and "Blättern" contain [b] and [t], as do the corresponding words "bald . . . Blüten." This stark parallelism in the consonants provides the hard fibre which supports the more delicate and living quality of the liquid *l* and nasal *n*. The *l*, in particular, is strangely mercurial and conveys the sense of the flow of sap described in the foregoing line. And in keeping with this, its labile nature, it refuses to remain where it is but slips from its place by the [t] back to the [b]: [b lt . . . bl t].

Equally intriguing is the behavior of the vowels which inhabit these words. The initial vowel of each pair is the [a] of the word "bald." In the first pair this vowel is slightly raised by *umlaut* to *ä;* in phonetic symbols [a] → [ɛ]. But in the second pair the [a] is not merely lightened—it abandons its original quality entirely and soars to the flutelike tone *ü* [y]. Yet can it do otherwise? After all, the Protean metamorphosis from leaf to blossom is the crowning example of enhancement, of heightening or "Steigerung" in Goethe's botany. Thus the plant's life-cycle, which we saw portrayed in the imagery of this passage, is reflected in the use of sounds, from the hard, 'earthlike' consonants through the 'saplike' flow of the *l* to the metamorphosis into leaves and finally, carried by the vowels, into the even more refined blossoms.

The phenomenon is subtler yet. We spoke of the consonants as earthlike. They form the firm structure which supports the liquids and vowels just as the plant's roots, themselves mineralized and earthbound, provide the solid basis which bears the burden of life. Phonetics itself speaks of the *l* as a "liquid." In the flow of the *l* from one side to the other within these words the watery element comes to expression. In the articulation of the vowels, however, the organs of speech allow for an uninterrupted flow of the breathstream. Through the vowels the element of air enters the body provided by the consonants and liquids. And in the metamorphosis of the vowels from [a] to [ɛ] and the powerful rise from [a] to [y] one senses a flaming-up of tonal color, a fiery element which is in perfect harmony with the "Steigerung" from the green leaf to the blossom enhanced by color. The flower opens to the sun and, in the terminology of the alchemists, begins a "sulphuric," burning process as it releases its pollen and fragrance into the atmosphere. Earth, water, air, fire—these are the four elements of nature into which the four parts of this Greek chorus enter. All four participate in the life-cycle of the plant and all four weave through the sound pattern of the words "bald mit Blättern, bald mit Blüten," building up out of the material of language a very exact tonal organism which in but four words precisely embodies the mysterious metamorphosis of this part of the spirit chorus into the world of plant life. Through patient observation Goethe the scientist learned to follow the transformations of Proteus, the leaf. Through his alert sense for language Goethe the artist was able to give this Proteus another medium in which to play his tricks.

A second group of the Greek chorus transforms itself into airy mountain spirits and echoes:

> Wir, an dieser Felsenwände weithinleuchtend glattem Spiegel
> Schmiegen wir, in sanften Wellen uns bewegend, schmeichelnd an,
> Horchen, lauschen jedem Laute, Vogelsängen, Röhrigflöten,
> Sei es Pans furchtbarer Stimme: Antwort ist sogleich bereit;
> Säuselt's, säuseln wir erwidernd, donnert's, rollen unsre Donner
> In erschütterndem Verdoppeln, dreifach, zehnfach hintennach.
> (9999–10004)

Once again we find a profusion of strikingly onomatopoetic effects as the chorus dissolves into spirits of the air who move in waves along the smooth rock cliffs and create the echoes for every sound of nature from the rustle of reeds to the boom of thunder. Let us look closely at the last two lines. The first of these is constructed in two halves with parallel content: the rustling reeds and the spirit echo, the roar of thunder and the spirit echo. The delicate *s*-sounds of "Säuselt's, säuseln . . . ," however, contrast vividly with the weighty *d* and *n* of "donnert's . . . Donner," whereby the contrasting intensity of the acoustical impressions breaks through the seeming parallelism of the line. The impression conveyed by "säuseln" is scarcely audible, while the thunder is likened to "Pans furchtbarer Stimme." Moreover, it is clear that in order to produce an echo off these cliffs the sighing rushes must be quite close at hand. As a result, the sound has but a short distance to go and the spirits produce the echo immediately: "Säuselt's, säuseln . . ." The thunder, however, may occur far in the distance, in which case it takes some time for the sound to traverse the intervening space and strike the rock walls. As a result the spirit echo is longer in coming, and the words "donnert's" and "Donner" are separated by two intervening words: ". . . donnert's, rollen unsre Donner." Goethe was a very exact observer of natural phenomena and his poetic use of language is correspondingly exact.

The final line picks up the rolling echo of thunder and multiplies it over and over as the spirit beings that inhabit the cliffs in various parts of the forest pass the echo on to each other until it grows faint and dies: "in erschütterndem Verdoppeln, dreifach, zehnfach hintennach." Goethe has painted the gradual dying-away of the echo very precisely in sound: "dreifach, zehnfach hintennach." The metrical foot is trochaic, yet the final unstressed syllable is lacking, whereby the internal rhyme -ach is carried twice by an unaccented, once by an accented syllable: "dreifach, zehnfach hintennach." This internal rhyme is itself an echo which is lengthened in the final stressed position and fades into the distance. The vowels of the three initial stressed syllables form the following sequence: *ei e i*. The powerful diphthong *ei*([ai]) of "dreifach" thus dissolves into its component parts in the two following words, the [a] heightened to the [e] of "zehnfach" and the delicate [ɪ] of "hintennach." But most astonishing of all is the metamorphosis of the initial consonants. The sequence begins with the vibrant voiced stop [d] of "dreifach." The voiceless alveolar [ts] of "zehnfach" is a metamorphosis of the voiced alveolar [d]. The voice has been lost and a rush of air has been introduced: a voiceless plosive. Finally, in "hintennach," all traces of weight and form have disappeared and we hear only a rush of air, a delicate breath: [h], as the last remnants of the echo pass away. Once again, as in the case of the tree spirits, Goethe combines a precise awareness of natural phenomena with a poetic vision which—literally—spiritualizes them. And he weaves a linguistic fabric in tones which in an exact and thoroughly alive way embodies the extraordinary events seen by his inner eye and heard by his inner ear.

With the close of this scene the women of the Greek chorus have all found their way into the elemental life of nature as spirits of the trees, the air, the water and the warmth which ripens the fruit of the vine. This is in a sense a process of death; the women no longer exist in human form. They have "died into" nature and exist henceforth as "spiritualized nature."

The theme of death and rebirth is woven into *Faust* on many levels. Faust himself goes through a process of "stirb und werde" on several occasions: the Easter night, "Anmutige Gegend," the descent to the Mothers, and the descent into the underworld in the company of the seeress Manto. Finally, in the fifth Act of Part II, he must confront the fact of his death on earth. In the opening three scenes of Act V daylight recedes and night gradually envelops Faust's world—a symbol of the approaching end of his physical existence. In "Mitternacht" he is blinded and in "Großer Vorhof des Palasts" death overcomes him. In the final scene "Bergschluchten" we witness his reawakening in the spiritual world. The transition scene between his death and reanimation is "Grablegung," in which the struggle for Faust's eternal being between the forces of heaven and hell culminates in the triumph of the angels: "*Sie erheben sich, Faustens Unsterbliches entführend*" (SD 11825). The angels drive off the infernal beings by strewing roses, traditional symbols of Christian love. The forces of love which they embody flow from the hands of holy penitent women:

> Jene Rosen aus den Händen
> Liebend-heiliger Büßerinnen
> Halfen uns den Sieg gewinnen,
> Uns das hohe Werk vollenden,
> Diesen Seelenschatz erbeuten.
> (11942–46)

The "penitent women" may be thought of as those who appear at the end of the scene as Magna peccatrix (Luke 7:36–50), Mulier Samaritana (John 4:7–30), Maria Aegyptiaca (*Acta Sanctorum*) and possibly also Gretchen, who appears as Una Poenitentium (SD 12069) in the service of the Virgin in Glory.

The roses are imbued with Christian love, yet they are also, after all, plants. In the context of our foregoing discussion, then, they may be termed "spiritualized nature." This comes clearly to expression in the fact that as they strew them the angels *address* them, in the second person plural familiar, as living beings who have a task to perform:

> Rosen, ihr blendenden,
> Balsam versendenden!
> Flatternde, schwebende,
> Heimlich belebende,
> Zweigleinbeflügelte,
> Knospenentsiegelte,
> Eilet zu blühn.
>
> Frühling entsprieße,
> Purpur und Grün!
> Tragt Paradiese
> Dem Ruhenden hin.
> (11699–709)

The roses are portrayed as unfolding and rushing into bloom. They are alive and are described in keeping with Goethe's own admonition in "Die Metamorphose der Pflanzen": "Werdend betrachte sie nun . . ." (l. 9). Through the forces of love which they now bear, the roses have the hidden power to heal ("Heimlich belebende"), a quality which gives these lines an extraordinary depth. They can inspire a feeling of reverence and thus through this spiritualized Christian context call forth in the reader a greatly deepened sense of that awe which, in his poem, Goethe expresses in contemplating the wonder of the blossom:

> Immer staunst du aufs neue, sobald sich am Stengel die Blume
> Über dem schlanken Gerüst wechselnder Blätter bewegt.
> (47–48)

Again let us examine the language. The first seven lines spoken by the angels are so constructed that the form of the verb gives exact expression to the content. The first four lines describe the qualities of the roses in a succession of five present participles: ". . . blendenden . . . versendenden . . . Flatternde, schwebende . . . belebende." The mood of these lines is gently lilting and airy and is carried by the dactylic foot with its one stressed and two unstressed syllables (— ⌣ ⌣). In the fifth and sixth lines, however, the present participle yields to the past participle, the liquid participial and adjective ending *-ende* to the harsher *-elte:* "Zweigleinbeflügelte,/ Knospenentsiegelte." These lines introduce the images of the stem and the bud. Stem and bud contrast with leaves and blossoms in that the stem is hard and the bud tightly formed. Both in a sense appear "rounded out," finished. And this is exactly the inner expressive potential of the *past* participle. It renders the sense of an activity which has been "rounded out," completed, and it thus happily contains the dry, voiceless [t] in contrast to the softer [d] of the present participle. We also notice that, curiously enough, these two lines are scarcely "lines" at all, for each is but one word. The sense of completeness is thus once again embodied formally, this time in the extreme conciseness of the single word which has here replaced the phrase.

We must not be fooled by appearances, however. The little stems are indeed "finished." But the buds, though tightly closed and hard, are not. Thus while the sixth line introduces the image of the bud, it also metamorphoses it into that of the rose which is "unsealed" and is poised on the threshold, ready to reveal itself in flower: "Knospenentsiegelte."

The plant has in a sense "died" into the bud, and all is anticipation. Then follows the miracle of the blossom, called forth by the angels' words: "Eilet zu blühn." The "crown" of the plant's being, the noblest metamorphosis, the "höchste Gestalt"[10] may now unfold in response to the angels' call. In keeping with this image of a sudden burst into bloom the verb itself goes through a powerful metamorphosis—from the permanence of the past participle into the dynamic call of the imperative: "Eilet . . ."[11] The three words "Eilet zu blühn" also reveal an extraordinary sound quality. The two past participles end, as we have seen, in the sounds *-elte*. The pure participial ending, without the appended adjective ending *e* is simply the *t*. This letter expresses very vividly the sense of completion rendered grammatically by the past participle. An action is finished and comes to rest in what is (in this case most appropriately) labeled a voiceless *stop*. The appended *e* modifies this sense of finality and seems to reach out for something more. The word "Eilet," purely from the standpoint of its component sounds, is a curious transformation of the preceding ending *-elte*. The initial *e* of that ending has been strengthened by the addition of the letter *i* and appears as a diphthong: *ei*, while the final *e* has slipped back between the *l* and the *t*. The two sound structures thus appear, backed up against one another in the poem, as "Knospenentsieg*elte,*/ *Eilet.*" But let us now look at what follows. In the past participle the action of the verb comes gradually to rest via vowel, liquid, voiceless stop in the sounds *-elte*, and a light suggestion of new life appears in the ending *e*. In the imperative the simple *e* is heightened to *ei* and the "hint of life" of the final *e* slips back into a position *before* the final [t]. Here the sound pattern comes *fully* to rest in the [t] which must now bear the burden of the powerful diphthong and the extra vowel in a sense "pressing" on it from behind; for after all, the word's meaning calls up the tendency to rush forward, whereas the

[10] "Die Metamorphose der Pflanzen," l. 44, HA I, 200.

[11] The reading of "Eilet" as an imperative form (cf. also "Tragt," l. 11708) is textually justified by line 11711 ("So haltet stand und laßt sie streuen."), which line is not followed by an exclamation point, yet is unambiguously imperative. The punctuation of these lines is the same in the Weimarer Ausgabe.

[t] forms a barrier to this motion. The growth force suggested by the imagery is too powerful, however, and in the initial consonant of the following word ("zu") the breath stream splits open the [t] and rushes forth with elemental power in the sound [s]. Thus the German *z* may be rendered phonetically as [ts]. The sense of hardness here finally yields to the power of new life and the sounds rush ahead into the powerful vowel *u* and its soaring metamorphosis through *umlaut*, *ü:* "Eilet zu blühn." In the following four lines the roses, greatly heightened as image by the specific mention of their colors, rain forth in a burst of paradisiacal life as the *u* and *ü*, further heightened to *ie* and *i*, tone forth as the principal vowels of the accented syllables in this hymn of renewal:

> Fr*ü*hling entspr*ie*ße,
> P*u*rpur und Gr*ü*n!
> Tragt Parad*ie*se
> Dem R*u*henden h*i*n.

Once again then, in this entire passage, we find that Goethe has woven a little "metamorphosis of the plants" in the medium of poetic diction. The content, the imagery come to precise expression through the threefold metamorphosis of the verb and through sounds which in the most intimate way embody the poet's vision. Once again the "Protean" life of the plant reveals itself to us both visually and acoustically. And once again the plant forms are envisioned as inwardly alive. The angels address them as beings. Can we help but recall the delicate weaving of sounds in the passage in Act III, as the women of the chorus, transformed into spirits of nature, slipped into the inner life of the plants? The same life is there: ". . . locken leise wurzelauf des Lebens Quellen . . ./ . . . bald mit Blättern, bald mit Blüten . . ."

In both instances we have before us a "spiritualized nature." Those spirits which entered the plant kingdom at the end of Act III now reappear, to speak out of the very inner nature of the plant, in Act V. The setting is different: there the ancient, mythological world of Greece, here the later world of imagery associated with a Christian heaven. The chorus of spirits, then, has itself gone through a striking metamorphosis, "dying into" nature in the pre-Christian context and being "reborn" in the Christian context.

This extraordinary vision of the transformation of the nature spirits appears once again, expanded and deepened, in the final scene "Bergschluchten." The scene opens on a setting of forests, rocks and desert as the abode of holy Anchorites. The first words are spoken by a chorus of these monks and call forth an echo from off the rocky cliffs:

> Chor und Echo. Waldung, sie schwankt heran,
> Felsen, sie lasten dran,
> Wurzeln, sie klammern an,
> Stamm dicht an Stamm hinan.
> (11844–47)

The scene is inwardly alive. The forest seems to sway, the cliffs to weigh heavily, the roots to grasp for a hold among trees and rocks. Here the "Chor und Echo" refer externally to the Anchorites. Yet as one reads on through the words spoken by the three holy fathers, up to the appearance of the Blessed Boys, one realizes that the images of nature to which this chorus and echo refer are at once outer and inner. "Chor und Echo" continue:

Woge nach Woge spritzt,
Höhle, die tiefste, schützt.
Löwen, sie schleichen stumm-
freundlich um uns herum,
Ehren geweihten Ort,
Heiligen Liebeshort.

The words of the Pater ecstaticus refer entirely to an inner experience:

Pater ecstaticus, *auf und ab schwebend.*
Ewiger Wonnebrand,
Glühendes Liebeband,
Siedender Schmerz der Brust,
Schäumende Gotteslust.
Pfeile, durchdringet mich,
Lanzen, bezwinget mich,
Keulen, zerschmettert mich,
Blitze, durchwettert mich!
Daß ja das Nichtige
Alles verflüchtige,
Glänze der Dauerstern,
Ewiger Liebe Kern.

Pater profundus, *tiefe Region.*
Wie Felsenabgrund mir zu Füßen
Auf tiefem Abgrund lastend ruht,
Wie tausend Bäche strahlend fließen
Zum grausen Sturz des Schaums der Flut,
Wie strack mit eignem kräftigen Triebe
Der Stamm sich in die Lüfte trägt:
So ist es die allmächtige Liebe,
Die alles bildet, alles hegt.

Ist um mich her ein wildes Brausen,
Als wogte Wald und Felsengrund,
Und doch stürzt, liebevoll im Sausen,
Die Wasserfülle sich zum Schlund,
Berufen, gleich das Tal zu wässern;
Der Blitz, der flammend niederschlug,
Die Atmosphäre zu verbessern,
Die Gift und Dunst im Busen trug—

Sind Liebesboten, sie verkünden,
Was ewig schaffend uns umwallt.
Mein Innres mög' es auch entzünden,
Wo sich der Geist, verworren, kalt,
Verquält in stumpfer Sinne Schranken,
Scharfangeschloßnem Kettenschmerz.
O Gott! beschwichtige die Gedanken,
Erleuchte mein bedürftig Herz!

Pater Seraphicus, *mittlere Region.*
Welch ein Morgenwölkchen schwebet
Durch der Tannen schwankend Haar!
Ahn' ich, was im Innern lebet?
Es ist junge Geisterschar.

(11848–93)

In *Goethe und Plotin* Franz Koch describes very accurately the delicately transfigured world of nature as it appears in the above lines: "Anachoreten in der Kulisse repräsentativer Naturelemente als einer 'Art von idealem Montserrat' verkörpern im Unisono aller Naturstimmen von 'Chor und Echo' das Ineinander von Geist und Natur: spiritualisierte Materie, die unterste Stufe des Aufstieges der Seele."[12] "Spiritualisierte Materie" is exactly the right term. It is what we have referred to in this study as "spiritualized nature." And when Koch speaks of the "Unisono aller Naturstimmen von 'Chor und Echo' " he makes a subtle and extremely important point. The chorus and echo are spoken outwardly by the Anchorites. Yet all is here also inward, and the voices of nature, the voices of the elemental spirits in forest ("Waldung, sie schwankt heran"), rocks ("Felsen, sie lasten dran") and water ("Woge nach Woge spritzt") themselves speak through the chorus and through the echo. And in the words of the pater profundus the elemental spirits of light and warmth also appear in the outward/inward landscape through the flash of lightning ("Der Blitz, der flammend niederschlug" 11879). Indeed, in the course of five lines the pater profundus speaks of all four abodes of the elemental spirits who, abandoning their forms as the Greek chorus, slipped into nature at the end of Act III—the plants (forest), rocks, water and warmth/light—there the light and warmth playing through the vineyard, here the lightning:

Als wogte *Wald* und *Felsen*grund,
Und doch stürzt, liebevoll im Sausen
Die *Wasser*fülle sich zum Schlund,
Berufen, gleich das Tal zu wässern;
Der *Blitz*, der flammend niederschlug,
(11875–79. Italics mine)

[12] Franz Koch, *Goethe und Plotin* (Leipzig, 1925), p. 220.

There is one basic difference, however, between the two scenes. The four groups of elemental spirits are now the bearers of the creative love, in the Christian sense, which is the object of the contemplation of the Anchorite monks:

> Sind Liebesboten, sie verkünden,
> Was ewig schaffend uns umwallt.
> Mein Innres mög' es auch entzünden,
> Wo sich der Geist, verworren, kalt,
> Verquält in stumpfer Sinne Schranken,
> Scharfangeschloßnem Kettenschmerz.
> O Gott! beschwichtige die Gedanken,
> Erleuchte mein bedürftig Herz!
> (11882–89)

The roses, too, strewn by the angels, are bearers of the forces of Christian love, of which the angels could also have said ". . . sie verkünden,/ Was ewig schaffend uns umwallt." For in these final scenes the atmosphere is completely permeated by that selfless love which reveals itself in the ascending hierarchy of beings and finds its most exalted expression in the mater gloriosa and the chorus mysticus. The world of the elemental spirits of nature is here inwardly illuminated by the higher spirituality of this love. In the words of the pater profundus: "So ist es die allmächtige Liebe,/ Die alles bildet, alles hegt" (11872–73).

In volume I of *Geisteswissenschaftliche Erläuterungen zu Goethes Faust* Rudolf Steiner points to precisely this "stirb und werde" of the Greek chorus which, as we have seen, "dies into" nature and reappears as "Liebesboten" in this Goethean-Christian heaven: "Die heidnischen Elementargeister verschwinden in die Natur hinein, und sie treten da, wo der Christus-Impuls sich mit der Erde lebendig verbunden hat, wiederum hervor."[13]

His intense investigation of the metamorphosis of plant forms enabled Goethe to imbue the "spiritualized nature" in *Faust* with a quality of now fragile, now intensely vibrant life. This expresses itself not only in the nature imagery and the subtleties of its embodiment in sound, but also in the extraordinary metamorphosis of the chorus itself. A close examination of the intricacies of these levels of metamorphosis and their interrelatedness renders the passages in Act III, in "Grablegung" and in "Bergschluchten" more accessible, more alive. In "Bergschluchten" it is this same "vegetative" principle of metamorphosis which structures the entire scene. Goethe wished to portray the unfolding of Faust's entelechy in the spiritual world—a task which required that the poet find a fitting medium in which to embody very etherial processes. The medium he chose was singularly appropriate: ever higher levels of *consciousness*. The lowest of these is the "spiritualisierte Materie" (Koch) of the opening passages and the highest the

[13] Rudolf Steiner, *Geisteswissenschaftliche Erläuterungen zu Goethes Faust* (Dornach, 1967), vol. I, *Faust, der strebende Mensch*, p. 164. This is the first of two volumes containing twenty-seven lectures on *Faust*.

inexpressible mysteries of divine love as celebrated by the chorus mysticus:

Das Unbeschreibliche,
Hier ist's getan;
Das Ewig-Weibliche
Zieht uns hinan.

(12108–11)

Between these two levels Faust's immortal self is passed from one being or group of beings to another in a metamorphosing ascent of ever more refined levels of consciousness. In this way the "spiritualisierte Materie" or "spiritualized nature" of the lowest level yields to ever higher forms of what Steiner terms a "spirituelle Szenerie":

> So tritt uns lebendig entgegen—und auf die Vorstellung dieses Lebendigen kommt es an—, daß Goethe Faustens Seele in die geistige Welt hinaufgeleitet, daß er aber dazu eine spirituelle Szenerie braucht. Wir können vermuten, wie die Natur zuerst in Bewegung gerät, wie sich das elementarische Leben aus der Natur heraus erhebt, wie dann die Naturwesen übergehen in die Bewußtseine, die immer höhere sind, mit der Seele übergehen in das Umfangen von geistigen Wesenheiten, wie es die seligen Knaben sind, und wie es dann sein können die Seelen der Büßerinnen und auch die Seele des Faust selber. In der ganzen spirituellen Szenerie steckt das darinnen. Und dann fortwährend wunderbare Steigerungen bis zum Schlusse hin, wo der Chorus mysticus das Weltgeheimnis ausspricht, wo wir sehen, wie unser geistiges Auge heraufgehoben wird in eine geistige Welt. Wir machen den Aufstieg mit von dem Stehen in der Natur und auf dem festen Boden des physischen Planes zu den geistigen Welten, in welche die Seele des Faust aufgenommen wird.[14]

The principle of metamorphosis is so basic to Goethe's thinking that it manifests itself in *Faust* on many levels.[15] Of particular interest to us here is the way in which the metamorphosis of the chorus and nature spirits, particularly the plant spirits, forms the foundation for the higher metamorphoses of the human spirit. The transformations and heightening which Goethe observes in the plant kingdom provide him with an archetypal form for the ascent of Faust's soul into the higher regions of the spiritual world. We therefore also find in "Bergschluchten" specific lines which describe the unfolding of Faust's entelechy. The "selige Knaben" liken the process to the emergence of the butterfly from the cocoon:

Freudig empfangen wir
Diesen im Puppenstand;
Also erlangen wir

[14] *Ibid.*, p. 161.

[15] A particularly helpful sketch of the manner in which Goethe's morphological principles of "Systole," "Diastole," and "Steigerung" may be seen to underlie the structure of *Faust* is presented by Humphry Trevelyan in "The Significance of Goethe's Science," *The Goethe Year*, Part 5 (London, 1949), pp. 26–32.

Englisches Unterpfand.
Löset die Flocken los,
Die ihn umgeben!
Schon ist er schön und groß
Von heiligem Leben.
(11981–88)

and the same "selige Knaben":

Er überwächst uns schon
An mächtigen Gliedern,
(12076–77)

Faust's destiny is spiritually united with that of Gretchen, who intercedes for him and leads him onward. She too speaks in metaphor of discarding the old sheath and emerging in "etherial raiment"; this image is itself a spiritualized metamorphosis of the cocoon and butterfly:

Sieh, wie er jedem Erdenbande
Der alten Hülle sich entrafft
Und aus ätherischem Gewande
Hervortritt erste Jugendkraft.
Vergönne mir, ihn zu belehren,
Noch blendet ihn der neue Tag.
(12088–93)

The further destinies of Gretchen and Faust are now closely entwined. At the highest level in the *Faust* poem the theme of metamorphosis thus expands from that of man alone to that of man and woman. The mater gloriosa:

Komm! hebe dich zu höhern Sphären!
Wenn er dich ahnet, folgt er nach.
(12094–95)

It is a long way from Goethe's botanical studies, from the precise descriptions of the transformations of "Proteus" upwards through seed, stem, leaf, bud, flower to the tremendous expansion of this image to embrace the developing human spirit, its encounter and union with another and the gradually ascending path which leads them to a higher world—a very long way.

Or is it?

Let us return to the poem "Die Metamorphose der Pflanzen," from which we took the starting-point for our discussion. The last lines of the poem systematically expand the concept of metamorphosis. From the transformations of the plant and the related caterpillar and butterfly the vision swells to a hymn on the growing, blossoming and fruition of human friendship and love:

Jede Pflanze verkündet dir nun die ew'gen Gesetze,
  Jede Blume, sie spricht lauter und lauter mit dir.
Aber entzifferst du hier der Göttin heilige Lettern,
  Überall siehst du sie dann, auch in verändertem Zug:
Kriechend zaudre die Raupe, der Schmetterling eile geschäftig,
  Bildsam ändre der Mensch selbst die bestimmte Gestalt.
O, gedenke denn auch, wie aus dem Keim der Bekanntschaft
  Nach und nach in uns holde Gewohnheit entsproß,
Freundschaft sich mit Macht aus unserm Innern enthüllte,
  Und wie Amor zuletzt Blüten und Früchte gezeugt.
Denke, wie mannigfach bald die, bald jene Gestalten,
  Still entfaltend, Natur unsern Gefühlen geliehn!
Freue dich auch des heutigen Tags! Die heilige Liebe
  Strebt zu der höchsten Frucht gleicher Gesinnungen auf,
Gleicher Ansicht der Dinge, damit in harmonischem Anschaun
  Sich verbinde das Paar, finde die höhere Welt.

(ll. 65–80)

Goethe the scientist, Goethe the poet: the two are one in Goethe the thinker. The concept formation as well as the vision are consistent throughout, as this study has sought to demonstrate in terms of but one limited aspect of *Faust*. Just as the plant seed falls into the earth and dies "as seed" while the new plant emerges, unfurls its leaves and opens its bloom to the sun, so also does Faust die in the dark night of the physical world, releasing his immortal self to unfold new organs of spiritual life and blossom into a higher world of effulgent light, accompanied by the soul most capable of helping him.

Goethe discovered the "Urpflanze" in Italy in 1787. On the sixteenth of April he went to the public park in Palermo with the intention of developing his "Nausikaa" into an expanded dramatic work. The following day he again went to the garden to spend the hours in the world that is Homer. But the profusion of plant life captivated his attention and he immersed himself in the contemplation which led to the botanical discovery: "Gestört war mein guter poetischer Vorsatz, der Garten des Alcinous war verschwunden, ein Weltgarten hatte sich aufgetan."[16] Approximately thirteen years later, in 1800, the "Prolog im Himmel" was written, in which the image of the plant as God's metaphor for the being of man was inserted into the slowly evolving manuscript of *Faust*. In the Prologue the Lord expresses unshakable confidence in man's potential to find the right way despite—and in a deeper sense because of—his tendency to err. As a cosmic Gardener, a divine Morphologist, God speaks gentle words of trust in the slow forces of growth—forces against which he knows even Mephisto cannot prevail:

[16] *Italienische Reise*, HA XI, 267. Cf. also the "Bericht" of July 1787, pp. 374–75.

> Wenn er mir jetzt auch nur verworren dient,
> So werd' ich ihn bald in die Klarheit führen.
> Weiß doch der Gärtner, wenn das Bäumchen grünt,
> Daß Blüt' und Frucht die künft'gen Jahre zieren.
> (308–11)

The metaphor gradually grew and matured in Goethe's poetic imagination until thirty years later, in the writing of the poem's final scene "Bergschluchten," it came at last to full fruition.

III

The Song of Lynkeus
"Zum Sehen geboren,/ Zum Schauen bestellt"

Zum Sehen geboren,
Zum Schauen bestellt,
Dem Turme geschworen,
Gefällt mir die Welt.
Ich blick' in die Ferne,
Ich seh' in der Näh'
Den Mond und die Sterne,
Den Wald und das Reh.
So seh' ich in allen
Die ewige Zier,
Und wie mir's gefallen,
Gefall' ich auch mir.
Ihr glücklichen Augen,
Was je ihr gesehn,
Es sei wie es wolle,
Es war doch so schön!
(11288–303)

As Faust's watchman, Lynkeus, sings his gentle song at the opening of the scene "Tiefe Nacht," Mephisto and his three Mighty Men are away committing upon the idyllic world of Philemon and Baucis that violence which they embarked upon at the end of the preceding scene and which the watchman will report momentarily. This report of three tragic and unnecessary deaths will introduce a final grisly debasement of Faust's character. The air is heavy with foreboding, yet the watchman poised atop his tower is awake to the beauty and mystery of nightfall. The eye sweeps the heavens and earth around, while the heart swells with gratitude and finds release in music. The watchman's song, in tones sweetly mellow, as of a muted trumpet, pierces the darkness of this "tiefe Nacht."

In its simplicity and grandeur this little lyric is one of the most haunting in Goethe's *Faust*. The rhymed couplets which directly precede and follow it are jarring by contrast with the poem's undulating amphibrachic meter. In the first instance the couplets speak of violence planned ("Nach überstandener Gewalt/

Versöhnt ein schöner Aufenthalt," 11280–81) and in the second of violence accomplished ("Welch ein greuliches Entsetzen/ Droht mir aus der finstern Welt!" 11306–07). All the more striking, then, are the gently lilting beat, the musicality and the strangely innocent-sounding sentiment of the watchman's song. So strangely innocent, indeed, that one eminent critic terms it "childlike."[1] Gentleness, innocence, yet also a ripeness, a mature ability to accept with gratitude what life has brought.[2] An odd combination indeed, this fusion of childhood's openness and the mellowed vision of age. Yet on closer examination we find that the breadth of this elusive mood springs from the poem's innermost structure. The song opens, after all, with reference to birth ("Zum Sehen geboren,") and concludes in retrospection, as the watchman draws together the threads of a life fully lived and finds it in his heart to accept what that life has been ("Es sei wie es wolle,/ Es war doch so schön!"). The poem's mood, then, is itself an expression of its content, both cradle-song and requiem, at once airily dance-like and ceremoniously restrained, in its trustfulness pure and in its wisdom ripe. It sings a little life-story, a lyrical autobiography *en miniature* that sparkles, jewellike, in a setting of darkness, wrongdoing and agony. There is magic in these lines, as though that transcendent harmony and order of the universe which ennoble the eye and grant vision to the heart were here able for a moment to pour into a world anguished by the blindness and malice of men.

Above all, this is a poem on the human eye, on sight, on insight and on vision. For Goethe the eye of man is sunlike:

> Wär nicht das Auge sonnenhaft,
> Die Sonne könnt' es nie erblicken;
> Läg' nicht in uns des Gottes eigne Kraft,
> Wie könnt' uns Göttliches entzücken?[3]

For Goethe the world of colors, as "deeds and sufferings of light,"[4] is intimately related to the eye; for the eye is creative. It continually produces inwardly the complementary after-image of the color seen. But more importantly, the colors are themselves a universe both sensory ("sinnlich") and moral ("sittlich"). They partake of both the physical and the spiritual. The creative human eye is the mediator of this awesome process.

[1] ". . . die kindlich selige Art, wie die ganz leicht gewordene Sprache die Dinge einfach aufzählt, das stellt die Haltung der weltseligen Weisheit dar:" Kurt May, *Faust II. Teil. In der Sprachform gedeutet* (München, 1962), p. 261.

[2] Cf. Dorothea Lohmeyer, who sees in Lynkeus the mature eye of old age: ". . . das Auge, . . . das . . . in einer Welt des Alters . . . das Dauernde, and das heißt das Unsinnlich-Geistige, zu erkennen vermag." Dorothea Lohmeyer, *Faust und die Welt* (Potsdam, 1940), p. 104.

[3] HA I, 367.

[4] "Die Farben sind Taten des Lichts, Taten und Leiden." "Didaktischer Teil, Vorwort," *Zur Farbenlehre*, HA XIII, 315.

The poem contains sixteen lines. The first eight speak primarily of the sensory world: the external world of nature, the objects perceived by the eye in nature ("das Sinnliche"). The last eight speak of the moral sphere: the inner experiences engendered by that contemplation, the eternal harmonies of the world, the soul's acceptance of what it has seen ("das Sittliche"). Thus the two primary qualities which for Goethe inform the world of color come into clear focus through the form of the poem. Moreover, the metrical foot, the amphibrach (⏑ — ⏑), neither hastens nor retards the flow of the lines. It sustains a mood of perfect balance corresponding to the balance of outer and inner worlds that comes to expression in the poem's content. The rhyme scheme divides the poem into four stanzas of four lines each. It is a simple progression of interlocking couplets: abab, cdcd, efef, ghih. For easy reference we shall follow the precedent of another critic in referring to these as "stanzas."[5] We note that the final four lines contain a flaw in the rhyme. We shall return to this presently. The poem celebrates man's faculty of sight, and it abounds in references to this faculty: "Sehen," "Schauen," "blick'," "Augen," "gesehn." Yet it is at the same time a little autobiography. The central theme develops its levels of meaning as the life-story unfolds.

The first stanza presents a fourfold picture of the singer's life, from birth to maturity. The first line speaks of life's beginnings. A physical body is provided which contains the organs of sight needed by the soul which will inhabit it: "Zum Sehen geboren." In the second line the mere ability to see ("Sehen") yields to the deeper faculty of envisioning ("Schauen"), as environment and circumstances provide soul and body with a specific task: "Zum Schauen bestellt." In the third line the human being replies actively to the possibilities provided by the physical organism and the tasks suggested by the surrounding world. Through the swearing of an oath he makes a specific commitment. By answering to the opportunities afforded him he enters upon his life's "calling" and steps into his place in the world: "Dem Turme geschworen." Finally, in line four, the full maturity of the ego rays forth as the world can now speak to man's self and the self can say "yes" in reply, can accept its destiny in the world: "Gefällt mir die Welt." This line places the crown of full manhood on the figure whose life unfolds in the foregoing lines. It is therefore entirely appropriate that whereas in the first three instances the verb stands only at the end of the line, and as the rather weak past participle ("geboren," "bestellt," "geschworen") here it appears as the first word in the line and in its active form ("Gefällt"). What is more, it is linked by a powerful internal rhyme with the last word, and man's active acceptance of his task in the world thereby combines formally with that world itself: "Gefällt"/ "Welt." This conscious act of uniting with the world is possible only through the fact that man is endowed with an ego. Thus interestingly enough this ego or self, the poem's "lyrical I," first makes its appearance in this line: "mir."

[5] Werner Kraft, "Goethes Türmerlied," *The Goethe Year*, Part 5 (London, 1949), pp. 52–56.

This first stanza is deceptively simple. In reality it is a miniature "vita," a "poem within a poem" which contains in germinal form the thematic outline of the larger poem, just as its four lines reflect the four-stanza structure of the lyric itself. This is entirely in keeping with Goethe's view that the individual part of an organism contains ideally the whole, just as the single leaf bears within it the potential to unfold into all the organs of the plant.

In the second stanza the theme of active seeing alternately swells to the farthest reaches of the starry heavens and contracts to the immediate surroundings. The vision is very exact and moves from the lifeless mineral kingdom ("Mond . . . Sterne") to that of vegetative life ("Wald") and finally to the kingdom of the beasts ("Reh") in a process of increasing animation. The realm of the stars is the awesome celestial world of the archangels in the "Prolog im Himmel." The surrounding forest is here the protective habitat of natural life whose representative is the peaceable deer. In this stanza the act of seeing moves rhythmically in a gentle systole and diastole, a perceptual breathing process. In the third line, for instance, the eye fixes first upon the single moon and then expands its focus to the multitudes of stars, whereas in the fourth line it first takes in the countless trees of the forest and finally comes to rest on the individual animal. And the gaze moves alternately from the distant sky ("Ich blick' in die Ferne,") to the world nearby ("Ich seh' in der Näh' "), then back to the heavens ("Den Mond und die Sterne,") only to return once again to the surrounding forest ("Den Wald und das Reh"). This perceptual outbreathing/inbreathing, outbreathing/inbreathing thus flows in harmony with the alternating single lines.

Or does it? Through enjambement the individual lines form a single extended sentence. Yet we notice that this is not really true, for the sentence's inner *logic* relates lines one and three ("Ich blick' in die Ferne, . . . Den Mond und die Sterne") and two and four ("Ich seh' in der Näh' . . . Den Wald und das Reh"). The enjambement of lines two and three creates a vision which is logically absurd: "Ich seh' in der Näh'/ Den Mond und die Sterne." Only by lifting ourselves out of the logic of syntax and hovering in the poetic logic of the stanza's parallel construction can we escape the seeming flaw in the thought-structure and rest in the poet's vision.

In stanza three it becomes clear that in a larger sense the apparent mistake in the syntactical logic of stanza two is not a mistake at all, for when the eye can pierce through external appearances it grasps the eternal laws which inform them ("Die ewige Zier"). Here "Sehen" becomes "Schauen" and all spatial differentiation yields to a vision of the whole: "So seh' ich in allen/ Die ewige Zier." In keeping with Goethe's classical world view and the Greek name "Lynkeus," scholars are in general agreement that the German "Zier" is here best understood as a rendering of *κόσμος*.[6] The word *κόσμος* means both order and ornament, for

[6] So, for instance, Friedrich-Scheithauer: "*Zier:* die Schönheit der weise gewordenen Welt; Zier gibt hier das griech. 'Kosmos' wieder." Friedrich-Scheithauer, *Kommentar zu Goethes Faust* (Stuttgart, 1968), p. 292.

to the Greek both were expression of the same reality, the beautiful order and the precisely ordered form of beauty. And as if by design, the vowel pattern of this crucial line in the poem ("Die ewige Zier") reflects in its microcosmic structure the symmetry and harmony of the macrocosmic order of which it speaks: *ie e i e ie*. No other line in the poem contains such a perfectly balanced vocalic structure. Here the poet's seeing has indeed become an envisioning and he is able to incorporate the transcendent symmetry and ordered beauty of his vision into the medium of language; but there is yet another dimension to this pattern. For if one renders these same vowels in phonetic symbols, as they are pronounced, the following sequence emerges: [i] [e] [i] [ɛ] [i]. The visible structure is here broken through by a slight tonal metamorphosis which breathes life into the otherwise perfectly symmetrical and therefore beautiful—but dead—form. This line, then, stands within the poem as the representative of that perfectly ordered and beautiful "Greek" universe which has revealed itself to Lynkeus' outwardly and inwardly active eye. And while the little cosmos of this line's vowel pattern presents to the reader's eye an aspect harmonious and balanced, but static, it tells the ear that this coldly beautiful exterior is but its surface, for within it is alive.

The third and fourth lines of stanza three pick up the theme of stanza one, line four ("Gefällt mir die Welt") and carry it a step further: "Und wie mir's gefallen,/ Gefall' ich auch mir." The singer who has found the harmonious universe pleasing now is consciously in tune with his own being. As Emrich points out, Lynkeus need not suffer Faust's blindness, for the inner light already lives within him.[7] Until this point the poem has dwelt largely on the esthetic, the harmony and perfection of cosmic laws, a theme further elaborated, with reference to the activity of sight, in the fourth stanza. Yet these last two lines of stanza three have to do not only with the esthetic but also with the ethical realm. The singer, through experiencing the universal order of things, is "pleasing to himself," i.e. he is at peace with himself. In view of this line, then, it is clear that "die ewige Zier" also refers ultimately to *all* that life has brought. This is the deeper dimension of meaning in the poem. Underneath the esthetic level there lies the ethical level, just as under the *sensory* impressions (stanzas 1 and 2) there lie the *moral* (stanzas 3 and 4). The watchman is now singing of his life, of life itself.

The verb "gefallen" is now also saturated with meaning on two levels. The most obvious is the esthetic: the pleasing aspect of the created universe. Beneath this lies the ethical: the man who finds the whole sweep of his life and his relationship to the world and to himself in the larger sense pleasing. For this life, this biography unfolds through the medium of time, and it is therefore through the flow of time that life brings man the opportunities and challenges which become his destiny. In this larger sense the line "Und wie mir's gefallen" refers to the

[7] "Denn auch Lynkeus kennt ja das innere Licht, er ist ganz 'Auge' im Sinn totalisierend alles 'Ferne und Nahe' preisender Übersicht. Ihm muß nicht die äußere Welt erblinden, sondern er trägt in sich den Augenblick, der Äonen umspannt." Wilhelm Emrich, *Die Symbolik von Faust II* (Frankfurt a. M., 1964), p. 403.

sequence of events which have molded this life.

That which has happened to the watchman comes to expression once more in the final two lines of stanza four: "Es sei wie es wolle,/ Es war doch so schön!" This very objective "es" refers to all that the eyes have seen, all that the heart and mind have gained as "in-sight." In this larger context it refers to all the impressions, events, experiences which have come to man from the outer world, as well as to all the impulses from the active inner realm of his thinking, feeling, envisioning. All these experiences, working upon man in the stream of time, have made him the individual he is, have molded his destiny. Yet for Goethe human destiny unfolds that pattern of experiences and events which lie hidden, prefigured as potential within his being from the start. Out of the world of the religious mysteries of Greek antiquity Goethe draws forth this picture of man's being, to which he gives expression in the "Urworte. Orphisch" under the heading "ΔΑΙΜΩΝ , Dämon":

> Wie an dem Tag, der dich der Welt verliehen,
> Die Sonne stand zum Gruße der Planeten,
> Bist alsobald und fort und fort gediehen
> Nach dem Gesetz, wonach du angetreten.
> So mußt du sein, dir kannst du nicht entfliehen,
> So sagten schon Sibyllen, so Propheten;
> Und keine Zeit und keine Macht zerstückelt
> Geprägte Form, die lebend sich entwickelt."[8]

It is in the sense of the view of destiny which Goethe makes explicit in these lines that the deeper meaning of stanza three, lines three and four ("Und wie mir's gefallen,/ Gefall' ich auch mir") comes into focus. My personal destiny is "geprägte Form, die lebend sich entwickelt." The events which befall me are, in this view, not foreign to my nature but rather are an integral part of my being. As they happen to me, I can learn to recognize their rightness. I am "pleasing to myself" when I understand that in the deepest sense all that the world has brought to me belongs to me, is a part of my spiritual self. In the sense of the "Urworte. Orphisch" I *am* my destiny, and my insight into this mystery fills my soul with peace: "Und wie mir's gefallen,/ Gefall' ich auch mir." The stanzas now reveal the fullness and depth of their underlying ethical meaning. By recognizing "die ewige Zier" as the transcendent order and beauty of the outer and inner worlds, of nature and human nature, the eye opens to the subtler moral laws, the riddles of man's destiny. The watchman can now say "yes" not only to the beauty of the world but to these laws as well.

We have seen that stanza three, line two ("Die ewige Zier") is the pivotal line of the poem. The line which precedes it ("So seh' ich in allen") speaks still of that physical sight which is described in the first half of the poem. The line which

[8] HA I, 359.

follows it ("Und wie mir's gefallen,") introduces the inner, moral dimension which is elaborated in the second half of the poem. This is curious, for that line which in the deepest sense is the central line of the poem occurs not in the center, but off center. It surely belongs at the center, yet it *cannot* occur there for the simple reason that there can be no central line in a sixteen-line poem. The center occurs between stanzas two and three, and is silence. Thus this pivotal line, the poem's true axis, finds its way into stanza three and establishes itself there as a divider between the two halves of the poem. The poem thus has on the one hand an "external" center which is immediately visible on the printed page as the point which divides the poem symmetrically into two equal halves, each containing two four-line stanzas. On the other hand, however, the poem contains an "internal" or hidden center which is very clearly established by the inner necessities of its content. The full scope and import of this discrepancy in the poem's form becomes clear as we examine the two unequal halves.

The "inner axis," the line "Die ewige Zier," divides the poem into two parts of unequal length. Nine lines precede and six follow it. The structure of three times three, or nine lines in the poem's first "half" is an expression on a higher level of the threefold rhythm of the amphibrachic foot (⌣ — ⌣) which underlies the entire poem. On the other hand, the two times three, or six-line structure of the second "half" of the poem is an amplification of the principle of six syllables per line which also runs through the poem from beginning to end. Through the placement of the central line, a principle of threefoldness which inhabits the poem on the metrical level is set free to penetrate the entire structure of the lyric.

The poem's outward formal structure is based on the number four (four stanzas of four lines each). It is perfectly symmetrical and it is static. With the placement of the thematically pivotal line slightly off center the world of the "ewige Zier," the tremendous living harmony of the *κόσμος* invades the poem, shines into it "from within." It breaks apart the static form, transmuting it into an intricate symphony of threefoldness. The dead, cube-like fourfold pattern yields before the thoroughly alive structural force introduced by these intimations of the Greek universe as winter's ice gives way to the rays of spring's sun. One then notices the astonishing fact that this animation of the balanced but frozen outer form of the poem through the simple appearance of the line "Die ewige Zier" in its position off center, is itself a reflection of what transpires within that short line itself. For as we saw earlier, that line's vowel pattern is outwardly, visually symmetrical and therefore coldly beautiful, yet through the unseen but *spoken* vowels it is animated, ensouled from within. The spoken vowels do for the visual image of the line's vowel pattern what the line itself does for the visual image of the poem as a whole. A life element transforms the entire form from within—a Goethean "open secret" if ever there was one.

The balance and grace of the poem's content and form, as well as the watchman's name, which echoes that of the similarly named figure in Act III, lend an

Hellenic aura to these stanzas. His position atop the tower[9] provides Lynkeus with that higher "point of view" from which he can recognize the eternal harmonies of the *κόσμος* and awaken to the *δαίμων* of his own being. In these several respects the poem is profoundly Greek.

Yet stanza four goes a step further:

> Ihr glücklichen Augen,
> Was je ihr gesehn,
> Es sei, wie es wolle,
> Es war doch so schön!

Up to this point the watchman has sung what has been revealed to him through his eyes. He has taken the eyes themselves for granted, however. Here he turns his gaze backwards to his eyes and he addresses them from "outside" ("ihr"). The eye was for Goethe the most exalted organ of the human body. He felt that the light itself had called forth the eye in order that the inner light of the soul might come forth to meet the light without.[10] The noblest organ of man has served Lynkeus well, and he acknowledges this. Line two of the stanza, "Was je ihr gesehn," refers on the one hand to the many acts of physical perception and on the other to that moral envisioning ("Schauen") which is possible when seeing takes place under the figure of eternity, of the "ewige Zier." In the last two lines Lynkeus' words seem to ring forth from a vantage point at the very end of life, and we fancy we hear through them the voice of the aged Faust looking back at the beauty and joy which have been his during his hundred tumultuous years. But Faust is nowhere to be seen, and it is Lynkeus who sings the final lines of the hymn in praise of sight: "Es sei wie es wolle,/ Es war doch so schön!" The first of these lines could refer to any life, for it speaks of the objective laws of any man's

[9] In the masque (Act I) Goethe places dame Viktoria, the winged "Göttin aller Tätigkeiten" (5456) atop a tower symbolizing the distant reach of her vision and influence. In the *Wanderjahre* (Book I, Ch. 10; HA VIII, 114 ff.) the symbol of the tower appears again, here as astronomical observatory, and Wilhelm is introduced to the venerable Makarie, whose occult abilities are so highly developed that she carries the entire solar system within her and lives consciously within it. For her the universal "ewige Zier" is a living intuitive reality. And in the *Lehrjahre* we discover that the complex events which have befallen the hero and have molded his destiny were guided by the quasi secret Society of the Tower ("Gesellschaft vom Turm"). When Wilhelm finally realizes this fact and is shown the scroll containing advice concerning his destiny it becomes clear that the "Turmgesellschaft" has had an understanding of the potential latent within him which must unfold as "geprägte Form, die lebend sich entwickelt." Just as Wilhelm, resting on the foundation of this Tower, is able gradually to come to a living awareness of his "calling," his destiny, his "*δαίμων*," so too does the watchman's tower provide for Lynkeus that foundation and elevated position from which he may gaze upon the universe, contemplate the mystery of its beauty and discover the deeper meaning of his own life, his destiny or "*δαίμων*."

[10] "Das Auge hat sein Dasein dem Licht zu danken. Aus gleichgültigen tierischen Hülfsorganen ruft sich das Licht ein Organ hervor, das seinesgleichen werde, und so bildet sich das Auge am Licht fürs Licht, damit das innere Licht dem äußeren entgegentrete." *Entwurf einer Farbenlehre*, HA XIII, 323.

unfolding destiny, of the pleasure and pain which are man's lot: "Es sei wie es wolle." But the last line is very personal and refers to this particular, individual life: "Es war doch so schön!"

Lynkeus addresses his eyes as "ihr glücklichen Augen." He can speak of them in this way because here he *distances* himself from them instead of simply using them. He is now conscious of his eyes and awake to what these organs have meant and mean to him. Can eyes be "happy" or "fortunate"? Here lies hidden the last deep secret in this poem. The physical eyes are organs of the body. But they are "fortunate" in that through their existence man is able to see. They give him the gift of sight, yet they themselves are selfless. Through them man is able to look into the beauty and order of the universe and thereby to find *himself* fortunate *in seeing*. If man is able, from the elevated position of his insight, not only to look back in gratitude at the wonders of the world which he has seen during life but also to awaken to a living sense of gratitude toward the physical body which has served him, a feeling of reverence may arise within him toward that body and the forces which have formed it. This mood of reverence and gratitude toward the sun-like organs of sight enables Lynkeus to address them as "ihr glücklichen Augen." Without them the gift of the beauties of nature would necessarily have been withheld from him. This sense of reverence and gratitude for one's own physical body is an expression within the poem of the reverence or "Ehrfurcht" referred to in the "pädagogische Provinz" as that underlying Christianity: "Nun ist aber von der dritten Religion zu sprechen, gegründet auf die Ehrfurcht vor dem, was unter uns ist; wir nennen sie die christliche, weil sich in ihr eine solche Sinnesart am meisten offenbart; es ist ein Letztes, wozu die Menschheit gelangen konnte und mußte."[11] In its perfected form this reverence bows down before poverty, scorn, suffering and even death. A stage in its awakening, however, is the attainment of a sense of gratitude toward those lower kingdoms of which the physical body of man is a part, and which provide a foundation upon which man's spiritual being may grow and develop. As though speaking from the very portal of death, our watchman looks back ("war") and, in objective acceptance of all of life's joys and sorrows, turns in gratitude toward the physical organism which served him. The thought is profoundly Christian and certainly also entirely Goethean in the sense of the passage quoted from the *Wanderjahre*.

Goethe's Iphigenia is a Greek, a Greek whose creator lived in the modern West. Unlike the Iphigenia of Euripides she listens not merely to the oracles but to her heart. Iphigenia is a Greek indeed, yet she is more. Similarly, the song of Lynkeus is very Greek, yet it is more. Its final message is that of the Christian "Ehrfurcht," which in its simple charity transfigures even those natural splendors of which the watchman sings so beautifully in the first half of the poem. This is the poem's second "open secret." It speaks to us of the mystery of the self ("Entelechie") which can only come to full fruition when it unfolds forces of selfless-

[11] *Wanderjahre*, Book II, Ch. 1; HA VIII, 157.

ness, inclining in gratitude before those kingdoms and beings which in certain respects may be its inferiors.

We recall that this last stanza in the poem is the only one which contains a faulty rhyme (ghih). Just as the deepest insight embodies itself in words, the poem's form gives way. The spiritual wisdom of the final stanza is profound, but the body is weak and the rhyme structure begins to disintegrate. What follows tells the story:

> Nicht allein mich zu ergetzen,
> Bin ich hier so hoch gestellt;
> Welch ein greuliches Entsetzen
> Droht mir aus der finstern Welt!

In Goethe's view man, among all creatures, is indeed "hoch gestellt." Through his upright stature he overcomes the burden of gravity and as a being endowed with thinking he towers above the beasts. But morally he is far from perfect. It is given to him to unfold the moral capacities latent within him:

> Edel sei der Mensch,
> Hilfreich und gut!
> Denn das allein
> Unterscheidet ihn
> Von allen Wesen,
> Die wir kennen.[12]

The *potential* for good lies slumbering within man. This is the deeper level of meaning of the *δαίμων*, the possibility for man to become what he has within him as potential. It shines into life with purifying splendor in certain elevated moments. But it is man's lot to err and to lose sight of his better nature. Goethe was under no illusions in this regard. Lynkeus' beautiful lyric is a reminder of what qualities man can evolve if he will. Such insights, however, are often but momentary beacons that illuminate the way and soon disappear from view as man, still far from the goal of spiritual freedom, falls victim once again to his lower nature.

Thus Lynkeus affords us a profound glimpse into what lives as unrealized spiritual potential in the human breast. And that means, in this specific context, in the breast of Goethe's representative of humanity, Faust. The true home of this spiritual potential, of Faust's entelechy, reveals itself after his death, in the final scene, "Bergschluchten." But for the moment Faust is still seriously entangled in the forces of his earthly destiny.

In the "Walpurgisnacht" Mephisto had said to Faust: "Du glaubst zu schieben und du wirst geschoben" (4117). And now once again Faust is pushed along by forces alien to his nobler self. He has already given Mephisto the order to remove Philemon and Baucis from his sight and the stage is set for the enact-

[12] "Das Göttliche," HA I, 147.

ment of the horrors which this order will conjure. The serene wisdom of which Lynkeus sings lives as promise within Faust, but Faust is not yet awake to this promise. In the last stanza Lynkeus' insight proves too deep for the body which is to contain it and the rhyme crumbles. The watchman must then contemplate and report the tragic consequences of Faust's last ghastly blunder. The sweet strains of the song pass away. For a moment all is silence. But the watchman's anguished voice must then proclaim the triumph of the hellish flames of destruction which sear the eye accustomed to beauty. Once again only music can loose the burden of a full heart. But song now resounds as dirge: "Was sich sonst dem Blick empfohlen,/ Mit Jahrhunderten ist hin."

And Faust plunges headlong into darkness, blindness, "tiefe Nacht."

IV

The Theme of Sacrifice and the Question of Faust's Redemption

Perhaps the most difficult question confronting the reader of Goethe's *Faust* is that of Faust's ultimate redemption. Because he has, directly or indirectly, several murders on his conscience, it has seemed to many readers inappropriate that he should be "saved." At the end of Part II Goethe introduces Faust's immortal soul into a spiritual world conceived in terms of traditional Christian imagery including penitent women, ascetic monks and the Virgin Mary. However, Goethe employs this imagery in his own unorthodox manner, so that it serves his purpose of giving form to the metamorphosis and "Steigerung" of Faust's immortal entelechy following his death.

Goethe had originally intended to include a scene depicting a heavenly court of judgment over Faust, including Christ as well as the evangelists and saints. Goethe abandoned this rather legalistically conceived treatment in favor of one more in keeping with his own belief in slow, organic transformation and ennoblement. It is therefore clear that the "Christian" conception of the end of *Faust II* is at the same time a very "Goethean"—i.e. *unorthodox* conception. From a certain point of view this fact is itself sufficient to induce the critic to assert that inasmuch as Faust does not fulfill the critic's criteria of that which constitutes being "Christian" one may properly deny that there is anything Christian about the outcome at all.

Two passages are bothersome to such a critic, in this connection. The first is the famous passage spoken by the angels who carry Faust's immortal parts:

> Gerettet ist das edle Glied
> Der Geisterwelt vom Bösen,
> Wer immer strebend sich bemüht,
> Denn können wir erlösen.
>
> (11934–37)

The last two lines speak clearly of *two* aspects of Faust's redemption: man's own active striving and the activity of supersensible beings who effect his salvation.

The second passage is Goethe's own commentary upon the above lines (and the four which follow them), as reported by Eckermann (6 June 1831):

"In diesen Versen," sagte er, "ist der Schlüssel zu Fausts Rettung enthalten. In Faust selber eine immer höhere und reinere Tätigkeit bis ans Ende, und von oben die ihm zu Hilfe kommende ewige Liebe. Es steht dieses mit unserer religiösen Vorstellung durchaus in Harmonie, nach welcher wir nicht bloß durch eigene Kraft selig werden, sondern durch die hinzukommende göttliche Gnade.[1]

This latter passage, with its clear reference to the role of divine Grace, is substantiated by words in *Dichtung und Wahrheit.* In the fifteenth Book Goethe explains why he became alienated from the Pietistic brotherhood:

> . . . Was mich nämlich von der Brüdergemeinde so wie von andern werten Christenseelen absonderte, war dasselbige, worüber die Kirche schon mehr als einmal in Spaltung geraten war. Ein Teil behauptete, daß die menschliche Natur durch den Sündenfall dergestalt verdorben sei, daß auch bis in ihren innersten Kern nicht das mindeste Gute an ihr zu finden, deshalb der Mensch auf seine eigenen Kräfte durchaus Verzicht zu tun, und alles von der Gnade und ihrer Einwirkung zu erwarten habe. Der andere Teil gab zwar die erblichen Mängel der Menschen sehr gern zu, wollte aber der Natur inwendig noch einen gewissen Keim zugestehen, welcher, durch göttliche Gnade belebt, zu einem frohen Baume geistiger Glückseligkeit emporwachsen könne. Von dieser letzteren Überzeugung war ich aufs innigste durchdrungen, ohne es zu wissen, obwohl ich mich mit Mund und Feder zu dem Gegenteile bekannt hatte . . .[2]

Goethe here draws a subtle and important distinction: he rejects the view that man is to renounce all striving of his own and to surrender himself entirely to divine Grace. But Goethe does not thereby reject the idea of Grace. He views it rather, entirely in keeping with his own morphological—even botanical—mode of thinking, as a revivifying force which awakens the seed of man's moral being and enables it to develop into a complete organism, a "tree of spiritual bliss." These lines from *Dichtung und Wahrheit* are thus a further elaboration of the thoughts expressed in the lines "Wer immer strebend sich bemüht,/ Den können wir erlösen." For this statement of Goethe's also delineates clearly the natural striving of man on the one hand and the role of Grace, the divine activity which answers that striving, on the other.

Confronted with the highly unusual employment of Christian imagery in the final act of *Faust II*, Wilhelm Emrich, in his significant study *Die Symbolik von Faust II*, finds it impossible to speak of the role of Grace, as Goethe here defines it, as Christian: "Im strengen Sinn also ist die Gnade von oben bei Goethe nicht christlich, denn sie gründet sich weder auf die Verwandlung und Abtötung eines sündigen Ich noch auf das Vertrauen auf einen göttlichen Erlöser. . . ."[3] Because Goethe does not explicitly fulfill these two theological criteria which Emrich

[1] Ernst Beutler, ed., *Goethe, Gespräche mit Eckermann*, Artemis Ausgabe (Zürich, 1949), p. 504.

[2] *Dichtung und Wahrheit*, Book 15, HA X, 43–44.

[3] Wilhelm Emrich, *Die Symbolik von Faust II* (Frankfurt a. M., 1964), pp. 418–19.

imposes upon the work, the "hinzukommende göttliche Gnade" is not Christian. What, then, is it? Emrich's explanation is very ingenious and quite in keeping with the views of modern psychology. What is more, it seems all the more plausible in that it leans upon the entirely correct statement that the religious symbolism has been entirely transformed into Goethean symbolism.[4] The explanation is as follows: "Die von oben kommende Liebe ist eben zutiefst Echo, Widerhall einer lebendig emporstrebenden "bildenden" Kraft und kann und darf nicht ihre "poetische Wirklichkeit" in ein autonom transzendentes Bereich verlagern . . . ohne die Einheit des ganzen zu stören."[5] The "hinzukommende göttliche Gnade," then, of which Goethe speaks, is nothing but an "echo" or projection of the individual's (Faust's) upward-striving powers. This interpretation nevertheless directly negates the first part of Goethe's statement: "Es steht dieses mit unserer religiösen Vorstellung durchaus in Harmonie, nach welcher wir *nicht bloß durch eigene Kraft selig werden* . . ." [italics mine]. Despite Goethe's own commentary, which expressly underlines the role of higher forces which he terms "Gnade" in this final act of *Faust II*, Emrich goes further and asserts: "Goethe leugnet also durchaus ein Versagen Fausts im sozial-ethischen und überhaupt moralischen Raum und eine entsprechende innere Notwendigkeit der 'Gnade.' "[6] Emrich is then quick to qualify this picture of the situation, however, and states very correctly: "Von Selbsterlösung oder rational fortschreitender Selbstoffenbarung im humanistisch-aufklärerischen Sinne kann . . . allerdings auch nicht die Rede sein. . . ."[7] The reader is by now thoroughly perplexed. The divine Love from above is "Echo, Widerhall einer lebendig emporstrebenden 'bildenden' Kraft." What is more, we are told: "Im Grunde vollzog sich Fausts Erlösung schon beim Umschlag der real-irdischen Vorgänge in transzendental-zeitlose im Bereich seiner Tätigkeit selber, d. h. im Augenblick des Durchbruchs des inneren Lichts und der Vision vom transzendentalen 'Eiland' mitten im Toben der Elemente.'[8] Yet we are not to view this as "Selbsterlösung."

As the above contradictions demonstrate, it is simply not possible to maintain that despite the Christian imagery the scene is not Christian in character and the role of the "hinzukommende göttliche Gnade," of which Goethe speaks, nothing but an "echo" of the force within Faust. Emrich himself makes a statement which points to the direction in which Goethe's intentions lie when he says: "Liebe ist niemals Selbstoffenbarung, sondern Geschenk."[9] This remark, which

[4] *Ibid.*, p. 417.

[5] *Ibid.*

[6] *Ibid.*, p. 418.

[7] *Ibid.*, p. 419.

[8] *Ibid.*, p. 418. Note that Emrich here argues in favor of "transcendental," "timeless" processes, whereas on the previous page (417) he argues *against* an "autonom transzendentales Bereich" of love.

[9] *Ibid.*, p. 419.

is not predicated upon any theological definitions but reveals Emrich's own deeper and entirely correct understanding of the *process* as such, provides a key whereby we may examine just such a process within the work itself and perhaps thereby come closer to an understanding of the manner in which Goethe, himself non-theological and undogmatic, may intend his remarks concerning "Gnade," as well as the Christian symbolism itself, to be understood.

Perhaps one of the principal problems in accepting the unorthodox admixture of Goethean thinking *and* Christian imagery in this scene is a semi-conscious assumption by many readers that the Christian elements have no business being assimilated into the fabric of Goethe's concept formation ("Werden," metamorphosis, "Steigerung," *et al.*) in the first place. To be "Christian," so such an argument goes, they must be so labeled, i.e. employed *explicitly*, rather than implicitly. To expect such a treatment by Goethe, who was quite unable to form any inner connection with Christianity as officially represented by the churches of the time, would be unrealistic. Yet the same Goethe, shortly before his death, says to Eckermann concerning Christ: "Ich beuge mich vor ihm, als der göttlichen Offenbarung des höchsten Prinzips der Sittlichkeit."[10] In the light of such a statement as this it is quite clear that it is more than the search for useful or esthetically satisfying symbols which informs Goethe's handling of the final act of *Faust*. To be sure, Goethe speaks of Christ as the "göttliche Offenbarung des höchsten Prinzips der Sittlichkeit," and not as the divine "Erlöser," which to some readers may be the essential condition of such a statement's credibility as an expression of truly "Christian" sentiment. Yet this, too, misses the point. Goethe acknowledged and admired the truth revealed in the *various* religions. The Old Testament was a favorite book from childhood, and the wisdom of the Near East finds expression in the efforts of his later years (*West-östlicher Divan*). Whether it was these religions, the Greek mysteries or the sun-worship of ancient Persia, Goethe sought in each the workings of the divine worlds. And Christianity takes its place for him in this company as one revelation among many.[11] Each one of these traditions Goethe employs in keeping with his own genius, i.e. in a "Goethean" manner. Hence the "Urworte Orphisch" are both "Goethean" *and* "Greek." It is my contention that in this same sense, the final scene of *Faust II* must be understood as both "Goethean" and "Christian." It is not only unnecessary to insist that it be exclusively one or the other—to do so simply distorts the scene's meaning.[12]

[10] *Gespräche mit Eckermann*, p. 771.

[11] Cf. "Die Geheimnisse," HA II, 271–84. In this connection cf. also the very interesting work by Richard H. Grützmacher, *Die Religionen in der Anschauung Goethes* (Baden-Baden, 1950).

[12] With respect to the "Goethezeit" in general, Korff makes this point very well: "Die Goethezeit ist nicht christlich, weil auch andere Religionen für sie die Geltung der Wahrheit haben; aber weil sie pantheistisch ist und Gott in allen Formen anzubeten die innere Weite hatte, ist sie *auch* christlich. Und das ist, was man neben dem Umgekehrten allerdings begreifen muß." H. A. Korff, *Geist der Goethezeit*,

The reverence Goethe felt toward the spiritual world itself enabled him to employ the Christian imagery as such, i.e. as "Christian," and his intellectual honesty required that he do so implicitly, rather than explicitly, thereby creating for the puzzlement of his readers an "open secret" of considerable compass. If we are to understand how divine Grace enters into Faust's destiny we must search for its manifestations *within* that destiny, rather than expect to find it tacked onto the end of the play as a *deus ex machina* expressly labeled "Christian." Ever since Faust's near encounter with suicide and his grateful exclamation on Easter Sunday ". . . die Erde hat mich wieder!" (784), his destiny develops through all that he encounters on earth. And the workings of divine Love are made possible on earth in part through the forces of *sacrifice*. In such processes in which sacrifice plays a role, and which weave between human beings, a medium becomes available whereby spiritual forces may find expression in the world of men. These forces, awakened and carried in the drama principally by Gretchen, mold the vessel which contains the spiritual sustenance needed by Faust. The guilt assumed by Faust in his involvement with Gretchen encompasses several murders, related to and including that of the girl herself. By any usual standards of guilt and just punishment these were surely sufficient to insure Faust's eternal damnation. Yet Goethe not only "saves" him—in the final scene he presents a transformed Gretchen who intercedes for Faust in the heavenly world. Thus through her sacrifice Gretchen becomes the vessel, the intermediary for the forces of divine Grace as they work into Faust's destiny.

There are two episodes in the drama, whose imagery itself suggests comparison, and which serve to illuminate the role of the theme of sacrifice. Let us begin with an examination of certain elements in these scenes. One is the scene "Wald und Höhle" in Part I and the other the Philemon and Baucis episode in Part II. The element common to both scenes, while treated differently in each case, is the theme of the sacrifice of innocent life to Faust's titanic nature, and Faust's realization of this sacrifice.

The famous monologue (3345–65) in which Faust, in "Wald und Höhle," describes his compulsion to destroy Gretchen's world, dates from the *Urfaust*. Its *Sturm und Drang* language embodies directly the message of uncontrolled erotic drives which through Mephisto's cynical needling have taken possession of Faust's consciousness. Gretchen is to be sacrificed to this desire, and Faust realizes to which spiritual forces the sacrifice will be brought: "Du, Hölle, mußtest dieses Opfer haben!" (3361). The line is reminiscent of Faust's words to Mephisto at the end of the second "Straße" scene: "Und komm, ich hab' des Schwätzens Überdruß,/ Denn du hast recht, vorzüglich weil ich muß" (3071–72). When possessed by consuming passion Faust abandons the struggle for self-control by invoking

5 vols. (Leizpig, 1964), I, 23. The true nature of Goethe's intention in the final scenes of *Faust* is perhaps stated most precisely by Grete Schaeder: "Die Szenen der 'Bergschluchten' sind 'christliche Landschaft' ohne christliches Bekenntnis zu sein." Grete Schaeder, *Gott und Welt* (Hameln, 1947), p. 402.

the simple rationalization of blind necessity.

The water-imagery, which serves as the metaphor for Faust's churning desire, is itself first suggested to him by Mephisto (3307–10). In the monologue at the end of the scene Faust recognizes these instinctual drives as the destructive force within himself which will undermine Gretchen's existence as the torrents of water undercut the alpine hut. It is important to note in what area of Faust's inner life the vision is rooted. The verb "untergraben" (3360) points to the gradual erosion of Gretchen's world by the flood of emotion, rather than its destruction through conscious intellectual decision. In contrast to this, the peaceful little world of Philemon and Baucis will fall to a destructive force in Faust which emanates as much from the mental sphere as from the emotions. Their removal to another site is premeditated, because their presence interferes with the abstract perfection of Faust's grand design for the area.[13] Indeed, the verb "untergraben" reappears, transformed, in this episode as the canals which Faust constructed as the crucial link between his palace and the outer world are referred to as "Gräben" (11092) or "Gräbchen" (11229). In both cases this act of digging ("untergraben," "Gräbchen") involves the destruction of innocent life and avenges itself with terrific poetic irony in the scene in which the blind Faust, himself at the point of death, confuses the digging of his grave ("Grab") with that of yet another ditch. Mephisto sums up this pathetic delusion with characteristic cynicism: "Man spricht, wie man mir Nachricht gab,/ Von keinem Graben, doch vom Grab" (11557–58).

Whereas Faust destroys both Gretchen and several of her family (Valentin, the baby, and indirectly also her mother) as well as Philemon, Baucis and the wanderer, Gretchen's sacrifice is unique. She alone is united with Faust in love and thereby participates in the sacrifice, whereas all the other figures are *sacrificed*, i.e. victimized by Faust's character. Perhaps an awareness of this very fact of Gretchen's love for him, which renders his destruction of her so peculiarly heinous, is at the root of the psychological reaction which attacks him: *Angst*. Thus Faust's double use of the verb "müssen" in the attempt to rationalize the coming mischief ("Sie, ihren Frieden mußt' ich untergraben!/ Du, Hölle, mußtest dieses Opfer haben!," 3360–61) is followed by the word "Angst": "Hilf, Teufel, mir die Zeit der Angst verkürzen!" (3362). In contrast to this "Angst" the aged Faust, having (again through machinations of Mephisto) sacrificed Philemon, Baucis and the wanderer, is attacked not by the immediacy of "Angst" but by the creeping paralysis of "Sorge," which gradually erodes his inner life. "Sorge" might be said to be not only the sister of "Mangel," "Schuld" and "Not" but

[13] Cf. Stöcklein's characterization of Faust's undertaking: "So hat das Kanalnetz und der umschließende Park absolutistisch-geometrischen Stiles seinen Mittelpunkt im Palast Faustens, des Autokraten. Ein Höchstausdruck von *Gestaltung, konzentrischer Anlage* tritt dort in das Symbol ein, wo es den Sinn von Fausts *gesamtem Tun* im Schlußbild seines Lebens konzentriert darstellt." Paul Stöcklein, *Wege zum späten Goethe*, 2nd ed. (Hamburg, 1960), p. 104.

also in a sense an older sister of "Angst"—older and born of experience.

The two scenes are also inwardly related through the image of the hut. The collapse of the alpine hut, the "Hüttchen auf dem kleinen Alpenfeld" (3353), which Faust sees as a metaphor for Gretchen's world, later becomes stark reality in the collapse of Philemon and Baucis' hut as it falls prey to the flames (11312). Similarly, the bell which in the scene "Kerker" announces Gretchen's execution (4590) is echoed in the "silvery tone" ("Glöckchens Silberlaut") of the old couple's bell as described by the wanderer (11072), a bell which Faust, however, cannot abide ("Verdammtes Läuten!," 11151; "Das Glöckchen läutet, und ich wüte," 11258).[14]

We spoke above of the fact that while both Gretchen and Philemon, Baucis and the wanderer are "sacrificed," i.e. victimized by Faust, Gretchen, through her love for him, participates in her demise. Her love for Faust finds expression in her last words before death, the final words of Part I: "Heinrich! Heinrich!" (4614), and she reappears to intercede for him at the end of Part II. Gretchen is only dimly, instinctually aware of the dangers surrounding her. She is naïve and trusting and only *feels* the presence of evil.[15] Philemon and Baucis, on the other hand, are very much more consciously aware of Faust's involvement with evil. Baucis comments upon Faust's reclamation project with insight into the role which magical (i.e. Mephistophelian) forces played in its realization: ". . . es ging das ganze Wesen/ Nicht mit rechten Dingen zu" (11113–14). Gretchen is troubled by the question as to whether Faust does or does not "believe" in God ("Glaubst du an Gott?" 3426), yet in her love for him does not recognize the selfishly erotic intentions which he harbors for her. Baucis, however, sees very clearly the ego-centered purposes which motivate Faust's designs on their property and labels them explicitly:

> Gottlos ist er, ihn gelüstet
> Unsre Hütte, unser Hain;
> Wie er sich als Nachbar brüstet,
> Soll man untertänig sein.
> (11131–34)

Ironically it is just Gretchen's lack of mature insight and healthy skepticism, i.e. her naïvely trusting nature which provides the "soul-atmosphere" in which her spiritual love for Faust may grow. It is this "weakness" of character which is also a definite strength. The fact that she preserves within her the paradisiacal light of

[14] L. A. Willoughby points to another connection between the hut image in "Wald und Höhle" and in the Philemon and Baucis episode, and notes: "Faust hates the 'Hütte,' not only because it is a blot on the landscape, but because it is a reminder of his guilt toward Gretchen." He points to the inner relationship of the figure of the wanderer with Faust's own being and notes the mythical overtones: "It is an example of the symbol becoming myth, taking on a ritualistic, religious meaning." L. A. Willoughby, "The Image of the 'Wanderer' and the 'Hut' in Goethe's Poetry," *ÉG*, 6 (1951), 219.

[15] Cf. 2753–58; 3469–94.

the innocence of childhood and pristine creation renders her immune to Mephisto's direct attack:

> Es ist ein gar unschuldig Ding,
> Das eben für nichts zur Beichte ging;
> Über die hab' ich keine Gewalt!
> (2624–26)

This divine presence within her provides her with that organ of perception whereby she is able to recognize and believe in the same goodness within Faust, despite what happens to her through his weaknesses. It is this which renders her sacrifice deeply significant for the future of Faust's entelechy.

Philemon, Baucis and the wanderer, unlike Gretchen, do not reappear as participants in the scenes following Faust's death. Nevertheless, the sacrifice of their lives is a monumental event in Faust's destiny. It represents a last tragic involvement with Mephisto's schemings. With reference to the metaphor of fire, Heinz Politzer has made the singularly keen observation that the serpent-symbol associated with Mephisto (Faust: "Schlange! Schlange!," 3324) appears, transformed, in the flames which consume the old couple's chapel and which are referred to as "schlängelnd" (11332): "Die Schlange hat sich als Glut in die Glut eingeschlichen."[16] This tragedy contributes to Faust's resolve to abandon his reliance upon magical assistance. It is out of the smoke of the couple's burning hut, chapel, and trees that the figure of Care ("Sorge") forms itself,[17] in the encounter with whom Faust is finally able to say (to himself): "Nimm dich in acht und sprich kein Zauberwort" (11423). It is this figure of Care who blinds Faust physically (11498), thereby bringing about indirectly the spiritual awakening on the threshold of death, which Faust expresses in the words: "Die Nacht scheint tiefer-tief hereinzudringen,/ Allein im Innern leuchtet helles Licht" (11499–500). The figure of Care is of course distilled out of the whole of Faust's life-experience, yet she bears the above-mentioned direct relationship to his last great "crime," the incineration of the three figures discussed. As such their death, which seems outwardly so unspeakably meaningless, contributes directly to the physically blinding breath of "Sorge" which, however, *awakens* Faust's spiritual sight (". . . im Innern leuchtet helles Licht"). This is a clear illustration of what is meant by the suggestion that the workings of divine Love (in this case the inward illumination) are made possible on earth through the forces of sacrifice.

In his discussion of Faust's struggles against the elemental forces of the sea Emrich equates Faust's entelechy with the "inner light." He refers to it as the " 'unsterbliche Entelechie,' die Goethe hier mythisch als 'inneres Licht' be-

[16] Heinz Politzer, "Vom Baum der Erkenntnis und der Sünde der Wissenschaft: Zur Vegetationssymbolik in Goethes *Faust*," *JDSG*, 9 (1965), 367.

[17] In ll. 11382–83, "Geboten schnell, zu schnell getan!—/ Was schwebet schattenhaft heran?" the rhyme itself forms a link between the figure of "Sorge" and "jenem Nachgefühl der Tat, das wir mit dem Wort 'Reue' bezeichnen wollen . . . ," as pointed out by Stöcklein, *Wege zum späten Goethe*, p. 118.

zeichnet. . . ."[18] I choose to interpret the "inner light" as on the one hand symbolizing Faust's entelechy and at the same time as an image for the spiritual perception which begins to dawn in Faust's consciousness as the outer, physical world grows dark. In this sense it is a first awareness before death of the light-filled spiritual world which in "Bergschluchten" "blinds" Faust by its very brightness as his entelechy rises ever higher. This light is the light of divine Love, and reaches Faust by way of the very forces of sacrifice of which we have spoken. It is therefore appropriate that in "Bergschluchten" it should be the principal bearer of these forces, "Die eine Büsserin, *sonst Gretchen genannt*," who speaks of the light's effect upon the awakening entelechy of Faust in the words: "Noch blendet ihn der neue Tag" (12093).

The events of the tragic deaths of the old couple and the wanderer are poetically related in yet another way to the spiritual events following Faust's death. This inner connection unfolds through a transformation of the color-symbolism and of the imagery of vegetation. The destruction of the old couple's hut is reported by the watchman Lynkeus (11304–35). The fire within the hut spreads to the linden trees which collapse, bringing down the little chapel in conflagration. The trees, symbols of the purity of vegetative nature, give shade and with a protective gesture enclose human life in this idyllic setting. It is then significant that they should destroy the chapel as they collapse. The violated natural order crushes the foundations of man's spiritual institutions.

It is Mephisto and his three henchmen ("Die Drei," SD 11282) who destroy this idyllic world with the help of Mephisto's "freundlich Element" (2300), fire. It is that element which Mephisto had earlier characterized as particularly suited to his destructive purposes: "Hätt' ich mir nicht die Flamme vorbehalten,/ Ich hätte nichts Aparts für mich" (1377–78). Not only the verb "schlängelnd" mentioned by Politzer gives expression to the devilish nature of the conflagration. The two colors mentioned are the colors of hell itself, red and black: "Flamme flammet, rot in Gluten/ Steht das schwarze Moosgestelle" (11320–21). In the following two lines Lynkeus renders this associative use of the two colors explicit through his comparison of the event with the image of hell: "Retteten sich nur die Guten/ Aus der wildentbrannten Hölle!" (11322–23). In this connection I should like to point out that the Apocalypse tradition in medieval art often portrays the beasts or demons associated with the forces of the Antichrist as separate black and red beings.[19]

[18] Emrich, *Symbolik*, p. 398.

[19] It is highly unlikely that Goethe was not aware of this widespread tradition. The colors red and black here quite naturally lend an "infernal" aura to the scene, just as does the verb "schlängelnd." Cf. 1) the manuscript of the *Apocalypse of Saint Sever* (an 11th century Latin manuscript in the Bibliothèque Nationale): *L'Apocalypse de Saint Sever*, ed. Émilr A. van Moé (Paris: Les Éditions de Cluny, 1943), plate 22 ("l'agneau"), showing two beasts, one brown-black, the other, a serpent, red; plate 24 ("le dragon enchainé"), the same. 2) *The Trinity College Apocalypse*, ed. Peter H. Brieger (London: Eugram-

The frame of the house stands as a black skeleton amid the flames' red glow—reminiscent of an eerie *Knochenmann* moving through a burning city. Even more striking is the picture of the glowing, hollow treetrunks which Goethe sketches in two short lines: "Bis zur Wurzel glühn die hohlen/ Stämme, purpurrot im Glühn.—" (11334–35). It is a nightmarish, grotesque vision à la Hieronymos Bosch. The treetrunks, symbols of innocent vegetation, have been burnt out, leaving hollow shells which glow "purpurrot." The red and black of hell have seized upon a last outpost of piety and harmony in the human community and have transformed it into a nightmare.

Philemon, Baucis and the wanderer are all victims of the holocaust. Yet once again, if we follow carefully the details at work in Goethe's poetic imagination, the imagery itself leads us to deeper meanings inherent in the scene. In this instance it is important to notice a subtle nuance in Goethe's employment of the color-symbolism. The color red ("rot"), which in line 11320 describes the glow of the smoldering black frame of the cottage, yields in line 11335 to the color "purpurrot," which describes the glowing treetrunks. The reader familiar with Goethe's color studies is at once struck by the introduction of the word "purpur." This is the alternate term which Goethe applies to the intensified red which represents the ultimate confluence, through "Steigerung" or heightening, of the polar opposites of yellow and blue. Goethe first describes this phenomenon in the essay "Versuch die Elemente der Farbenlehre zu entdecken. Der Beiträge zur Optik viertes Stück" (1793) and speaks of this color "welche alle andern an Pracht und zugleich an Lieblichkeit übertrifft; es ist der Purpur."[20]

"Purpur," also referred to as "Rot," occupies a position of peculiar eminence in Goethe's imagination. In his discussion of the "sinnlich-sittliche Wirkung der Farbe" Goethe refers to this color as "diese höchste aller Farbenerscheinungen."[21] Not only does he associate it with the dignity of age and also the charm of youth;[22] he assigns to it the apocalyptic role of that color which should illuminate heaven and earth on the day of judgment.[23]

In the scene "Großer Vorhof des Palasts" Faust speaks his last words on earth, and dies. In the first scene following his death, "Grablegung," Mephisto conjures up grisly visions of hell as he and his devils ("Dickteufel," "Dünnteufel") prepare

mia Press, 1967), folio 14 *verso*, p. 34, a depiction of St. John facing two versions of the beast from the sea, one each black and red; folio 19 *verso*, p. 40, showing the dragon red, the beast black. 3) Fra Angelico, *The Last Judgment*, Museo di S. Marco, Florence, in Robert Hughes, *Heaven and Hell in Western Art* (New York: Stein and Day, 1968), p. 207.

[20] Cotta (1902 edition), XXII, 105. Quoted from Peter Schmidt, *Goethes Farbensymbolik* (Berlin, 1965), p. 58.

[21] *Zur Farbenlehre*, paragraph 794, HA XIII, 499.

[22] *Ibid.*, paragraph 796, p. 500.

[23] "Das Purpurglas zeigt eine wohlerleuchtete Landschaft in furchtbarem Lichte. So müßte der Farbeton über Erd und Himmel am Tage des Gerichts ausgebreitet sein." *Ibid.*, p. 500.

to capture Faust's soul. They are interrupted by an inpouring of light ("*Glorie von oben rechts*," SD 11676) and the heavenly hosts strewing roses. As they do so, they speak of the paradisiacal, springlike rejuvenation they bring to Faust:

> Frühling entsprieße,
> Purpur und Grün!
> Tragt Paradiese
> Dem Ruhenden hin.
> (11706–9)

Here, then, we again encounter the word "Purpur," this time thoroughly transformed as it lights up with pristine delicacy in the spiritual world, in the presence of Faust's earthly remains, after the midnight hour. "Purpur," the color of the glowing treetrunks, and "Grün," the color of the vegetative life destroyed by the conflagration, are both metamorphosed into the color of the roses strewn to drive off Mephisto and his associates. The angels refer to Faust as "dem Ruhenden," for he is dead only in the earthly world and his entelechy will soon awaken in the realm of spirit. The words "Frühling entsprieße" virtually reanimate the linden trees as the fires of Mephisto's realm are warded off. The colors "Purpur und Grün" represent a highly significant polarity within Goethe's conception of color relationships. They were introduced early in Part II in the scene "Lustgarten" as Mephisto flattered the emperor into fancying himself lord of the elements, for Goethe associates these shades with the water of the sea.[24] What is more, they represent for Goethe, as does the sun, the objective manifestation of divine spiritual reality in the phenomenal world of nature. In a passage of extraordinary beauty in his *Farbenlehre*, Goethe discusses these two colors as follows:

> Wenn man erst das Auseinandergehen des Gelben und Blauen wird recht gefaßt, besonders aber die Steigerung ins Rote genugsam betrachtet haben, wodurch das Entgegengesetzte sich gegeneinanderneigt und sich in einem Dritten vereinigt, dann wird gewiß eine besondere geheimnisvolle Anschauung eintreten, daß man diesen beiden getrennten, einander entgegengesetzten Wesen eine geistige Bedeutung unterlegen könne, und man wird sich kaum enthalten, wenn man sie unterwärts das Grün und oberwärts das Rot hervorbringen sieht, dort an die irdischen, hier an die himmlischen Ausgeburten der Elohim zu gedenken.[25]

In the light of the above passage it becomes clear that for Goethe the colors green and red, even from the standpoint of his color studies, impart a particularly deep spiritual quality to the image of the roses. This fact coincides precisely with the *thematic* significance of the rose symbol, for the roses "burn" the spirit of negation, Mephisto, by virtue of their own pure spirituality. The angels had

[24] Cf. ll. 6009–10. Cf. also the *Farbenlehre*, paragraph 164, *Ibid.*, p. 364.

[25] *Zur Farbenlehre*, paragraph 919, p. 521.

themselves received the roses from penitent women, as the "jüngere Engel" later explain:

Jene Rosen aus den Händen
Liebend-heiliger Büßerinnen
Halfen uns den Sieg gewinnen,
Uns das hohe Werk vollenden,
Diesen Seelenschatz erbeuten.
(11942–46)

This detail is of particular significance, for it points to the fact that the penitent women are able to offer, through the form of the roses, spiritual forces of which even the angels are in need if they are to fulfill their task. What manner of forces are these? They are forces of love which are attained through sacrifice. The four "sinful" women whom Goethe introduces in the final scene, Magna peccatrix, Mulier Samaritana, Maria Aegyptiaca and Una poenitentium, *sonst Gretchen genannt*, appear here by virtue of the fact that they have become penitents ("Büßerinnen") and earned for themselves a new nearness to divine Love through the sacrifice of their lower natures.

It is interesting that just as Faust is railing against the old couple's hut and complaining bitterly that it is not yet his, the image of *thorns* occurs, in the figure of speech "Ist Dorn den Augen, Dorn den Sohlen" (11161). In a similar turn of phrase he later exclaims to Mephisto: "Dir Vielgewandtem muß ich's sagen:/ Mir gibt's im Herzen Stich um Stich" (11235–36). Faust is consumed by a greedy desire to possess the property, and the greed doubles back upon him as a reflected egotism which he experiences as stabbing thorns. It is a foretaste of the pain suffered by the titan who crushes others in his path, for lack of control of his passion and desire. This is rendered very explicit by the two lines which follow the second passage quoted above: "Mir ist's unmöglich zu ertragen!/ Und wie ich's sage, schäm' ich mich" (11237–38).

The healing of this condition may be effected through the intervention of the Grace of which Goethe speaks to Eckermann in connection with Faust's situation. These forces of redemption gain access to the sphere of men's destinies through the transformation of lower instincts by penitence and self-sacrifice, as is shown in the metaphor of the roses, which derive their forces not from the angels, but from the penitent women who have extricated themselves from the egotism of exaggerated sensuality. The image of the thorns, which paralyze man's entire being, from his eyes ("Dorn den Augen") to the soles of his feet ("Dorn den Sohlen") is therefore inwardly related to the rose-imagery, just as the self-inflicted pain of egotism is related to the love which can heal it.

The scenes following Faust's death reveal an endless wealth of secrets pertaining to his life during the previous action of the play. This fact is indicated in the words of the "chorus mysticus":

Alles Vergängliche
Ist nur ein Gleichnis;
Das Unzulängliche,
Hier wird's Ereignis;
(12104–7)

One of the most impressive evidences of this principle is the recurrence and heightening of the theme of death and resurrection.[26] Faust's suicide wish in Part I, associated with the Easter events and the image of Christ lowered into the grave (749 ff.), is followed by the sunrise of the Easter morning and the reanimation of Faust's existence on earth through the Easter chorus. In Part II Faust himself dies and is buried, and his entelechy is gradually reanimated following the spiritual sunrise announced as a "Glorie von oben" (SD 11675). The two scenes are related in the manner of an octave, even from the formal standpoint, for both the Easter chorus of Part I ("Christ ist erstanden!," 737 ff.) and the angelic hosts of Part II ("Folget, Gesandte," 11676 ff.) break in upon the scene of death and negation with the same gentle dactylic rhythm. The first scene presents Faust's earthly experience of a "realistic," human Easter chorus and as such is an example of "das Vergängliche," "das Unzulängliche" of which the chorus mysticus speaks. Faust's experience in spirit realms after death is the higher "Ereignis" (12107) of which the previous episode was only a parable, a "Gleichnis." The parable's meaning is first truly revealed in the final scene. Yet even this "revelation" is prefigured as *both* Goethean and Christian in the words of the disciples in the first scene. The disciples speak of Christ's Resurrection using the Goethean term "Werdelust":

Hat der Begrabene
Schon sich nach oben,
Lebend Erhabene,
Herrlich erhoben,
Ist er in Werdelust
Schaffender Freude nah,
Ach, an der Erde Brust
Sind wir zum Leide da!
(785–92)

The words are unmistakably Goethean. Yet let us note the vowel pattern of the first four lines. The accented vowels are as follows:

a a
o o
e a
e o

[26] Cf. the discussion by Jantz of the work's structure: Harold Jantz, "Patterns and Structures in *Faust:* A Preliminary Inquiry," MLN, 83 (1968), 359–89. Jantz points to four important places in *Faust* at which "we have a darkness before dawn," a "death before resurrection," 366–67. Jantz subsequently terms this element of the play a "fourfold movement from death to resurrection," 385.

Can it escape our notice that the very lines describing the burial and Resurrection of Christ contain, each one twice, the two vowels which in the Book of Revelations He uses to describe Himself ("Ich bin das A und das O, der Anfang und das Ende")? In the two following lines each vowel recurs once again in a derivative form of the verb "erhaben," its upward-rising thrust musically enlivened by the metamorphosed *e* of the two adverbs "lebend" (the resurrected life itself) and "herrlich" (the radiance of that life). Such intimate details as this reveal how profound Goethe's treatment of such a theme really is. The Goethean-Christian quality of the final scene of Part II is concretely prefigured in the Goethean-Christian tenor of lines such as these which are related to it both thematically and formally as we have seen. The word "Werdelust" itself becomes "Ereignis" in the final scene as Faust's "immortal parts" ("Unsterbliches," SD 11934), or entelechy are borne upward by the angels, blessed boys, etc. The whole event stands under the signature of *becoming* ("Werdelust"), of the principle of metamorphosis from "Puppenstand" (11982) to new life.

In view of the foregoing it should now be possible to interpret the sacrifice of Philemon, Baucis and the wanderer somewhat more deeply, or inwardly. The event of their death is part of the heavy guilt which, as "Sorge," blinds Faust outwardly, releasing the "inner light." After his death it adheres to his innermost nature, forming part of the "Erdenrest" (11954) which the perfected angels themselves tell us can only be removed by the power of eternal Love ("Die ewige Liebe nur/ Vermag's zu scheiden," 11964–65). This eternal Love works *through the sacrifice itself* and is embodied symbolically in the roses. This is reflected not only in the transformation of the use of color, but also in the image of dust. The smoke which formed itself into the figure of Care is itself reanimated by the Love borne by the hosts of angels, as they tell us on their first appearance: "Sündern vergeben,/ Staub zu beleben" (11679–80).

The perennial question as to whether or not Faust is worthy of being "saved," especially after having committed three additional murders immediately preceding his death, is improperly put. Speculation as to its "rightness" or "wrongness" implies a specific judgment of the legalistic type which Goethe abandoned with his earlier thought of a judgment scene in Heaven. At bottom, Goethe's world outlook is concerned less with absolute judgments than with the processes of transformation and becoming ("Werden"). In the sphere of ethics this is perhaps best characterized by the term "positive Fruchtbarkeit" used by Viëtor in a passage which superbly summarizes Goethe's posture and also recognizes that it is not basically at odds with that of a non-dogmatic Christianity:

> So steht Goethe mit seiner Ansicht, daß von der Art des Lebens hier das Fortleben abhänge, in einer alten Tradition, zu der auch der christliche Glaube in Beziehung steht. Aber Goethe gibt der Überlieferung eine neue Wendung, in der seine Auffassung von der Bestimmung des Menschen sich ausdrückt. Nicht ein Leben nach den Geboten, nicht moralische Reinheit an sich gibt ein Anrecht auf persönliches Fortleben. Es ist die Entschiedenheit unseres Wollens und die Kraft

unseres Handelns, die positive Fruchtbarkeit, die wir lebend entfaltet haben,—dies ist es, was uns hier Personalität gewinnt und sie uns drüben bewahrt.[27]

In another passage Viëtor sums up very explicitly this union of "classical" and Christian elements in Goethe's world view:

> Auf dem Höhepunkt der Epoche, in der die moderne, säkulare Kultur zum letztenmal blühte, hat Goethe ein Bild des Menschen errichtet, in dem das klassische Ideal mit dem in dem christlichen Zeitalter geschaffenen Menschenbild sich verbindet. Die moralische Humanität, die auf die Autonomie des Gewissens gegründet ist, geht eine Ehe ein mit dem Geist der homerischen Antike, die den Menschen noch in ursprünglicher Einheit mit der Natur zeigt.[28]

The vegetative metaphor "positive Fruchtbarkeit" is reminiscent of Goethe's botanical studies, whose thought-processes are characteristic of the whole tone of his thinking. It is Schiller whom we have to thank for the epigram which most concisely illustrates the Goethean hope that man may bring about consciously, in the moral sphere, the metamorphoses and spiritual blossoming which the plant achieves unconsciously:

> Das Höchste
>
> Suchst du das Höchste, das Größte? Die Pflanze kann es dich lehren:
> Was sie willenlos ist, sei du es wollend—das ist's.[29]

This process is possible for man through the polarity of interacting earthly striving and divine Grace: "Wer immer strebend sich bemüht,/ Den können wir erlösen." The following two lines point expressly to this role of Love extended to man from above: "Und hat an ihm die Liebe gar/ Von oben teilgenommen." The question as to whether or not this Love is justified in extending itself to such a wayward soul as Faust, is irrelevant. For Goethe it does so, with the same organic necessity with which sunlight shines upon the plants. Man, in contrast to the plants, however, must learn to cooperate with the "sunlight." The most eminent representatives of German classicism were not so naïve as to equate the moral striving of man with the growth of the plant. The latter process is, also for Schiller, a symbol drawn from the natural world. This symbol must find expression in the *conscious* striving of man, lest he remain "der Unbehauste" as whom Faust sees himself in "Wald und Höhle" (3348).[30] In this scene Faust quite honestly senses the magnitude of the sacrifice he is demanding in his treatment of Gretchen

[27] Karl Viëtor, *Goethe* (Bern, 1949), p. 482.

[28] *Ibid.*, p. 528.

[29] Friedrich Schiller, *Sämtliche Werke*, 5 vols. (München and Leipzig, Hanser, 1958), I, 243.

[30] In the *Versuch, die Metamorphose der Pflanzen zu erklären* (1790) Goethe does not expand upon the symbolical associations of man's inward perfection which may be read out of the metamorphoses of plant forms. Nevertheless, he clearly had such an analogy in mind, as it is revealed in his private notes. Cf. Ronald Gray, *Goethe the Alchemist* (Cambridge, 1952), Chapter IV. Gray points to the specific

—hence his self-characterization as "der Gottverhaßte" (3351) and his rationalization "Du, Hölle, mußtest dieses Opfer haben!" (3361).

Gretchen, through her sacrifice, is the central bearer of the Love which links Faust to the divine creation. In her destiny as well, the signature of the archetypal juxtaposition of death and dawn plays a key role. What is more, the apocalyptic associations we have discussed in connection with the Easter chorus and its fulfillment at the end of the play also extend to the "structural octave" of Gretchen's death scene ("Kerker") and her reappearance at the end of the play. Her words "der letzte Tag" ("Tag! Ja es wird Tag! der letzte Tag dringt herein;" 4580) are an unmistakable reference to the day of judgment and find fulfillment in the "revelation" of her higher spiritual existence as "una poenitentium" in the final scene of Part II. Similarly, the prayer before the *physical statue* of the "mater dolorosa" in the scene "Zwinger" ("Ach neige,/ Du Schmerzenreiche," 3587–88) appears as a revelation of the workings of Grace itself in the transformed version spoken before the *spiritual being* of the "mater gloriosa" in the final scene ("Neige, neige,/ Du Ohnegleiche," 12069–70). Through repeated examples of this sort we find that the final scene of Part II provides a positively apocalyptic unsealing, or revelation, of the spiritual *Urbilder* of earthly experiences presented earlier in the poem.[31]

Faust's involvements in guilt and destruction are undeniably severe. The fact that Goethe saw fit to lead him upwards despite these transgressions rests in the optimism of the eighteenth century and, more pertinently, in the spiritual resources of the author. More pertinently, for the reason that the upward path of man's entelechy as Goethe here portrays it is not automatic and therefore not naïvely optimistic in its conception. The vegetation symbolism, the power of conscious striving within the entelechy—these are all forces inherent in Nature as Goethe conceived it. Yet this is no Leibnizian ideal construct, in which the monads all of necessity interact to represent the "best possible world." It is rather a world fraught with illusion, guilt, error and death—a world-picture which can only retain its upward progression through the intervention of divine Love, as this is repeatedly shown, from the "Stimme von oben" (SD 4612) at the end of Part I to

analogy with the process of self-sacrifice, an analogy inherent in the transitional stage from leaves to calyx: "Nothing was more natural, within the framework of alchemical beliefs, than that such an ennoblement should derive from complete self-sacrifice, through 'death and rebirth' " (p. 81). Gray subsequently sums up Goethe's use of the analogy of the plant seed in words which illuminate the underlying intent of the Schiller epigram quoted above: "In the seed of the plant, the alchemist, as well as Goethe, had an almost perfect analogy for the organic growth of the divine image in Man. This was perhaps a symbol in full accordance with Goethe's definition" (p. 132).

[31] From a different angle Jantz also arrives at the conclusion that the treatment of the end of the drama is appropriate. He notes that innumerable critics have objected to the Christian conclusion as though it were somehow out of harmony with the rest of the work, "an old man's unfortunate whim. . . ." Yet Jantz demonstrates that it is "exactly the kind of ending the poet had planned at an early stage." "Patterns and Structures in Faust," MLN, 83, 383 ff.

the workings of the spiritual world "von oben" (11939) at the end of Part II.

Faust is in a very real sense a representative of that which it has become fashionable to call "man's state," and Goethe was fully conscious of the role played in the life of every human being by the sacrifices brought, willingly or unwillingly, by others with whose destinies he is connected. A proper understanding of the way in which Goethe weaves the mystery of sacrifice into his work renders all abstract argumentation about the work's Christian or non-Christian character superfluous. Once the function of this theme is studied in depth the Christian imagery of the end of Part II no longer appears as traditional décor employed to clothe the essential, and non-Christian theme of "Werden." Both elements are found to be intimately related in the poetic exemplification of a unified world outlook. What could possibly be a more fitting fulfillment of the Goethean theme of "Werden" than its ennoblement in the Christian sense, through the *spiritual growth* which springs forth from the consequences of sacrifice? Against this background Goethe's optimism is revealed in its fullness, and that means in its maturity. It is an optimism born not of naïveté but of the insight of a spirit well acquainted with grief and renunciation.

In the *Märchen* Goethe presents the theme in its quintessential form. The bridge over the river is established just through the green snake's sacrifice of its own being, whereby it literally "lays the foundation" for something new. It is a sacrifice consciously undertaken, rather than passively suffered. To the old man's question "Was hast du beschlossen?" the snake replies: "Mich aufzuopfern, ehe ich aufgeopfert werde, . . ."[32] In the *Faust* drama the theme is given its purely Christian form in the chorus of angels who speak of Christ as "der Liebende" who has withstood the test of conscious sacrifice:

> Christ ist erstanden!
> Selig der Liebende,
> Der die betrübende,
> Heilsam' und übende
> Prüfung bestanden.
> (757–61)

Sacrifice on this scale does not compel obeisance but rather is a source of deeply creative forces of love; in the words of the old man in the *Märchen*: "Die Liebe herrscht nicht, aber sie bildet, und das ist mehr."[33] Faust does not "believe" the words of the song, yet through them and through the music, forces are freed within him which reanimate the spirit, drive forth the tears and return him to the earth (784). It is on the earth that he must live out his life and survive the test ("Prüfung") of his own existence. Even such a powerful and encompassing entelechy as Faust finds this too great a task to be accomplished during his hundred

[32] HA VI, 233.

[33] *Ibid.*, p. 238.

allotted years. Goethe once made the statement: ". . . um sich künftig als große Entelechie zu manifestieren, muß man auch eine sein."[34] This is quite an order indeed, even for such a titan as Faust. It is not easy to say how Goethe intended that the process of "Werden" should be resolved. The earth being a likely place upon which to work at it, it is perhaps not unthinkable that the entelechy might contemplate a return visit. Mephisto, at any rate, does not underestimate this, for him, sobering thought. In a paralipomenon to the scene "Grablegung" he contemplates just this possibility, and he therefore seems concerned to make haste in announcing to God that he has won the wager:

> So ruhe denn an deiner Stätte.
> Sie weihen das Paradebette
> Und eh das Seelchen sich entrafft
> Sich einen neuen Körper schafft
> Verkünd ich oben die gewonnene Wette.
> Nun freu ich mich aufs große Fest
> Wie sich der Herr vernehmen läßt.[35]

Should Faust once again feel the call of the haunting phrase ". . . die Erde hat mich wieder" and return to pick up the threads of his strivings, Mephisto would be just as disquieted by this as he is by the gentle onslaught of heavenly beings. For in either case he is most definitely the "loser," and Mephisto is one being in the world-order who is certainly not known for an inclination to sacrifice. And particularly not when the object of the sacrifice is an entelechy of the magnitude of Faust, to whom Mephisto himself refers as his "großer, einziger Schatz," his "hohe Seele" (11829–30), the soul of man.

[34] *Gespräche mit Eckermann*, 1 September 1829, p. 371.

[35] Paralipomenon 94. Weimarer Ausgabe XV/2 (1888), 187.

V

"Des Menschen Kraft, im Dichter offenbart" Thoughts on the Sources of Poetic Creativity in View of Goethe's Image of Man

In an issue devoted to the arts, the *Saturday Review* for 15 July 1972 features an essay by Professor B. F. Skinner entitled "On 'Having' a Poem."[1] The article is adapted from a lecture delivered at the New York Poetry Center on 13 October 1971 and is referred to on the cover as "A Startling Vision of the Poet." The vision is startling indeed, for Skinner propounds the thesis that the poet produces his work of art in the same way in which the hen produces an egg. The question which Skinner undertakes to answer is stated as follows: "Does the poet create, originate, initiate the thing called a poem, or is his behavior merely the product of his genetic and environmental histories?"[2] Skinner assumes that the question of spiritual creativity is of the same order as that of biological phenomena and therefore undertakes to answer it by drawing an analogy to the process of reproduction in the human mother and in the hen. The analogy was suggested to him by a remark of Samuel Butler to the effect that "a poet writes a poem as a hen lays an egg, and both feel better afterwards."[3]

The human mother, Skinner asserts, is "a place, a locus in which a very important biological process takes place."[4] Through her the genes of her parents are passed on to the child, but she makes "*no positive contribution*" to the process, for in this view: "To have a baby is to come into possession of it." The mother, then, is passive, the process in essence automatic. The conclusion is drawn by analogy: "The poet is also a locus, a place in which certain genetic and environmental causes come together to have a common effect." The poet, Skinner assumes, is as little aware of the origins of his creative efforts as is a hen of the origins of hers. This leads him to propose that it is illegitimate to speak of a

[1] B. F. Skinner, "On 'Having' a Poem," *Saturday Review*, 15 July 1972, pp. 32–35. Originally published in *Cumulative Record: A Selection of Papers*. 3rd ed. (New York, 1972), pp. 345–55. The following references are to this book.

[2] *Cumulative Record*, p. 351.

[3] *Ibid.*, p. 350.

[4] *Ibid.*, p. 352.

creative mind at work in the poet: "And because the poet is not aware of the origins of his behavior, he is likely to attribute it to a creative mind, . . ."[5] The lines of the argument are clear, and Skinner sums them up as follows: "Writing a poem is the sort of thing men and women do as men and women, having a baby is the sort of thing a woman does as a woman, and laying an egg is the sort of thing a hen does as a hen." The three events are assumed to be of the same order and are thus all treated on exactly the same level. This has the appearance of objectivity, yet it is a statement which clearly contains a great deal of hidden philosophy. Be the logic of the assertion what it may, Skinner hastens to reassure us that its implications are benign: "To deny a creative contribution does not destroy man *qua* man or woman *qua* woman any more than Butler's phrase destroys hen *qua* hen. There is no threat to the essential humanity of man, the muliebrity of woman, or the gallity of *Gallus gallus*." All is well. The "essential humanity of man" is not threatened by equating him with a hen. Of course not, for the concept of the humanity of man which Skinner advances here does not embrace factors of a higher order than those of biology. If higher attributes do not exist it is nonsense to assume that they are threatened. Skinner continues: "What is threatened, of course, is the autonomy of the poet. The autonomous is the uncaused, and the uncaused is miraculous, and the miraculous is God." Here, finally, is the full thrust of the argument: by the simple assertion that the act of spiritual creativity in man is in all essential respects equal to the biological generation of a human baby or of the hen's egg Skinner undertakes to dispense once and for all with the "uncaused," the "miraculous," indeed even with "God." We leave it to our readers individually to consider the implications of this image of man and the logic of the concept-formation advanced on its behalf. The point is that this way of thinking has gained a conspicuous following in recent years and does indeed—Skinner is quite right—pose a threat to the autonomy of the poet. One may in fact be justified in considering the implications of its considerable influence to pose a threat to what generations of men schooled in the Judeo-Christian tradition have commonly felt to comprise "the essential humanity of man."

Goethe has long been considered one of the eminent spokesmen of the western tradition. Not, to be sure, in the sense of any orthodoxy, but in terms of the broad spectrum of attitudes and values which are the very life blood of his humanism. *Faust* is itself a documentation of his lifelong struggle to achieve ever greater clarity of insight into "the humanity of man," particularly of modern western man in his struggle for self-determination and for spiritual autonomy. The picture of man and of the poet advanced by Professor Skinner represents a clear-cut attack on the image of the human being which lies at the heart of Goethe's life work. Goethe's commitment is to spiritual freedom and dignity. In the sublime process of artistic creativity he sees the manifestation of genius. In the

[5] *Ibid.*, p. 354.

same process Skinner sees mindless causality. The image of man as poet which Skinner presents speaks for itself. We shall take its challenge as occasion to reflect on the image of man as poet and as creative thinker which Goethe presents, particularly in *Faust* and in his posture as natural scientist. The subject is vast and we shall have to restrict the scope of the discussion. We shall see a picture emerging, however, which we shall place before the reader and which may serve as a stimulus to rethink Goethe's view of man in the light of that other view whose uncritical acceptance could be the undoing of much that we hold dear in western culture.

Goethe, himself a highly conscious artist, was fully aware of that aspect of the creative process which takes place largely subconsciously, manifesting itself virtually as a force of nature. He experienced this force in himself and observed it in others. In Byron, for instance, he saw this elemental poetic creativity at work. He describes it to Eckermann as follows: "Zu seinen Sachen kam er, wie die Weiber zu schönen Kindern; sie denken nicht daran und wissen nicht wie."[6] The image is reminiscent of Skinner's, yet Goethe refers the thought to a faculty which he terms "inspiration" and which he contrasts to the faculty of "reflection." Thus he prefaces the above statement with the words: "Aber alles, was er produzieren mag, gelingt ihm, und man kann wirklich sagen, daß sich ihm die Inspiration an die Stelle der Reflexion setzt." Goethe was particularly shattered by the news of Byron's death, for he saw in the English poet a reflection of the gifted young man that he had once been himself—the surging power, self-confidence, idealism and spontaneity which had characterized the storm and stress period, the early Sesenheim poems, the great hymns and the elemental fire of *Werther* and *Götz*.

In the sixteenth Book of *Dichtung und Wahrheit* Goethe describes this "talent as nature" which had worked through him so powerfully as a young man:

> Ich war dazu gelangt, das mir inwohnende dichterische Talent ganz als Natur zu betrachten, um so mehr, als ich darauf gewiesen war, die äußere Natur als den Gegenstand desselben anzusehen. Die Ausübung dieser Dichtergabe konnte zwar durch Veranlassung erregt und bestimmt werden, aber am freudigsten und reichlichsten trat sie unwillkürlich, ja wider Willen hervor.
>
> Durch Feld und Wald zu schweifen,
> Mein Liedchen weg zu pfeifen,
> So ging's den ganzen Tag.[7]

At this time of life Goethe lived so intensely with his *feelings* in the world of nature that he experienced his own being as a part of that world and his innate creative talents as a part of the host of productive forces which are at work within it. These forces of creativity often broke forth with such power that Goethe felt he had

[6] Conversation of 24 February 1825. Ernst Beutler, ed., *Goethe, Gespräche mit Eckermann*, Artemis Ausgabe (Zürich, 1949), p. 149.

[7] *Dichtung und Wahrheit*, Book 16, HA X, 80.

little or no conscious control of them. Awakening in the night he often felt carried by an unfathomed surge of inspiration and struggled to capture it on paper:

> Auch beim nächtlichen Erwachen trat derselbe Fall ein, und ich hatte oft Lust, wie einer meiner Vorgänger,[8] mir ein ledernes Wams machen zu lassen, und mich zu gewöhnen, im Finstern, durchs Gefühl, das, was unvermutet hervorbrach, zu fixieren. Ich war so gewohnt, mir ein Liedchen vorzusagen, ohne es wieder zusammen finden zu können, daß ich einigemal an den Pult rannte und mir nicht die Zeit nahm, einen quer liegenden Bogen zurecht zu rücken, sondern das Gedicht von Anfang bis zu Ende, ohne mich von der Stelle zu rühren, in der Diagonale herunterschrieb. In eben diesem Sinne griff ich weit lieber zu dem Bleistift, welcher williger die Züge hergab: denn es war mir einigemal begegnet, daß das Schnarren und Spritzen der Feder mich aus meinem nachtwandlerischen Dichten aufweckte, mich zerstreute und ein kleines Produkt in der Geburt erstickte.[9]

Goethe refers to this mysterious type of poetic creativity as "somnambulent," or trance-like ("nachtwandlerisches Dichten"). And the results of it surprised him, just as his description of them may surprise us: "Für solche Poesien hatte ich eine besondere Ehrfurcht, weil ich mich doch ohngefähr gegen dieselben verhielt, wie die Henne gegen die Küchlein, die sie ausgebrütet um sich her piepsen sieht." Back to the hen! Byron, says Goethe, gave birth to his poems as women to their children, and Goethe sometimes thought of his own creations as little chicks hatched by the mother hen. This points to a reason why Skinner's thesis has a certain appeal: the images he uses contain a grain of truth. Yet as always the mistaking of a partial truth for the whole truth is much more dangerous than the presentation of an untruth, for an untruth is more easily recognized. And a partial truth presented in the form of an *image* is particularly powerful, for it eludes logical conceptualization and works on in the reader or listener purely visually.

The fundamental differences underlying Skinner's and Goethe's use of these images is revealed by a closer look at the contexts in which they appear. Skinner uses the metaphors as illustration of a general law of poetic creation and therefore speaks of "the poet." In the case of both Byron and of his own "somnambulent" activities Goethe employs the imagery to characterize a specific, indeed unusual situation. Moreover, a careful look at the wording in each case proves that Goethe had more in mind than a simple mechanical process. In the first instance he speaks of two mental faculties of man, "Inspiration" and "Reflexion" and cites Byron as an illustration of the preeminence of the first. Thus Byron's bringing forth poems as a mother her children here means something utterly different from Skinner's notion that the mother is "a place, a locus in which a very important biological process takes place," a process to which she makes "*no positive contribution*." And in the passage in *Dichtung und Wahrheit* Goethe is careful to distance

[8] The reference is to Petrarch.

[9] *Dichtung und Wahrheit*, HA X, 80–81.

himself from his own metaphor by inserting the word "ohngefähr" into the comparison he draws: ". . . weil ich mich doch ohngefähr gegen dieselben verhielt, wie die Henne . . ." Moreover, the hen in Goethe's simile is not merely a passive "locus," she has provided the warmth needed to hatch the eggs and now contemplates the living beings which have been born ("um sich her piepsen sieht"). Most importantly, however, Goethe stands before the whole phenomenon not in cold detachment but in reverence: "Für solche Poesien hatte ich eine besondere Ehrfurcht. . . ." The mood engendered imparts itself also to the choice of language. There is a touch of humor and also a sense of warmth in the diminutive "Küchlein" and the verbs "ausgebrütet" and "piepsen." Goethe uses the simile of the hen with conscious restraint to illustrate a particular variety of only semiconscious creative activity and he does so with reverence. Skinner uses the same image to cover all cases and he does so with the avowed intent of doing away with any phenomena which remind him of the "uncaused," the "miraculous," or "God." The two stances are utterly different. Indeed, Goethe views the quiet reverencing of that whose cause is not yet apprehended as the highest good of man the thinker: "Das schönste Glück des denkenden Menschen ist, das Erforschliche erforscht zu haben und das Unerforschliche ruhig zu verehren."[10] Goethe's use of the image of the hen differs from that of Skinner in the underlying context in which it rests. And this context, the author's intent, is crucial in reading his use of such an image. This importance of taking into account what lies behind a thought or an action is clearly stated by Ralph Waldo Emerson as follows: "The sentiment from which it sprang determines the dignity of any deed, and the question ever is, not what you have done or forborne, but at whose command you have done or forborne it."[11]

If much of the young Goethe's poetic creation was, in his own words, "somnambulent," it was nevertheless felt to be an *activity*, and he felt it to be nourished from those two great founts from which he drew strength and inspiration for the rest of his life's work: nature and love. Both themes spring forth in the Sesenheim period with a freshness that is eternal. The theme of nature:

> Wie herrlich leuchtet
> Mir die Natur!
> Wie glänzt die Sonne!
> Wie lacht die Flur!

The theme of love:

> O Lieb', o Liebe,
> So golden schön
> Wie Morgenwolken
> Auf jenen Höhn,

[10] *Maximen und Reflexionen*, no. 719, HA XII, 467.

[11] Ralph Waldo Emerson, "Experience," *Essays, Second Series*, Centenary Edition (Boston and New York, 1903), III, 72.

and the exclamation of gratitude for the fact that love has set moving not only the secret life of nature but also the singing voice of the poet:

Wie ich dich liebe
Mit warmen Blut,
Die du mir Jugend
Und Freud' und Mut

Zu neuen Liedern
Und Tänzen gibst.
Sei ewig glücklich,
Wie du mich liebst.[12]

Nature and love are two streams which fed Goethe's poetic genius throughout his life. They flow through his great poem on the struggles of modern man, *Faust*, and in a deep sense they underlie his efforts in the scientific fields. But the important point is that they did not simply coagulate in him to form poetry but that they fed his creative genius. A whole generation felt this innate, sovereign power of creativity in man so strongly that it gave its name to the age: "die Geniezeit." It was a rebellion against convention and rigidity and it soon led to such a blaze of emotionalism and egotism that the word "Genie," seriously misapplied to cover any whim or excess, necessarily went out of fashion. The point had been made, however. The poet possessed a spark of divine life which he could kindle to bright flame. Goethe was fascinated throughout his life by this very element in man—the eternally active, incalculable, unpredictable force of the self. He later often referred to it as "das Dämonische" and in his last years he refined and purified the concept and called it by the Aristotelean term "entelechy," the being having its goal (τέλος) in itself. We shall now turn our attention to certain structural elements, themes and images in *Faust* which illuminate Goethe's picture of the nature of poetic genius and its creative activity.

It is significant that the character Faust does not appear on the stage until the official opening scene of Part I, "Nacht." The scene is preceded by a threefold introduction: "Zueignung," the "Vorspiel auf dem Theater" and the "Prolog im Himmel." The three serve to prepare the reader for what is to come, so that he does not step abruptly from the world of everyday commerce into the sanctuary of the dramatic poem. In this sense they form an "entrance hall," or an "entrance gate." It was just such an image which Goethe had in mind when, in 1798, he began publication of the journal *Die Propyläen*, whose name refers to the entrance gate of the Acropolis in Athens. The sentiment expressed in the two opening paragraphs of the "Einleitung in die Propyläen" describes very well one of the principal functions of the three introductory scenes in *Faust:*

> Der Jüngling, wenn Natur und Kunst ihn anziehen, glaubt mit einem lebhaften Streben bald in das innerste Heiligtum zu dringen; der Mann bemerkt, nach langem

[12] "Maifest" (1771), HA I, 30–31.

Umherwandeln, daß er sich noch immer in den Vorhöfen befinde.

Eine solche Betrachtung hat unsern Titel veranlaßt. Stufe, Tor, Eingang, Vorhalle, der Raum zwischen dem Innern und Äußern, zwischen dem Heiligen und Gemeinen kann nur die Stelle sein, auf der wir uns mit unsern Freunden gewöhnlich aufhalten werden.[13]

The realm of art is holy, its sanctuary to be entered only after due preparation and by way of an entrance hall in which the eye blinded by the sun and tumult without is able to adjust itself to the darkness and solemnity within. In *Faust* we are led in steps from the world of the poet's consciousness into the world of the theater in which his work is to be produced and finally into the inner being of that work itself.

The "Zueignung" is inner monologue. We are inside of the poet's mind and all is in flux: "Ihr naht euch wieder, schwankende Gestalten." The figures arise and fall, emerge and recede. It is a realm of the Mothers in which Goethe finds the forms of a world long gone, the figures who accompanied the writing of the first versions of *Faust* and into whose world he now (1797) descends to receive inspiration to continue. The Dedication is a confession, a revelation of what the process of poetic creation had come to mean to the mature Goethe. It contrasts markedly with the brilliant spontaneity, haste and semi-conscious outpourings described as his youthful "nachtwandlerisches Dichten." The process is now highly conscious—an almost reluctant reopening of the past, an extreme effort of the will, exerted in painful probings of the inner life. Here, too, a work of art wishes to come to birth, but it will not happen spontaneously. This inner realm, the source of inspiration, will be entered only knowingly and by dint of struggle. We recall Mephisto's characterization of the world surrounding the Mothers: "Um sie kein Ort, noch weniger eine Zeit" (6214). Here too, in the Dedication, Goethe must descend into the past and into surroundings long since disappeared from his view, overcoming the limits of both space and time. It is a purely spiritual realm ("Geisterreich," 26) and to wrest from it the inspiration for art involves the conscious acceptance of the pains of birth: "Mein Leid ertönt der unbekannten Menge" (21). The pain is intense as the being of the poem hovers as music on the air: "Es schwebet nun in unbestimmten Tönen/ Mein lispelnd Lied, der Äolsharfe gleich . . ." (27–28). Just as in the stunning "Trilogie der Leidenschaft" music brings solace to the agony of a heart in grief, transmuting sorrow into song, so here does the heart find comfort in the Aeolian strains which herald the birth of art from that timeless inner world which releases its children to the light only against the toll of tears:

Und mich ergreift ein längst entwöhntes Sehnen
Nach jenem stillen, ernsten Geisterreich,

[13] "Einleitung in die Propyläen," HA XII, 38. Cf. also Gerhard Storz, who refers to these three introductory scenes as the "Propyläen vor dem Bezirk der Faustdichtung." Gerhard Storz, *Goethe-Vigilien* (Stuttgart, 1953), p. 150.

Es schwebet nun in unbestimmten Tönen
Mein lispelnd Lied, der Äolsharfe gleich,
Ein Schauer faßt mich, Träne folgt den Tränen,
Das strenge Herz, es fühlt sich mild und weich;
Was ich besitze, seh' ich wie im Weiten,
Und was verschwand, wird mir zu Wirklichkeiten.
(25–32)

The new *Faust* hovers before Goethe's inner eye and ear as does Homunculus before Faust—a being as yet purely spiritual, abiding the time when it may find embodiment.

The earnest tone of the "Zueignung" finds relief in the "Vorspiel auf dem Theater," in which the motif of the embodiment of the poet's work in the world of the theater comes to expression in quintessential form. The mood is light and comic throughout, for the one serious figure, the poet, whom we need not identify with the Goethe of the "Zueignung,"[14] is so painfully idealistic as to evoke our gentle smiles. The poet represents the inward, ideal realm of art, the theater director the external, insensitively pragmatic and unabashedly mercenary world of the businessman who must please a clamoring public. Between the two stands the "lustige Person," a clown who cannot be referred to any character in *Faust*, but who fits perfectly into this little "phenomenology of the theater," for it is he who stands between poet and public and brings *life* onto the stage in word and gesture. As such he is truly the "soul" of the theater. The as yet unembodied "spirit" of the drama—any drama—lives first in the lonely inner world of the poet's consciousness. Through the high art of acting, represented here in charming

[14] Cf. Oskar Seidlin, "Ist das 'Vorspiel auf dem Theater' ein Vorspiel zum 'Faust'?" in *Von Goethe zu Thomas Mann* (Göttingen, 1963), pp. 56–64. Seidlin advances strong evidence to suggest that Goethe may originally have intended the "Vorspiel auf dem Theater" as a "Vorspiel" to the *Zauberflöte*. There are clear echoes of the world of the theater director Serlo in *Wilhelm Meisters Lehrjahre* and the tone of the entire scene is reminiscent of the spontaneity of the *commedia dell'arte*. What is more, certain of the paralipomena to the scene point to the *Zauberflöte* as do certain specific lines of the director (233–38). Although there is thus strong reason to believe that the scene may refer in a number of ways to the fairy-tale world of the *Zauberflöte*, Goethe placed it at the beginning of his *Faust*. It is this placement which is of particular interest to us in the present study. One can understand the role of the "Vorspiel" in *Faust* if one takes it as a picture of the world of the theater as such, with its "soul," the "lustige Person," and its double reference: on the one hand inward, in the figure of the poet, and on the other hand outward, in the director. As such the scene is a commentary on the forces which go into the performing of *any* work on the stage, and its humorous tone serves the essential purpose of leading the reader via a touch of comic relief from the profoundly serious sentiments of the "Zueignung" into the forces portrayed in the "Prolog im Himmel."

Aspects of this subject are discussed, particularly with reference to the older *Faust* literature, by Stuart Atkins: "A Reconsideration of Some Unappreciated Aspects of the Prologues and Early Scenes in Goethe's 'Faust,' " *MLR*, 47 (1952), 362–73 and in the subsequent exchange with D. J. Enright, under "Miscellaneous Notes," *MLR*, 48 (1953), 189–94. On the question of the possible relationship of the "Vorspiel" to the *Zauberflöte* cf. also Alwin Binder, *Das Vorspiel auf dem Theater. Poetologische und geschichtsphilosophische Aspekte in Goethes Faust-Vorspiel* (Bonn, 1969), pp. 183 ff.

spontaneity by the "lustige Person," it is "ensouled" in the medium of joy and sadness, and through the—however unenlightened—efforts of the director it finds "embodiment" in the physical house of the theater with all its trappings and appurtenances. These, says Goethe, are the three ingredients, the triad of forces which are necessary if the work of art is to be brought from the world of inspiration into its physical incorporation in the theater. The statement contained in this scene may refer to *Faust* or to another work intended for the stage, for its threefold structure contains an archetype of the destiny of any dramatic work from the inner to the outer, from the purely spiritual to the manifest, physical world. In its essentially comic tone of exaggerated indignation alternating with buffoonery and materialistic self-interest it casts a welcome bridge of restrained levity from the deeply serious "Zueignung" to the world of cosmic mysteries revealed in the "Prolog im Himmel" in which the one specific drama which is to unfold in the subsequent scenes and acts is introduced on a grand scale.

In the Prologue the new work of art heralded by the poet's searchings in the Dedication has arrived, has been born in the world, on the stage. Its first revelation is not yet darkened by the night of the physical surroundings which envelops Faust in the following scene, "Nacht." There we see Faust literally imprisoned in physical matter: narrow Gothic walls, books, bones and dust. And his spirit, too, is fettered to the realm of dead phenomena by the strictures of science. In the Prologue the realm of darkness is first described by the archangel Gabriel who gazes down upon the rotating earth: "Es wechselt Paradieseshelle/ Mit tiefer, schauervoller Nacht" (253–54). It then rises from the depths and makes its appearance in the person of Mephistopheles. The external realm of darkness on earth thus finds here its inner counterpart: moral darkness.

In the Prologue the work of art which is *Faust* is "born" on the stage. The scene is a bridge from the cosmic to the terrestrial, from light to darkness, and through the discussion of Faust, who has not yet appeared on stage, prepares us for the enactment of this man's destiny. It is a last glance back into the luminous realms of cosmic harmonies in which, the Lord assures us, Faust's entelechy has its true home and to which it will return at the end of Part II of the poem. This light-filled realm of the spirit is also that from which the poet has drawn his inspiration. This we shall see substantiated by the use of the symbol of *gold* in Part II. The celestial world of the Prologue is thus not only the world out of which Faust's entelechy is born, it is also that out of which the being of poetry is born.

The three introductory scenes are indeed an "entrance hall" into the body of the poem. They also form an extraordinary progression which leads us step by step from the poet's inner world of spiritual forms, the forms which he must capture as "schwankende Erscheinung" (348) in the Mother-ground of the cosmos, to their final embodiment in the external world of the stage. The Prologue crowns this threefold process as *Faust* begins to unfold its being in physical incorporation on the stage, yet in doing so still appears windowed on the world from which it has come.

In these three great steps the being, the Idea of *Faust* comes to birth. The young Goethe was inspired at times in spontaneous, unexpected ways and was then astonished to contemplate the little "chicks" he had hatched. The scenes of the *Urfaust* may in some slight measure have arisen in this way. The mature Goethe proceeds more reflectively, more consciously. Inspiration is wrested from sorrow and tempered by pain and one senses an element of intensely conscious inner struggle which Skinner does not describe as a factor in the creative process. In a discussion of Shakespeare in "The Hero as Poet" Goethe's translator and friend Carlyle shows appreciation for the unconscious depths which well up in the process of creativity as a force of nature. Yet he also shows a clear understanding of the central role of the sorrow and struggle which lie hidden behind the wisdom revealed in great art:

> It is Nature's highest reward to a true simple great soul, that he get thus to be *a part of herself.* Such a man's works, whatsoever he with utmost conscious exertion and forethought shall accomplish, grow up withal *un*consciously, from the unknown deeps in him;—as the oak-tree grows from the Earth's bosom, as the mountains and waters shape themselves; with a symmetry grounded on Nature's own laws, conformable to all Truth whatsoever. How much in Shakespeare lies hid; his sorrows, his silent struggles known to himself; much that was not known at all, not speakable at all: like *roots*, like sap and forces working underground! Speech is great; but Silence is greater.[15]

We have now identified two sides of the process of artistic creation which transcend facile descriptions of the confluence of genetic and environmental histories in the poet: inspiration, whose organs are fashioned in man now by joy ("Maifest"), now by suffering ("Zueignung"), and: productive effort, struggle and work. Carlyle describes them with reference to Shakespeare. In *Representative Men* Emerson describes the second, the role of unceasing toil, with specific reference to Goethe: "This cheerful laborer, with no external popularity or provocation, drawing his motive and his plan from his own breast, tasked himself with stints for a giant, and without relaxation or rest, except by alternating his pursuits, worked on for eighty years with the steadiness of his first zeal."[16] The two sides of the act of poetic creation come to expression in *Faust*, Part II in connection with the allegorical figure who represents poetry. He appears in the masque in Act I as the Boy Charioteer ("Knabe Lenker") and reappears in Act III as Euphorion.[17] The symbol which carries the motif of inspiration in Part II is gold. In the masque Faust as Plutus and Mephisto as Avarice ("Geiz") refer not only to material wealth. They also represent the problem of the attainment and use of the spiritual wealth of insight and creativity. The Boy Charioteer scatters

[15] Thomas Carlyle, "The Hero as Poet," *The Works*, Centenary Edition (New York, 1897), V, 289.

[16] Emerson, *Representative Men*, Centenary Edition, IV, 289.

[17] Goethe himself identifies the two figures as identical. Cf. the conversation with Eckermann for 20 December 1829. *Gespräche mit Eckermann*, pp. 379–80.

gold jewelry to the crowd and he refers to the flames of inspiration which are also his to bestow: "Auch Flämmchen spend' ich dann und wann,/ Erwartend, wo es zünden kann" (5588–89). Plutus refers to him as his son (5629) and as "... Geist von meinem Geiste" (5623). But the true spirit of poetry has its home in another world and finds itself alienated in society. It is a sentiment which recurs in various forms from *Werther* to *Tasso* to the poet in the "Vorspiel auf dem Theater" and *Faust* II. The Boy Charioteer needs a realm of isolation and quietude. His father Plutus describes this sphere:

> Nun bist du los der allzulästigen Schwere,
> Bist frei und frank, nun frisch zu deiner Sphäre!
> Hier ist sie nicht! Verworren, scheckig, wild
> Umdrängt uns hier ein fratzenhaft Gebild.
> Nur wo du klar ins holde Klare schaust,
> Dir angehörst und dir allein vertraust,
> Dorthin, wo Schönes, Gutes nur gefällt,
> Zur Einsamkeit!—Da schaffe deine Welt.
>
> (5689–96)

In a secluded world, in isolation and perhaps, as in the "Zueignung," also in loneliness—here the poet can receive inspiration and "create a world." In *Dichtung und Wahrheit* Goethe describes the importance he attached to this "Einsamkeit" for the genesis of his works: "Ich fühlte recht gut, daß sich etwas Bedeutendes nur produzieren lasse, wenn man sich isoliere. Meine Sachen, die so viel Beifall gefunden hatten, waren Kinder der Einsamkeit. . . ."[18]

In Act III the higher, idealized sphere far beyond the scenes of external happenings rises before our eyes as the birthplace of Euphorion. Once again the symbol of gold is associated with poetic inspiration. The child carries a golden lyre—the emblem of his art—and Phorkyas describes the flaming golden light which suggests the intensity of his spiritual strength and inspiration:

> Denn wie leuchtet's ihm zu Haupten? Was erglänzt, ist schwer zu sagen,
> Ist es Goldschmuck, ist es Flamme übermächtiger Geisteskraft?
> Und so regt er sich gebärdend, sich als Knabe schon verkündend
> Künftigen Meister alles Schönen, dem die ewigen Melodien
> Durch die Glieder sich bewegen . . .
>
> (9623–27)

The gold of inspiration is the one outstanding characteristic of Euphorion, activity the other. Indeed, his urge to activity is so strong that it oversteps its proper bounds and leads to his death. Euphorion also owes his existence to activity—the creative encounter of Faust's soul with the forces of beauty personified in Helen. The activity comes to expression in the speech lesson in which Helen learns the art of rhyming:

[18] *Dichtung und Wahrheit*, Book 15, HA X, 48.

Helena. So sage denn, wie sprech' ich auch so schön?
Faust. Das ist gar leicht, es muß von Herzen gehn.
Und wenn die Brust von Sehnsucht überfließt,
Man sieht sich um und fragt—
Helena. wer mitgenießt.
(9377–80)

Neither Faust nor Helen is here passive, a mere "locus" from which poesy springs forth unearned. The soul exercises its sensibilities in a delicate listening and responding. The point is that the soul is *active* and creates the possibility for Euphorion, the being of poetry, to enter the world.

The picture of poetic creation presented both in the introductory scenes of *Faust* and in those concerning the Boy Charioteer and Euphorion describes poetry as a living being born of the soul of a poet who is much more than an onlooker. The process is alive and the artist makes a very definite "positive contribution." The touchstone of Goethe's approach, which distinguishes it unmistakably from that of Skinner, is the poet's sense of the reality of the inner world as a world of spiritual *life* from which he draws his inspiration and whose forces find embodiment through the *medium* of the thoughts and images given to him as a treasure of life-experience. This realm of productive spiritual forces is sublime, as is the light-filled world of the Prologue. But it is also dangerous if approached by man in haste, egotism, or lack of preparation. Goethe portrays this factor in Faust's self-inflated conjuration of the Earth Spirit, his dangerous trip to the Mothers and the Emperor's disastrous experience with the chest of gold.

There is one quality which is the essential prerequisite for approaching the world of spiritual creativity. Gretchen has it in her naïve way but Faust never fully achieves it during his life. Yet it must be attained by the seeker after insight. The quality is *selflessness*. And in Goethe's view all men are capable of its development:

> Wer sich mit irgendeiner Kenntnis abgibt, soll nach dem Höchsten streben! Es ist mit der Einsicht viel anders als mit der Ausübung: denn im Praktischen muß sich jeder bald bescheiden, daß ihm nur ein gewisses Maß von Kräften zugeteilt sei; zur Kenntnis, zur Einsicht aber sind weit mehrere Menschen fähig, ja man kann wohl sagen, ein jeder, der sich selbst verleugnen, sich den Gegenständen unterordnen kann, der nicht mit einem starren, beschränkten Eigensinn sich und seine kleinliche Einseitigkeit in die höchsten Werke der Natur und der Kunst überzutragen strebt.[19]

It is this quality of selflessness, of being able to "subordinate oneself to the objects" under investigation, which also lies at the heart of Goethe's stance as natural scientist. It is out of this posture that he can say that the highest good of man as thinker is to investigate what he can and quietly to reverence what he cannot investigate. It is this same stance which sustains Goethe's sense of appreciation for what is called *genius*. Skinner is at great pains to abolish the notion of genius,

[19] "Einleitung in die Propyläen," HA XII, 51.

ridding the discussion of any overtones of the "miraculous" and the "divine." Goethe, as noted above, begins as a young man in the apotheosis of genius and in the course of his life deepens and refines his view of it, settling in his advanced years on the Leibnitzian "monad" and the Aristotelian "entelechy" to describe the spiritual essence of man, before which he felt the profoundest reverence.

Skinner's equation of poet/woman/hen proceeds from his own idea of the cognitive mode appropriate to the scientist. Goethe, too, was a scientist. His science is unorthodox and more controversial than Skinner's. Yet an understanding of it is essential to an understanding of his image of the creative human being. A look at a number of concepts underlying Goethe's view of nature will enable us to clarify how he is able to sustain his commitment to the concept of creative genius.

We have noted at the beginning of this study that the seeming objectivity of Skinner's point of view is open to serious question. His uncritical equation of the creative faculties in man, woman and hen rests on a spurious logic and contains considerable unspoken bias. Goethe, too, is accused of being subjective, rather than objective, in his natural scientific works. In the *Farbenlehre* he is as much concerned with the role of the human eye in his experiments as with that of the prismatic phenomena. He speaks of both the "sensory" ("sinnlich") and the "moral" ("sittlich") effects of the colors within the same context. The science of the future will have to decide to what degree Goethe was in error and to what degree he may have anticipated later developments in science. The point here is that Goethe's method does not admit of the strict separation of the spheres termed "objective" and "subjective." He felt understood and complimented when the psychologist Heinroth, in his *Anthropologie*, referred to Goethe's thinking as "gegenständlich." The word may be translated as "objective," yet the meaning is thereby perhaps more obscured than revealed. For Goethe realizes that Heinroth recognizes in his thinking an inner activity which *unites* with the outer objects of nature in an active way ("tätig"):

> . . . ja er bezeichnet meine Verfahrungsart als eine eigentümliche: daß nämlich mein Denkvermögen *gegenständlich* tätig sei, womit er aussprechen will: daß mein Denken sich von den Gegenständen nicht sondere, daß die Elemente der Gegenstände, die Anschauungen in dasselbe eingehen und von ihm auf das innigste durchdrungen werden, daß mein Anschauen selbst ein Denken, mein Denken ein Anschauen sei; welchem Verfahren genannter Freund seinen Beifall nicht versagen will.[20]

In the botanical writings, in particular, one observes this faculty of thinking which enters deeply into the metamorphoses of plant forms and takes them into itself. It is indeed "Denken" as "Anschauen" or "Anschauen" as "Denken." The categories "subjective" and "objective" are reunited on a higher level in this activity which Heinroth terms "gegenständlich."

[20] "Bedeutende Fördernis durch ein einziges geistreiches Wort," HA XIII, 37.

In addition to the concepts "subjective" and "objective" one must examine those of "causality" and "chance" in connection with Goethe's view of man. It is the concept of *causality* which Skinner employs to set up the sequence of biological events which he advances as the analogy for the process of poetic creativity in man. It is this principle which underlies his effort to throw out the poet's autonomy. In a chapter entitled "Genius, Its Causes and Incidence" in the book *The Science of Culture* the anthropologist Leslie A. White advances a similar causal line of reasoning in order to explain the phenomenon of genius: "We are convinced that the great man is best understood as an effect or manifestation rather than as a prime mover."[21] This statement, which is characteristic of a significant stream of contemporary thinking, is diametrically opposed to Goethe's view of genius as the expression of the entelechy, a spiritual being which he definitely considered a "prime mover."

The concept of *chance*, which in itself has no positive content but is employed to cover those phenomena for which there appears to be no causal explanation, is now used to explain that which in the Goethean sense may be viewed as an aspect of the functioning of the entelechy. Thus White continues in his treatise on genius: "Whether an individual of exceptional natural endowment achieves the distinction of genius or not depends therefore very much upon the *accidental time of his birth*. Should *chance* place him somewhere along the slope of a developing pattern his chances of distinction will be relatively slight."[22] The concept of chance is here clearly invoked in support of this view of human psychological endowment. White then concludes his chapter on genius with the surprising statement that: "To explain culture history psychologically is of course to lean on mystery, *to appeal to chance*, to invoke 'that invisible and unimaginable play of forces within the nervous system,' to account for significant events and eras."[23] On the one hand we are asked to view chance as the factor upon which the emergence of genius depends. On the other hand we are warned against explanations of cultural history which "appeal to chance." Surely Goethe's Aristotelian concept of entelechy is no more difficult to think through than this self-contradictory discussion of the negative concept of chance advanced by White to support his claim to have explained the causes of genius: "The culturologist . . . , by working upon the supra-psychological, supra-sociological level of culture, by explaining culture in terms of culture, really makes it intelligible. And in explaining culture he explains the causes and incidence of genius as well."[24]

[21] Leslie A. White, *The Science of Culture* (New York, 1971), Chapter VIII, "Genius, Its Causes and Incidence," p. 190.

[22] White, p. 217. Italics mine.

[23] *Ibid.*, p. 232. Italics mine.

[24] *Ibid.*, p. 232.

Goethe was fully aware of the role of chance in human life. In the "Urworte. Orphisch" (1817) he draws on ancient Orphic mystery wisdom in his description of five forces which mold human life on

Goethe's thinking is "gegenständlich" and it seeks always to find concepts appropriate to the order of phenomena under investigation. He is fully aware of the usefulness of the concept of causality in its proper sphere of applicability. In his botanical studies, for instance, he employs the concept by describing the fact that the idea of the plant comes to expression in numerous ways which are determined, caused by various external conditions. The same plant will develop certain organs in the valleys and others on mountain slopes. But his thinking does not cling to this concept and seek to explain *all* phenomena by means of it. This is the significant point. In the case of the plant Goethe's thinking penetrates through the level of causality, unites in a dynamic way with the exact laws of morphology at work in the plant forms and discovers in them a set of laws of a *higher* order which he terms the "Urpflanze." For Goethe the external causalities are a real factor in the world. *But they are not the only determining factor.* The other determining factor is the plant as "monad," the plant as living idea or "type" which comes to expression in the sequence of forms in the physical world. This is a clear illustration of the very essence of Goethe's thinking—of a cognitive posture which is in vivid contradistinction to that of such thinkers as Skinner and White. For Goethe there are always two sides to all phenomena, especially in the life-sciences: the "external" and the "internal," the percepts and the concepts arrived at through their investigation by thinking. For the spiritual archetype of the plant is not equal to the sum total of the conditions necessary for the plant's manifestation in the world. The "Urpflanze" is entirely spiritual in nature and is gradually arrived at by a thinking which does not juggle concepts of chance but which holds to the phenomena themselves and lets them reveal their inner laws. Such a thinking is "gegenständlich," and once it has grasped the living reality of the "Urpflanze" it is fully conscious of the laws in which all the phenomena rest and which also contain, potentially, additional phenomena not yet manifest outwardly in the physical world:

> Die Urpflanze wird das wunderlichste Geschöpf von der Welt, um welches mich die Natur selbst beneiden soll. Mit diesem Modell und dem Schlüssel dazu kann man alsdann noch Pflanzen ins Unendliche erfinden, die konsequent sein müssen, das heißt, die, wenn sie auch nicht existieren, doch existieren könnten und nicht etwa malerische oder dichterische Schatten und Scheine sind, sondern eine innerliche Wahrheit und Notwendigkeit haben. Dasselbe Gesetz wird sich auf alles übrige Lebendige anwenden lassen.[25]

earth: ΔΑΙΜΩΝ, "Dämon," ΤΥΧΗ, "Das Zufällige" (chance), ΕΡΩΣ, "Liebe," ΑΝΑΓΚΗ, "Nötigung," and ΕΛΠΙΣ, "Hoffnung." In the sense of the poem all five forces together provide the basic conditions of man's life. The role of chance is an important one but not by any means the sole one. Cf. "Urworte. Orphisch," HA I, 359–60. The same subject is discussed in connection with Goethe's natural scientific thought and his poetry by Andreas B. Wachsmuth in "Goethes naturwissenschaftliches Denken im Spiegel seiner Dichtungen seit 1790," *Geist und Zeit*, no. 5 (Düsseldorf, 1959), 32–52.

[25] *Italienische Reise*, Neapel, 17 May 1787, HA XI, 324.

Our discussion of the mode of thinking which distinguishes Goethe's view of man from that of such thinkers as Skinner has moved from the problem of subjective vs. objective knowledge through a consideration of the concepts of causality and chance to that characteristically Goethean idea, the "type." We must now ask ourselves how it is possible objectively to *know* such a spiritual thought. For surely our commonly exercised faculty of discursive, logical thought does not participate in ideas of this living nature. Must they then be considered to be by definition subjective? Goethe did not consider them so. One may view his position as entirely justified if one takes into consideration a further concept necessary to an understanding of Goethe's science. This is the concept of the development of subtler and higher organs of perception. For just as Goethe recognized the evolution of forms within nature, from the simple to the complex, from the primitive to the refined, so too did he view man's cognitive faculties as alive and capable of evolution. This is the point at which Goethe's world view expands into qualitatively quite different spheres from those accessible to only one type of concept formation.

Goethe's view of man's faculties of cognition is itself in an inward sense "evolutionary." When, as in the case of the "Metamorphose der Pflanzen," thinking is exercised in a living way, as "anschauende Urteilskraft," the thought organism itself grows and develops ever more refined organs of insight: "Der Mensch kennt nur sich selbst, insofern er die Welt kennt, die er nur in sich und sich nur in ihr gewahr wird. Jeder neue Gegenstand, wohl beschaut, schließt ein neues Organ in uns auf."[26] This Goethean thinking, however, requires an intense exertion of the will, for it must enter deeply into the phenomena and in an exact way follow and describe their dynamic flow. The temptation is to abandon the phenomena and rush into theorizing about them: "In der Geschichte der Naturforschung bemerkt man durchaus, daß die Beobachter von der Erscheinung zu schnell zur Theorie hineilen und dadurch unzulänglich, hypothetisch werden."[27] Goethe sees the true theory as a factor of the phenomena themselves, a factor which will reveal itself to the scientist who remains within them with his thinking: "Es gibt eine zarte Empirie, die sich mit dem Gegenstand innigst identisch macht und dadurch zur eigentlichen Theorie wird."[28] The phenomena are violated not only by abstract theorizing but also by being investigated mechanically when they are by nature dynamic: ". . . Denn eben, wenn man Probleme, die nur dynamisch erklärt werden können, beiseiteschiebt, dann kommen mechanische Erklärungen wieder zur Tagesordnung."[29] The result of this misapplication of the principal of causality to processes of a higher nature is repeated errors: "Der eingeborenste Begriff, der notwendigste, von *Ursach'* und *Wirkung*, wird in der

[26] "Bedeutende Fördernis durch ein einziges geistreiches Wort," HA XIII, 38.

[27] *Maximen und Reflexionen*, no. 547, HA XII, 440.

[28] *Ibid.*, no. 509, p. 435.

[29] *Ibid.*, no. 596, p. 446.

Anwendung die Veranlassung zu unzähligen, sich immer wiederholenden Irrtümern."[30] Perhaps the most glaring error to which such an application, willy-nilly, of principles of causality in the life sciences and in psychology can lead is the tendency to confound the levels on which one is operating. One begins to assert that virtually all events in nature and man are exclusively mechanical, for in not tailoring one's concepts to the quality of the phenomena one has stunted the growth of the higher organs of cognition. Yet all true science in the Goethean sense depends upon the development of these organs. If much in present-day science does violence to what we consider the dignity of man Goethe's world view suggests that it is due to the fact that in our examination of the phenomena of nature we have often neglected to pursue an ongoing criticism of the method with which we conduct the investigations. Thus we have failed to *refine* that method. But only by applying increasingly refined, subtle methods of investigation can we, in this view, hope to unfold the organs of understanding needed to do justice to the higher phenomena. In the essay "The Poet" Emerson formulates this very thought in terms which are entirely in keeping with Goethe's view: "Since every thing in nature answers to a moral power, if any phenomenon remains brute and dark it is because the corresponding faculty in the observer is not yet active."[31]

If, in the Goethean and Emersonian view, there is a higher reality in the activity of thinking why do many scientists today not acknowledge it? Goethe's unequivocal answer is that in not having developed the necessary *organ*, Emerson's "corresponding faculty," they do not *experience* the higher reality. In "Der Sammler und die Seinigen" Goethe writes brilliantly to this very point:

> *Gast.* Es ist die Art der Herren Philosophen, daß sie sich hinter sonderbaren Worten, wie hinter einer Ägide, im Streite einherbewegen.
>
> *Ich.* Diesmal kann ich wohl versichern, daß ich nicht als Philosoph gesprochen habe, es waren lauter Erfahrungstatsachen.
>
> *Gast.* Das nennen Sie Erfahrung, wovon ein anderer nichts begreifen kann!
>
> *Ich.* Zu jeder Erfahrung gehört ein Organ.
>
> *Gast.* Wohl ein besonderes?
>
> *Ich.* Kein besonderes, aber eine gewisse Eigenschaft muß es haben.
>
> *Gast.* Und die wäre?
>
> *Ich.* Es muß produzieren können.
>
> *Gast.* Was produzieren?
>
> *Ich.* Die Erfahrung! Es gibt keine Erfahrung, die nicht produziert, hervorgebracht, erschaffen wird.[32]

For every experience man must develop the requisite organ of cognition. This is one fundamental concept which underlies Goethe's method. The complementary

[30] *Ibid.*, no. 593, p. 446.

[31] Emerson, "The Poet," *Essays, Second Series*, p. 15.

[32] "Der Sammler und die Seinigen," HA XII, 85.

concept is also put forth in this passage: that of productivity, of intense activity exercised in the cognitive process. Just as it is Faust's unceasing striving which enables him to obtain Helen and just as it is his productive interaction with her as he teaches her to rhyme which finally consummates their union and calls forth the being of poetry, so too is it the intense exercise by the scientist of the faculties of cognition which calls forth the higher organs of thought. Once this strength has been found and activated the Goethean mode of cognition recognizes no a priori limits to knowledge. By patient and earnest development of his faculties the scientist makes himself *worthy* of a higher cognitive participation in the creative inner life of nature—the "type," the "entelechy." With reference to a passage from Kant Goethe gives us a powerful confession of his belief in this possibility of man to transcend with his thinking the apparent limitations of his knowledge of nature:

> Zwar scheint der Verfasser hier auf einen göttlichen Verstand zu deuten, allein wenn wir ja im Sittlichen, durch Glauben an Gott, Tugend und Unsterblichkeit uns in eine obere Region erheben und an das erste Wesen annähern sollen; so dürft' es wohl im Intellektuellen derselbe Fall sein, daß wir uns, durch das Anschauen einer immer schaffenden Natur, zur geistigen Teilnahme an ihren Produktionen würdig machten. Hatte ich doch erst unbewußt und aus innerem Trieb auf jenes Urbildliche, Typische rastlos gedrungen, war es mir sogar geglückt, eine naturgemäße Darstellung aufzubauen, so konnte mich nunmehr nichts weiter verhindern, das *Abenteuer der Vernunft*, wie es der Alte vom Königsberge selbst nennt, mutig zu bestehen.[33]

Productive inner *effort*, then, is the key to the development of the higher organs of understanding:

> Im Reich der Natur waltet Bewegung und Tat, im Reiche der Freiheit Anlage und Willen. Bewegung ist ewig und tritt bei jeder günstigen Bedingung unwiderstehlich in die Erscheinung. Anlagen entwickeln sich zwar auch naturgemäß, müssen aber erst durch den Willen geübt und nach und nach gesteigert werden. Deswegen ist man des freiwilligen Willens so gewiß nicht als der selbständigen Tat; diese tut sich selbst, er aber wird getan . . .[34]

This systematic schooling and application of the will which may be activated from within by the entelechy is the very factor which in Goethe's view lies at the heart of what we know as "genius." It is also the very factor which is conspicuously absent in the picture of man as creator advanced by Skinner and by White. These two researchers describe very elaborately the factors which impinge on man from *without*. But they stop at this point, apply the purely causal mode of thinking, and do not experience a reality in what in Goethe's view can develop spiritually from *within*. Yet this latter development can lead to an experience of

[33] "Anschauende Urteilskraft," HA XIII, 30–31.

[34] *Maximen und Reflexionen*, no. 1203, HA XII, 528.

the reality of genius in the immortal entelechy of man, rather than to a desire to "explain" it out of existence. In a passage penned as a comment on the *Psychologie zur Erklärung der Seelenerscheinungen* (1824) by the philosopher Ernst Stiedenroth, Goethe has stated his case in utmost clarity. It reads almost as though it had been written in reply to Skinner and to White:

> Alle Wirkung des Äußern aufs Innere trägt er unvergleichlich vor, und wir sehen die Welt nochmals nach und nach in uns entstehen. Aber mit der Gegenwirkung des Innern nach außen gelingt es ihm nicht ebenso. Der Entelechie, die nichts aufnimmt, ohne sich's durch eigene Zutat anzueignen, läßt er nicht Gerechtigkeit widerfahren, und mit dem Genie will es auf diesem Wege gar nicht fort; und wenn er das Ideal aus der Erfahrung abzuleiten denkt und sagt: das Kind idealisiert nicht, so mag man antworten: das Kind zeugt nicht; denn zum Gewahrwerden des Ideellen gehört auch eine Pubertät.[35]

It is this "puberty," the realization of new sources of productivity within the cognizing soul of man, which the entelechy may develop and unfold and which lead it to the perception of higher truths ("zum Gewahrwerden des Ideellen"). At this level the assumed limits to scientific cognition are overcome. The Divine, the creative Intelligence lights up in the living thinking of man the scientist: " 'Die Natur verbirgt Gott!' Aber nicht jedem!"[36]

Goethe rejoices in the firm conviction that spiritual forces are present in nature and may be discovered by the scientist who is careful to metamorphose his method in keeping with the nature of the facts with which he is dealing. Skinner proceeds on the basis of a very rigid method and is pleased to offer an explanation of the facts which does away once and for all with the need to speak of "God." In a discussion of Skinner's *Beyond Freedom and Dignity* Noam Chomsky writes in *The New York Review of Books:*

> The task of scientific analysis is not—as Skinner believes—to demonstrate that the conditions to which he restricts his attention fully determine human behavior, but rather to discover whether in fact they do (or whether they are at all significant), a very different matter. If they do not, as seems plausible, the "task of a scientific analysis" will be to clarify the issues and discover an intelligible explanatory theory that will deal with the actual facts.[37]

Chomsky's criticism is cutting: Skinner applies a limited set of deterministic conditions to the complexities of human behavior without concerning himself with the question as to whether they explain that behavior fully or whether indeed they are even significant. Simple explanations are close at hand and easily

[35] *Ibid.*, no. 276, p. 403.

[36] *Ibid.*, no. 3, p. 365.

Goethe quotes the words "Die Natur verbirgt Gott!" from Jacobi's *Von den göttlichen Dingen*.

[37] Noam Chomsky, "The Case against B. F. Skinner," *The New York Review of Books*, 17, no. 11 (30 December 1971), p. 19.

grasped. Yet their uncritical application to phenomena carries with it a serious burden of responsibility for the possible distortion and therefore debasement of higher truths. Goethe formulates this thought as follows: "Die nächsten faßlichen Ursachen sind greiflich und eben deshalb am begreiflichsten; weswegen wir uns gern als mechanisch denken, was höherer Art ist."[38] The scientist who would not fall into the error of oversimplification and distortion must remain as critical of his own methodology as he is of the facts which arrest his attention. Then he may develop that organ of thought which perceives their true relationships. Truth is not given to man without his having awakened this organ: "Zum Ergreifen der Wahrheit braucht es ein viel höheres Organ als zur Verteidigung des Irrtums."[39] And Goethe, says Emerson, has "a certain gravitation towards truth."[40]

The highest forms of truth to which the scientist can aspire are in Goethe's view of a purely spiritual nature. Thus, for instance, the colors red and green, as they appear through intensification and mixing, remind him of the heavenly and the earthly expressions ("Ausgeburten") of the creative Elohim.[41] Orthodox science today balks at such a statement and contends that experiences of a qualitative nature must be subjective. The answer implicit in Goethe's position is, as we have undertaken to show, that a rigorous distinction between subjective and objective experience is ultimately untenable and that the scientist may gradually bridge this chasm if he develops higher organs of thought which can perceive qualitative experience with the same precision with which the common organs of logical thinking perceive the truths of quantifiable experience. Where, says science, is the *proof?* Out of the very fibre of Goethe's mode of thinking Emerson replies: "The physicians say they are not materialists; but they are:—Spirit is matter reduced to an extreme thinness: O *so* thin!—But the definition of *spiritual* should be, *that which is its own evidence*."[42] And many, he continues, stand at the edge of these insights yet do not muster the courage to take the next step: "Our friends early appear to us as representatives of certain ideas which they never pass or exceed. They stand on the brink of the ocean of thought and power, but they never take the single step that would bring them there."[43] In our own times, however, there are those in the scientific community itself who do find the courage to take this next step, and who suggest that Goethe's method is worthy of reexamination. Thus in an address delivered at the "Berliner Germanistentag" in 1968 under the title "Die Naturwissenschaft Goethes. Eine Gegenüberstellung Goethescher und modern-exakter Naturwissenschaft," the eminent Zürich physicist Walter Heitler speaks in unambiguous language of the validity of

[38] *Maximen und Reflexionen*, no. 595, HA XII, 446.

[39] *Ibid.*, no. 293, p. 406.

[40] Emerson, *Representative Men, op. cit.*, p. 275.

[41] *Zur Farbenlehre*, Didaktischer Teil, "Sinnlich-sittliche Wirkung der Farbe," HA XIII, 521.

[42] Emerson, "Experience," *Essays, Second Series*, p. 53.

[43] *Ibid.*, pp. 56–57.

Goethe's science. Not only is a true science of qualitative experience possible; the phenomena under investigation are spiritual realities and the Goethean approach to them is itself an *organ* of their apprehension:

> Es kann kein Zweifel sein, daß der Weg der kritischen Anschauung zu echter wissenschaftlicher Erkenntnis führt, und zwar in einem Feld, das gerade der analytischen Denkweise unzugänglich ist: im Feld der Qualitäten und der Gestaltzusammenhänge, die nicht quantitativ faßbar sind. Vor allem müssen wir Goethe zustimmen, daß die "Urbilder," der "Bauplan" usw. geistige *Realitäten* sind, die unserem Erkennen zugänglich sind und die wir als Teil des geistigen Inhalts der Naturdinge ansehen dürfen. Wenn wir wollen, so können wir sie als Abglanz des Schöpfergeistes betrachten, der sie geschaffen hat—womit wir der Goetheschen Auffassung als göttlichem Organ näherkommen.[44]

Heitler gives full credit to Newtonian science as applied within a specific context, yet he warns against limited vision and simplistic notions of "objectivity." He points to the fact that all modes of cognition require an organ of perception, a fact which, as we have seen, lies at the root of the Goethean epistemology:

> Der Galilei-Newtonsche Weg führte zu einer stets wachsenden Abstraktion, zu einer Loslösung der Wissenschaft vom Menschen, im Namen einer nicht recht verstandenen Objektivität. Objektiv sollte nur sein, was mit dem Menschen gar nichts zu tun hat, und das, glaubte man, sei nur das Meßbare und Analysierbare. Als ob nicht *jeder* Zugang zur Welt um uns ein menschliches Organ erfordern würde, in diesem Fall eben das Messen und abstrakte Denken! Vor dieser Abstraktion warnte Goethe. Eine Welt, in deren Gedankenbild der Mensch nicht mehr vorkommt, ist keine heile, ganze Welt mehr, keine Welt, in der Menschen wohnen können.[45]

Heitler is refreshingly unambiguous in presenting the facts as he sees them. Either man begins to take the Goethean approach to science seriously or he is in danger of falling victim to those forces of abstraction which may deprive him of his place in the world. The conclusion to which this contemporary physicist comes, a physicist who is in a position to be fully aware of orthodox science's objections to Goethe's work, is also straight to the point:

> Wenn es uns . . . gelingen sollte, Wissenschaft in Goethescher Richtung weiterzuentwickeln, auch weit über das hinaus, was bis jetzt thematisch und umfangmäßig vorliegt, dann hätten wir ein Gegengewicht, das uns helfen würde, der Versuchung Mephistos zu widerstehen, in der Newtonschen Wissenschaft und Technik das alleinige Heil zu erblicken.[46]

Behind the two images of the poet discussed in this essay there lie two very

[44] Walter Heitler, "Die Naturwissenschaft Goethes. Eine Gegenüberstellung Goethescher und modern-exakter Naturwissenschaft," *Der Berliner Germanistentag 1968*, ed. Karl Heinz Borck and Rudolf Henss (Heidelberg, 1970), p. 21.

[45] *Ibid.*, p. 22.

[46] *Ibid.*, p. 23.

different views of man. The view advanced by Skinner and White is essentially mechanistic. It would explain all phenomena—physical, biological, psychological and spiritual in terms of such concepts as causality and chance. Inherent in it is its proponents' clearly articulated effort to rid the culture of the traditional concept of genius. The picture of man advanced by Goethe is dynamic and developmental. This comes to expression poetically in the strivings of Faust and in the picture which, in the introductory scenes of *Faust*, Goethe gives of the genesis of the work of art. This picture is further elaborated by such scenes as those we have discussed in which the Boy Charioteer and Euphorion embody a commentary on the nature of creative spiritual activity which by far transcends the limits of even the subtlest web of causalities. Through the words of a great poet there speaks the force of a powerful human entelechy. In the words of the poet in the "Vorspiel auf dem Theater": "Wer sichert den Olymp? vereinet Götter?/ Des Menschen Kraft, im Dichter offenbart" (156–57).[47] We have also seen that Goethe's vision of man as poet stands not in isolation but is buttressed by the epistemological mode which informs his natural scientific inquiries. Goethe was ever a whole man, a man of universal interests, and each aspect of his universe emanates from the same integrated organism of thought.

We have seen that Goethe's picture of man flows from a thinking which at every level subjects its activity to sharp methodological criticism. What is more, this thinking rests in an attitude of patience and reverence toward the phenomena it seeks to understand.[48] And its exponent considers the concept of genius central to his vision of science, art and history. Skinner speaks with the voice of an increasingly prominent group of researchers within our contemporary culture. Goethe seems to speak with the voice of the past. Yet despite its shortcomings Goethe's stance contains a method capable of further development. In the past poetic inspiration was greeted quite naturally as the gift of a divine being, the muse, whom the bard invoked to move him to song. In his "A Defence of Poetry" Shelley describes that naïve ancient condition:

> In the infancy of the world, neither poets themselves nor their auditors are fully aware of the excellence of poetry: for it acts in a divine and unapprehended manner, beyond and above consciousness; and it is reserved for future generations to contemplate and measure the mighty cause and effect in all the strength and splendor of their union.[49]

[47] Cf. A. Binder (n. 14, *Das Vorspiel auf dem Theater*, pp. 38–39), who sees line 157 defined as genius ("Genie"). He also concludes that the "Vorspiel" is of such a general nature as to refer to all "Bühnenwerke" and specifically also to Part II of *Faust* (pp. 185–87).

[48] Goethe's violent polemics against Newton seem to belie this statement. They are unfortunate and have done much to interfere with an open-minded evaluation of his *Farbenlehre*. Here it is important, however, that one separate Goethe's attitude toward Newton from his attitude toward nature. He allows himself to engage in polemics toward the person of Newton, but he maintains a calm and reverential attitude toward the *phenomena*.

[49] Percy Bysshe Shelley, "A Defense of Poetry" (1821), *Shelley's Literary and Philosophical Criticism*, ed. John Shawcross (London, 1909), p. 129.

For centuries man has lived on the rich heritage of this tradition. Today this sense of direct inspiration has largely been lost. In the loss, however, lies the positive gain of a sense of freedom and self-determination. A return to the older instinctive consciousness would be inappropriate. The Romanticists looked back at it longingly and hoped to find ways to regain the lost sense of divine animation in nature and man. Goethe, with his Greek eye for proportion and balance, sensed the very real dangers which inhere in an overly enthusiastic Romantic subjectivity and he reacted strongly against it, labelling it unhealthy. The schism which this reaction inaugurated has adhered to the image of Goethe in German criticism to this day. He is referred to as a "classicist," in clear contradistinction to the Romantics. English criticism, however, has noticed the distinctly Romantic aspects in Goethe's outlook and in the English-speaking world he is usually considered one of the great Romantic poets. There is a certain deeper sense in which this English evaluation precisely hits the mark. The Romanticists frequently turned to the past or to the world of dream and visionary experience in their anxiety to regain the lost wellsprings of poetic imagination. Goethe, after his arrival in Weimar, subjected himself to the discipline of mind required by the natural scientist. His approach to science is such, however, that it seeks step by step, as in the case of his botany, to evolve a *new* pictorial consciousness. This new consciousness is to unfold in precise adherence to the laws of growth which inform nature herself and it remains at all times under the complete conscious control of the investigator. It may be termed a new *exact* imaginative consciousness. In this specific sense Goethe may be said to have inaugurated a new, *conscious* Romanticism embracing both the arts and the sciences and characterized by a precise yet labile, metamorphosing methodology. It contains within it the seeds of a new culture, yet its cultivation and development will depend upon the best efforts of men and women of great inner discipline and strength—faculties of a powerful (in Goethe's language) entelechy, qualities which have always been associated with what is called genius. And those persons who see the possibilities inherent in such a new and exact Romanticism will find themselves called upon to work together to evolve the insights which will one day reunite the arts and the sciences on a higher level. For the day of the single genius who gives his name to an age is also largely a thing of the past. Goethe had only the first presentiments of the effects which the mechanization of thought and the standardization and regimentation of life would begin to have on mankind in the twentieth century. Yet he already recognized that solutions will only be forthcoming when men call forth the qualities of genius latent in *every* man and woman and apply them in concert to the high tasks at hand. In the *Märchen* the old man with the lamp, coming to the assistance of Lilie, says: "Sei ruhig, schönes Mädchen! Ob ich helfen kann, weiß ich nicht; ein einzelner hilft nicht, sondern wer sich mit vielen zur rechten Stunde vereinigt."[50]

[50] *Das Märchen*, HA VI, 230.

There are influential voices in our contemporary culture whose view of man threatens to abolish the concept of genius. Goethe's, however, seeks to retain it. With reference to both nature and art he writes: "Die Natur wirkt nach Gesetzen, die sie sich in Eintracht mit dem Schöpfer vorschrieb, die Kunst nach Regeln, über die sie sich mit dem Genie einverstanden hat."[51] With reference to the dramatic poet's art he says: "Ein dramatisches Werk zu verfassen, dazu gehört Genie. Am Ende soll die Empfindung, in der Mitte die Vernunft, am Anfang der Verstand vorwalten und alles gleichmäßig durch eine lebhaft-klare Einbildungskraft vorgetragen werden."[52] Genius is here portrayed as a synthesizing eye for the whole. It is the elevated ability to give form, and as such it is able to direct the application of the soul's faculties of feeling ("Empfindung"), reason ("Vernunft") and understanding ("Verstand") to the task before it. Behind this world of inspiration there stands a reality which Goethe calls "Wahrheit," the truth toward which Emerson says that Goethe has "a certain gravitation." In the last stanza of that other "Zueignung" in ottava rima (1784) which Goethe wrote as an introduction to the "Geheimnisse" and which, in 1787, he published at the head of his collected *Schriften*, this reality appears as an allegorical figure: Truth. The figure steps up to and endows him with the gift of poetry:

> "Ich kenne dich, ich kenne deine Schwächen,
> Ich weiß, was Gutes in dir lebt und glimmt!"
> So sagte sie, ich hör' sie ewig sprechen,
> "Empfange hier, was ich dir lang' bestimmt!
> Dem Glücklichen kann es an nichts gebrechen,
> Der dies Geschenk mit stiller Seele nimmt:
> Aus Morgenduft gewebt und Sonnenklarheit,
> Der Dichtung Schleier aus der Hand der Wahrheit.[53]

This is *Goethe's* "startling vision of the poet," his vision of the forces which underlie the process of poetic creativity.

Goethe's picture of man not only has room for the concept of genius, it celebrates genius. Men may believe that the sciences and the arts are nothing but a product of purely human forces, but this, he says, is not so. Through the works of a Mozart, Raffael or Shakespeare there blow other winds. The *Gespräche mit Eckermann* close with a profoundly moving tribute to what Goethe viewed as the reality of genius. Under the date of 11 March 1832, eleven days before Goethe's death, Eckermann writes:

> "Wenn man die Leute reden hört," sagte Goethe, "so sollte man fast glauben, sie seien der Meinung, Gott habe sich seit jener alten Zeit ganz in die Stille zurückgezogen, und der Mensch wäre jetzt ganz auf eigene Füße gestellt und müsse sehen, wie er ohne Gott und sein tägliches unsichtbares Anhauchen zurecht komme. In

[51] *Maximen und Reflexionen*, no. 723, HA XII, 467.

[52] *Ibid.*, no. 919, p. 495.

[53] "Zueignung," HA I, 152.

religiösen und moralischen Dingen gibt man noch allenfalls eine göttliche Einwirkung zu, allein in Dingen der Wissenschaft und Künste glaubt man, es sei lauter Irdisches und nichts weiter als ein Produkt rein menschlicher Kräfte.

Versuche es aber doch nur einer und bringe mit menschlichem Wollen und menschlichen Kräften etwas hervor, das den Schöpfungen, die den Namen Mozart, Raffael oder Shakespeare tragen, sich an die Seite setzen lasse. Ich weiß recht wohl, daß diese drei Edlen keineswegs die einzigen sind und daß in allen Gebieten der Kunst eine Unzahl trefflicher Geister gewirkt hat, die vollkommen so Gutes hervorgebracht als jene Genannten. Allein, waren sie so groß als jene, so überragten sie die gewöhnliche Menschennatur in eben dem Verhältnis und waren ebenso gottbegabt als jene.

Und überall, was ist es und was soll es?—Gott hat sich nach den bekannten imaginierten sechs Schöpfungstagen keineswegs zur Ruhe begeben, vielmehr ist er noch fortwährend wirksam wie am ersten. Diese plumpe Welt aus einfachen Elementen zusammenzusetzen und sie jahraus jahrein in den Strahlen der Sonne rollen zu lassen, hätte ihm sicher wenig Spaß gemacht, wenn er nicht den Plan gehabt hätte, sich auf dieser materiellen Unterlage eine Pflanzschule für eine Welt von Geistern zu gründen. So ist er nun fortwährend in höheren Naturen wirksam, um die geringeren heranzuziehen."

Goethe schwieg. Ich aber bewahrte seine großen und guten Worte in meinem Herzen.[54]

The last sentence is telling, for it expresses the mood in which the gentle and long-suffering Eckermann was able to receive Goethe's words—the only mood in which such words can take root, grow, and reveal their inner life: "Ich aber bewahrte seine großen und guten Worte in meinem Herzen."

And from the English-speaking world we have the words of Emerson, that gentle sage of Concord, who understood Goethe very deeply—not uncritically, but with profound admiration. As though anticipating the blindness and deafness which have closed in on us in the twentieth century Emerson admonishes us to look once again to Goethe and from his work to draw courage in our struggle to bring to birth a loftier image of man: "Goethe teaches courage, and the equivalence of all times; that the disadvantages of any epoch exist only to the fainthearted. Genius hovers with his sunshine and music close by the darkest and deafest eras."[55]

[54] Conversation of 11 March 1832. *Gespräche mit Eckermann*, pp. 772–73.

[55] Emerson, *Representative Men*, p. 290.

VI

Zoilo-Thersites
Another "sehr ernster Scherz" in Goethe's *Faust II*

One of the most bizarre figures in Goethe's *Faust II* makes an unheralded entry during the "Mummenschanz," undergoes a sudden transformation, and is not seen again during the remainder of the drama. This is the thoroughly unpleasant Zoilo-Thersites, who wears the double mask of Zoilus, the unfair, vicious critic of Homer, and Thersites, the Homeric character who heaped abuse upon his fellow Greeks at Troy. Rounding out a procession of allegorical figures (Fear, Hope, Prudence, Victory) this double-faced monstrosity unleashes a venomous verbal barrage that clearly justifies the assumption that it is Mephistopheles, the spirit of negation, who has donned the dual mask and exits by means of a magical transformation.[1]

By appearing in such a costume, Mephistopheles takes an initial step toward the attainment of an aspect of ugliness that will culminate in his assuming the guise of Phorkyas, enabling him to function more effectively in the realm of the esthetic (Acts II and III). The problem of the *raison d'être* of Zoilo-Thersites, however, still needs examination and clarification. The figure seems to be the expression of little more than a bit of Goethean whimsey, largely unrelated to the remainder of the work. Yet the treatment of the imagery and the structural handling of this episode within the drama lead one to conclude that the unlovely creature is directly related to certain aspects of Faust's experience of the world. The present study will undertake to point to those specific connections with the imagery and structure of *Faust II* which suggest that when Goethe created Zoilo-Thersites he was very conscious of the organic inner workings of his poetic imagination.

Because it provides a direct connection between Zoilo-Thersites and the whole problem of the esthetic experience in the drama, the image of the egg is of particular interest. The masked figure's transformation into snake and bat proceeds via an intermediate stage in which it contracts into the form of an egg:

[1] Thus, for instance, Erich Trunz: "In der Maske des *Zoilo-Thersites* steckt Mephistopheles, der hier sich selber spielt." HA III, 541.

Wie sich die Doppelzwerggestalt
So schnell zum eklen Klumpen ballt!—
—Doch Wunder!—Klumpen wird zum Ei,
Das bläht sich auf und platzt entzwei.
Nun fällt ein Zwillingspaar heraus,
Die Otter und die Fledermaus;

(5474–79)

Curiously enough, the image of the egg occurs once again in the course of the work, in the scene "Innerer Burghof" (Act III), where Faust describes the birth of Helen of Troy, daughter of Leda and Jupiter in the form of a swan:

Als mit Eurotas' Schilfgeflüster
Sie leuchtend aus der Schale brach,
Der hohen Mutter, dem Geschwister
Das Licht der Augen überstach.

(9518–21)

A strange coincidence, indeed, that an image so fraught with meaning should be used by Goethe in just these two connections. What then of the chronology of their creation? Act III, the "Helen Act," was completed in the year 1826 and was published the following year as *Helena: Klassisch-romantische Phantasmagorie. Zwischenspiel zu Faust* in volume IV of the *Ausgabe letzter Hand*. Goethe then proceeded with the work on the scenes at the Emperor's court, which he completed in 1827 and which appeared the following year in volume XII of the *Ausgabe letzter Hand* (lines 4613–6036). Thus the sequence of occurrence of the egg image in the play does not reflect the sequence of its creation. Goethe first introduced the image in what is clearly the more weighty context—that of the third act. Its subsequent introduction in connection with Zoilo-Thersites cannot possibly have occurred without Goethe's conscious realization that he was using a motif in Act I which he had already incorporated into the third and central act. Thus we have a sound basis for viewing as significant certain thematic and metaphoric parallels that link the figure of Zoilo-Thersites with the problem of beauty, the realm of the esthetic which figures so centrally in Faust's quest.

Before proceeding to an analysis of the imagery associated with Zoilo-Thersites we shall examine the figure's incorporation into the composition of the whole and in this structural context seek a clue to the character's function in the drama. For the placement of the Helen act within the entire poem provides the background against which Zoilo-Thersites' place within the masque reveals its inner necessity. It is not accidental that Goethe placed this act at the center of *Faust II;* its position is in keeping with the importance attributed by German Classicism to the "esthetic education" of man as that sphere of experience which brings into balance the various sides of human nature. In *Über die aesthetische Erziehung des Menschen in einer Reihe von Briefen* (1795) Friedrich Schiller expressed in philosophical terms the central function of the esthetic as it mediates between the physical and the spiritual. Similarly, the central position which Goethe assigns to the figure of Helen reflects the importance attributed to the esthetic experience in the harmonious development of the human personality, *der Mensch*, as an ideal of German Classicism.

All the more significant, then, is the aspect presented by the vision of the birth of this symbolic figure and the image of the egg from which she emerges. The vision is heightened through the adjective "leuchtend": "Als mit Eurotas' Schilfgeflüster/ Sie leuchtend aus der Schale brach" (9518–19). The radiance of the esthetic experience, indicated here in the myth of Helen's birth, finds powerful symbolic expression in the words of the watchman Lynkeus. He is overwhelmed by her beauty, which he likens to the sight of the blinding sun itself: "Diese Schönheit, wie sie blendet,/ Blendete mich Armen ganz" (9240–41). Such are the depths of symbolic and thematic meaning associated with the image of the egg in the heart of the drama.

If the image of the egg is evoked as a mythical recollection of the origin of beauty just at the point in the poem when Faust is deeply immersed in the central experience of the esthetic, what is the structural context in which the image is again introduced within the masque? It lies midway between the two main episodes of the scene. Before Zoilo-Thersites enters, the parade of characters passing in review presents an allegory of human society and of the natural and social elements on which it is founded.[2] First to appear are the representatives of the world of nature (gardeners, grain and fruit, and flowers, associated with both the natural and the artificial sphere of beauty), since it forms the basis upon which human community is able to develop. There follow characteristic representatives of society (mother, daughter, woodsmen, clowns, parasites, a drunk, a satirist), who are succeeded by mythological figures (the Graces, Fates, and Furies) as personified forces in the souls and destinies of those who make up the fabric of society. This allegory then reaches its peak through the entrance of the elephant with Fear (chained), Hope, Prudence as guide, and, lastly, the winged Victory atop her tower on the elephant's back, celebrated as "Göttin aller Tätigkeiten" (5456). The phenomenon "society"[3]—in its outward manifestation, as well as the inner psychological forces which contribute to its development and ennoblement —is here revealed before the onlookers in the cheerful irony of masquerade.

The appearance of Zoilo-Thersites interrupts the allegory at its peak. The rest of the masque presents a second group of figures which symbolically reveal the inner mysteries of the creative process of man's spirit. Hence the figures are representative of this process: Boy Charioteer (Poetry, genial inspiration),

[2] For a detailed discussion of the problem cf. Wilhelm Emrich, *Die Symbolik von Faust II*, 3rd ed. (Frankfurt a. M., 1964), pp. 131 ff.

[3] Cf. Dorothea Lohmeyer, *Faust und die Welt* (Potsdam, 1940), pp. 29–35.

Plutus-Faust (Wealth, not only material, but more pertinently the spiritual wealth which inspires creativity), its opposite Avarice-Mephisto,[4] and finally Pan—the Kaiser with his whole retinue. The scene presents the profound and mysterious alchemy of creativity which centers on the inexhaustible symbol of gold,[5] image of the hidden inspirative (and also potentially dangerous) forces of the world. As the (supposedly) inspired head of society the Emperor embodies the stance of the creative individual in relation to these forces, which are of central significance not only for the realm of art, but for that of any truly creative activity. The Emperor's lack of the spiritual maturity and insight needed to cope with these forces finds symbolic expression at the end of the masque in the conflagration, an episode reminiscent of Faust's brash and incomprehending attempt to conjure the Earth Spirit. Whereas the first group of figures in the masque appear merely as conventional and rather detached allegories (the Fates rendered virtually harmless through the irony of reversed roles), the second group unfold before our eyes a symbolic world of sobering innerness and intensity. That the Emperor himself is here subjected to what would be, were it not magic, a positively dangerous dose of self-knowledge underscores the contrast. The deeper and more mysterious nature of this second half of the masque is sensed by the Herald, who, at the approach of the dragon-drawn chariot, exclaims "Mich schaudert's" (5520). His apprehension subsequently proves well founded.

The disruptive entry of Zoilo-Thersites must be viewed with reference to its position between these two main episodes of the masque. The figure's abusive language and gruesome transformation serve to startle and shock the spectators; like the Herald himself they are in a state of confusion. As the mysterious chariot approaches, the Herald realizes that something will be disclosed which transcends his limited understanding: "Aber was nicht zu begreifen,/ Wüßt' ich auch nicht zu erklären" (5508–9). Clearly, then, the figure of Zoilo-Thersites is introduced at precisely that point in the masque when a forceful deepening of both imagery and theme is about to take place. The masque as conventional revue is enriched by the dramatic dialogue (Herald, Boy Charioteer, Plutus) which introduces the theme of poetry (the esthetic realm) and culminates in the symbolic treatment of the problem of creativity with the appearance of the Emperor-Pan. Powerful and mysterious inner forces of the creative process are to be made known, and the almost apocalyptic quality of this revelation is evident in the spiritual shock which heralds its advent.

Of the new group of figures the first to speak is the Boy Charioteer, representative of poetry and son of Plutus-Faust. The identity of the boy, revealed by

[4] That Faust wears the mask of Plutus, and Mephistopheles that of Avarice, is verified by Goethe: "Daß in der Maske des Plutus der Faust steckt und in der Maske des Geizes der Mephistopheles, werden Sie gemerkt haben." Conversation of 20 December 1829. Ernst Beutler, ed., *Goethe, Gespräche mit Eckermann*, Artemis Ausgabe (Zürich, 1949), p. 379.

[5] Cf. Emrich, pp. 185 ff. and 267 ff., who treats of this symbol as it is woven into the entire drama.

Goethe as Euphorion,[6] establishes a parallel between this scene and the birth of Euphorion to Helen and Faust in Act III. Can there then by any question of coincidence in the occurrence of the egg image at this point in the masque? The inner structural laws of the work reveal its artistic necessity as a prefiguration of the thematics of the Helen act. In both instances this image occurs at a point at which a profound deepening and an enrichment of the theme of creative production, art and poetry manifest themselves. The stylized appearance of Faust with his son Euphorion (whose identity, as is consonant with the nature of the masque, is veiled through a change in name) in Act I will be transformed into living experience in Faust's union with Helen and the birth of their son in Act III.

We are now in a position to return to the image of the egg and to investigate the complex imagery associated with Zoilo-Thersites. We hope that this close textual investigation may show that what appears to be a surprising structural correspondence between this character and the theme of beauty in Act III is anchored in an objective and subtle transformation of motifs.

The underlying phenomenon that characterizes the nature of Zoilo-Thersites is duality. The character's very name is a composite of two separate personalities and finds expression in the double-faced mask. Moreover, he (they? it?) appears on the borderline between the two main episodes of the masque. This Janus-headed quality is further enhanced by the curious fact that the whole appearance of Zoilo-Thersites falls into two halves: the words of abuse directed at the representatives of the allegory just past are spoken by the character himself, whereas his transformation, brought about by the Herald's magic, is described by the latter. The two speeches are nearly identical in length (fourteen and thirteen lines, respectively).

Entering with the twofold cry "Hu! Hu!" the figure swiftly lets it be known that he is enraged at the sight of Victory with her pair of white wings (5461). Since Zoilo-Thersites cannot tolerate noble and commendable activities he defines his purpose in true Mephistophelean fashion as the restoration of chaos. Yet, in keeping with the nature of his present embodiment, this son of Chaos expresses his purpose not in chaotic form, but in polarities: "Das Tiefe hoch, das Hohe tief,/ Das Schiefe grad, das Grade schief" (5467–68). Thus the first speech, Zoilo-Thersites' direct statement of his purposes, is interlaced with a web of polar opposites. Similarly, the description of his magic transformation, effected and reported to us indirectly by the Herald, develops the dual imagery with all the consistency of its own bizarre logic. The "Doppelzwerggestalt" (5474) forms itself into an egg. Yet the hatching of the egg reveals not a single creature, but the gruesome "Zwillingspaar" (5478), snake and bat. It is truly a Mephistophelean parody on the theme of metamorphosis so central to Goethe's world view—a metamorphosis which leads here not to a heightening and ennoblement of being,

[6] *Gespräche mit Eckermann*, p. 379.

but to a "butterfly" more grotesque than the "caterpillar" which preceded it. Appropriately enough, therefore, the egg does not gently crack and slowly release its burden: "Das bläht sich auf und platzt entzwei" (5477). This too is an unnatural event. The snake and bat, emerging from the exploding egg, proceed to leave the scene, each in its own appropriate manner, echoing the polarity of "hoch/tief" in Zoilo-Thersites' speech. The Herald describes their exit: "Die eine fort im Staube kriecht,/ Die andre schwarz zur Decke fliegt" (5480–81).

The weird parody on the themes of beauty and of metamorphosis developed in Act I is directly related to the person of Mephistopheles through the recurrence of a number of images during the latter's ill-fated attempts to befriend the Lamiae in Act II (7696 ff.). Mephisto grasps one of these weird sisters, only to find that she has turned into a lizard with snakelike hair (7774–75), while the third, rather obese member of this group explodes in a fashion described by the verb "platzen," precisely the word used to characterize the exploding egg: "Doch ach! der Bovist platzt entzwei" (7784). Whereupon the Lamiae, disenchanted with the Nordic intruder, transform themselves into bats which silently describe gruesome circles about his head (7785–90). The connection between this episode and the Zoilo-Thersites theme in Act I is then rendered abundantly clear by Mephisto's comment on the masquelike character of his unhappy encounter with the Lamiae:

> Ist eben hier eine Mummenschanz,
> Wie überall, ein Sinnentanz.
> Ich griff nach holden Maskenzügen
> Und faßte Wesen, daß mich's schauerte.
> (7795–98)

Though both episodes center about a Mephistophelean parody of beauty and transformation and are clearly related through shared motifs (snakes, bats, masque), they are characterized by a subtle distinction. In Act I, Mephisto is himself a masked actor, and he plays a role within the courtly masque. In the "Klassische Walpurgisnacht," which unfolds the fairy-tale world of forms that lead up to the highest embodiment of beauty in the person of Helen, Mephisto appears as a would-be active participant, rather than as a role-player. Whereas Faust is able to appear as a masked actor in Act I and shed his mask entirely in order to become a true participator in the inner events of Acts II and III, Mephisto finds himself unable to take this decisive step into the realm of the living experience of the beautiful. Hence the shadowy distortion of the theme of beauty, which he has himself presented (as Zoilo-Thersites) in the masque, returns to haunt him "from outside" in the form of the Lamiae. The pseudo-metamorphosis into snake and bat in Act I also returns for Mephistopheles as a tragicomic and ironic motif in his fruitless attempt to find his way into the classical environment. Finally he is forced to undergo a pseudo-metamorphosis par excellence in borrowing the form of Phorkyas, i.e. in simply putting on another mask.

The above discussion has, we hope, elucidated the structural and thematic significance of the Zoilo-Thersites figure for our understanding of Mephistopheles' encounters with the theme of beauty. In the case of Faust himself, the significance of the episode lies at a deeper level, as we have sensed in noting the recurrence and structural placement of the egg image. To uncover the deeper connections inherent in this complex of imagery, we shall now place the Zoilo-Thersites episode against the larger background of the question of beauty in the Hellenic setting of Act III.

At the beginning of his long hymn in praise of Sparta Faust recalls Helen's mythical birth. The stanzas paint an idealized landscape in which nature and man exist in paradisiacal harmony beyond the ravages of time: "Ein jeder ist an seinem Platz unsterblich:/ Sie sind zufrieden und gesund" (9552–53). And the landscape itself, in its very contour, is extraordinary—so extraordinary indeed that Goethe coins a new word to describe it: "Nichtinsel" (9512) for "Halbinsel." Attached to the mainland only by a narrow isthmus, this region of the Peloponnesus represents a delicately balanced middle position between the two polar opposites of all landscape, land and water. We are at once reminded of the principle of duality associated with the egg image in Act I, and we find it once again woven into the very heart of the Helen episode as an archetypal landscape, the setting for the union of Leda and Jupiter and the resultant shining birth of Helen.[7]

Here Goethe touches upon a deep truth concerning the nature of the esthetic experience, for all works of art hover between the poles of rest and motion, of form and formlessness. Even so seemingly static an art form as architecture contains a musicality and inner dynamic in its proportions. The liveliest musical composition, on the other hand, may be considered art, rather than noise, by virtue of its formal structure. This archetypal polarity, touchstone of the esthetic experience, forms the natural context (land/sea) for the myth of Helen's birth; because the forces involved are here organically related and inwardly necessary, a miraculous transformation is able to take place. The duality-ridden pseudo-metamorphosis of the egg in Act I, viewed against this background, appears as a shadowy negative prefiguration of a profound truth subsequently revealed. Indeed, many details of the Zoilo-Thersites episode—apart from the bats, snakes, and principle of polarity—find their corresponding positive reflection in the scenes of Acts II and III. Zoilo-Thersites' tirade against winged Victory, for example, echoes themes to come:

> Mit ihrem weißen Flügelpaar
> Sie dünkt sich wohl, sie sei ein Aar,
> Und wo sie sich nur hingewandt,
> Gehör' ihr alles Volk und Land;
> (5461–64)

[7] The organic relationship of art and nature through inherent developmental laws shared by both is the cornerstone of the classical esthetics of Goethe since the Italian journey. The appropriateness of seeing in the landscape configuration of Act III an archetypal element directly related to the Helen myth is thus obvious. Cf. Emrich's discussion of the esthetic problem (*Symbolik*, pp. 226–361).

Not only does the association of a radiant heroine with the white wings of a bird bear an odd resemblance to the image of Helen, begotten by Jupiter in the form of a swan and popping forth from an egg; the resemblance is even more concrete. Zoilo-Thersites' cynical reference to the figure's queenly nature ("Gehör' ihr alles Volk und Land") becomes positive reality in the case of Helen, whom Faust elevates to the status of "Spartas Königin" (9463). What appears in the masque as a distorted "bad dream" disappears from sight and is reborn in the raiments of esthetic perfection in the timeless inner world of Faust's Hellas.

It will now be clear why Goethe chose to introduce two Greeks as a guise for Mephistopheles in the heart of the masque. When the Zoilo-Thersites episode is seen as a negative prefiguration of the problem of the esthetic, it is obvious that a thematic connection exists between this episode and the poetic reality of Faust's union with Helen in Sparta. The choice of the name Zoilo-Thersites casts a light upon the structural relationship between the two episodes we have been discussing. We recall that the realm of Arcadia is so idealized that men live in a paradisiacal state. Faust observes: "Wir staunen drob; noch immer bleibt die Frage:/ Ob's Götter, ob es Menschen sind?" (9556–57). Do not the names Zoilus and Thersites, in their negative way, point to figures who enjoy the stature of demigods in the consciousness of ancient Greek civilization? For Zoilus was the pedantic belittler of Homer, the latter a demigod by virtue of his quasi-anonymous, nearly mythological fame, while Thersites is the uncharitable companion of the Greeks, demigods by virtue of their heroic deeds as celebrated by the poet. The entire Zoilo-Thersites episode presents a prefiguration of central motifs of the mythological birth of beauty in the outward, critical-ironic distortion of their reflection in the magic mirror of Mephistopheles' nature. Quite unwittingly, the latter serves as a vehicle whereby Goethe plants the seeds of poetic imagery which, having had time to sprout and grow during the intervening "Klassische Walpurgisnacht," will blossom into true imaginative visions of organic necessity in the inward realm of Sparta, the soul-landscape in which Faust will unite his being with the forces of beauty.

Mephisto must assume a Greek aspect in Act I so that the function of this episode, the introduction of the themes associated with the mystery of the birth of the esthetic in the human soul, may be effected. That these themes are cruelly distorted in the make-believe world of the masque is quite in keeping with Mephistopheles' desire to make a mockery of just those deeper mysteries of man's soul which are too important for him to ignore. It is also in keeping with Goethe's uncanny artistic sensitivity, for he knew that an experience of spiritual depth and radiance often sends before it a negative shadow-image which heralds its coming. He also knew that an encounter with this shadow-image serves to jolt the soul out of its apathy and prepare it for a more conscious reception of deeper truths. In this subtle spiritual law there is just a touch of the apocalyptic, an element that shows itself quite clearly in another scene in *Faust II*. At the beginning of Act II,

Mephistopheles, entering Dr. Wagner's laboratory, rings a bell to announce his arrival. The clang of the bell is accompanied by upheavals and tremors in the very foundations of the building. It is the opening scene of the act in which occur the creation of Homunculus, his revelation of the content of Faust's dream-life, and the ensuing journey into the inner world of the "Klassische Walpurgisnacht."[8]

The deed of spiritual creativity consummated by Faust in his poetic union with Helen of Troy results in the birth of Euphorion. Is it any wonder that an event of such inner depth and power should similarly cast an after-image (which is literally a fore-image) into Act I? The reader is made aware—although unknowingly at first—of a mystery which will only later be revealed in its full ramifications. By means of a shock in the middle of the masque the theme of beauty is introduced in a distorted form, and the Boy Charioteer can make his entry. Only in Act III does the symbolism attain maturity, and only then does the son of Faust step forth onto the stage in his real nature, without a mask and having acquired his own name: Euphorion. This principle, whereby a theme once introduced reveals its full content only in the further course of the play, is a basic esthetic law which can be observed throughout *Faust*.[9]

Whereas the appearance of Zoilo-Thersites stands structurally and thematically in the middle of the masque and bears a direct relationship to the appearance of Helen in the drama as a whole, the episode must remain just that: an episode. By reason of its Mephistophelean origin it cannot be fruitful. The imagery therefore remains caught in the tension of dualities, the polar quality of contrasting darkness and light. In Act III, however, it is able to unfold within a harmonized context. Polarity, here expressed in the archetypal contrast of land and sea, no longer remains unresolved. On the contrary, it now provides the very conditions which make it possible for the egg not to explode, but to hatch, revealing the archetype of beauty. The hopeless black/white quality of the earlier episode is overcome through the fullness of life—a variegated, rainbow-drenched landscape: Sparta-Arcadia. In this scene it is possible for Faust to appear as himself, without the mask. For the nature of the appurtenance called the "mask" points to the true distinction between the two scenes. Through the medium of the mask Mephistopheles is able to perpetrate a nasty joke which points negatively to certain esthetic secrets. But the true spiritual processes of which this joke is a caricature cannot reveal themselves through a medium such as the mask, which is a detached contrivance for which the English language has coined the singularly apt term "false face." The true nature of the beautiful can no more reveal itself through this medium than it can through the mere phantom image of Helen

[8] Emrich points out clearly the apocalyptic "ring" of the scene (*Symbolik*, p. 249).

[9] Thus, for instance, Faust's vision of Gretchen in the "Walpurgisnacht" becomes reality in the dungeon scene and the conjuration of the Earth Spirit begins to reveal its secrets in such scenes as "Anmutige Gegend" in Part II, where the forces of nature heal the soul and Faust begins to comprehend their language through the colors weaving in the rainbow.

gleaned from the Mothers. An attempt to seize upon this shade must end in an explosion.

Similarly, Zoilo-Thersites presents a mere reflected image (and a distorted one, at that) of a mystery of the birth of beauty within the soul. But this mystery cannot express itself in the "Scheinwelt" of a conventional revue. The true revelation of the mystery is possible only in the "Welt des schönen Scheins," the live, organic world to which Faust attains only by dint of a protracted inner quest. In this timeless landscape of the soul beauty comes to birth through sound (rhyme), through a musical heightening of the inner attunement to language. Language in the everyday sense is transcended and the magic of pure tone blends Faust's and Helen's souls. Yet even here the process becomes progressively inward until, ultimately, the word falls silent ("Ich atme kaum, mir zittert, stockt das Wort" 9413) at the supreme moment of union, which is entirely spiritual in nature.

The introduction of the egg symbol and its many associations remains unproductive in the masque; and Faust himself appears in this scene merely as a masked actor. When the image is reintroduced in Act III the mere reflections are long since discarded and the archetypal reality reveals itself through the soul's marriage with the forces of beauty. No longer a mere actor in a—however profound—conventional review, Faust now appears as neophyte in an unfolding drama of self-knowledge. But the very fact that the imagery has been introduced in its distorted and shocking form in Act I prepares us for the reality (Act III) of which it is a shadow-image. Thus we now experience this reality the more fully. The shock effect of the pseudo-metamorphosis of Zoilo-Thersites, which throws even the Herald into confusion, has a curiously wakening, liberating effect which lets us hearken to the true nature of Helen's appearance.

The grotesque-serious quality of the Zoilo-Thersites episode recalls Goethe's own reference to Part II of the drama as "sehr ernste Scherze."[10] In a subtle way Mephistopheles' grotesque appearance in the middle of the masque helps to prepare the reader for the richer unfolding of what Schiller calls the "esthetic education of man," the development of the forces of artistic awareness at the center of man's nature, as this mystery reveals itself in the course of Faust's inner travels. Here again we see the irony and comic-tragic nature of Mephistopheles. For him there can be no deepened awareness, no true understanding of beauty. He cannot shed his mask; he can only exchange one mask for another—that of Zoilo-Thersites for that of Avarice, that of Avarice for that of Phorkyas. He is doomed to remain the tragic "Narr im Spiele." Yet by unwittingly serving a positive purpose in helping the audience to awaken to an important coming dimension of Faust's inner development he once again shows himself true to his nature as "Ein Teil von jener Kraft,/ Die stets das Böse will und stets das Gute schafft" (1335–36).

[10] To Wilhelm von Humboldt, 17 March 1832, *Goethes Briefe*, HA IV, 481.

VII

Faust's Blindness and the Inner Light
Some Questions for the Future

In the scene "Mitternacht" (Part II, Act V) the ever striving one-hundred-year-old Faust finds himself imprisoned in a splendid isolation of his own making. In his anxiety to fill out the last gap in his "Weltbesitz" he has involved himself in the murder of Philemon, Baucis and their guest and is set upon by the shadowy hag Dame Care ("Sorge"). The scene's title, "Mitternacht," recalls that of the opening scene of Part I, "Nacht," in which Faust's consuming desire had been to pierce the veil of sensory phenomena and merge with the spiritual:

. . . Ich fühle mich bereit,
Auf neuer Bahn den Äther zu durchdringen,
Zu neuen Sphären reiner Tätigkeit.
(703–5)

He was prepared to pay with his life for transcendence:

Ja, kehre nur der holden Erdensonne
Entschlossen deinen Rücken zu!
Vermesse dich, die Pforten aufzureißen,
Vor denen jeder gern vorüberschleicht.
(708–11)

Only the intervention of the powerful spiritual impulse proclaimed by the Easter chorus stays the hand that lifts the poison and Faust is given back to the earth ("O tönet fort, ihr süßen Himmelslieder!/ Die Träne quillt, die Erde hat mich wieder!" 783–84). The spiritual insight for which Faust longs so fervently will not be had through an act of self-negation, however noble its conscious intent. It will be attained only gradually and its price is suffering. The archetype of this trial of earthly existence is suggested in the words of the chorus of angels:

Christ ist erstanden!
Selig der Liebende,
Der die betrübende,
Heilsam' und übende
Prüfung bestanden.
(757–61)

Christ is risen, say the angels, but He is risen after having seen through the trial ("Prüfung") of earthly life and of death—the trial whose accomplishment gives the Resurrection its meaning.

In "Mitternacht" the ancient Faust once again fronts the prospect of death: "Es klang so nach, als hieß' es—Not,/ Ein düstres Reimwort folgte—Tod" (11400–401). He has indeed passed through the trial of a full life on earth and he stands now at the portals of that spirit world for which he had earlier longed and which will unfold before his inner eye in the last scene, "Bergschluchten." Yet it is high irony that Faust, face to face with death, has now lost interest in that spiritual awakening which he had so ardently sought:

> Der Erdenkreis ist mir genug bekannt,
> Nach drüben ist die Aussicht uns verrannt;
> Tor, wer dorthin die Augen blinzelnd richtet,
> Sich über Wolken seinesgleichen dichtet!
> Er stehe fest und sehe hier sich um;
> Dem Tüchtigen ist diese Welt nicht stumm.
> Was braucht er in die Ewigkeit zu schweifen!
> Was er erkennt, läßt sich ergreifen.
>
> (11441–48)

Faust has indeed taken on the "Prüfung" of life in the earthly world. And he has tasked himself so thoroughly that the full might of his expansive entelechy has now united with the details of his plan for a new society. It is a grand design for an earthly paradise. It is also alarmingly dependent upon the personality of its originator. Faust realizes this but in his egotistical zeal is quick to forget that it is at bottom a totalitarian premise: "Daß sich das größte Werk vollende,/ Genügt *ein* Geist für tausend Hände" (11509–10). The plan, then, is impressive, the accomplishments many, yet these have been attained at the price of increasing self-deception, illusion and blindness to the delicate spiritual laws which alone can impart to such an enterprise the qualities commonly termed "humanitarian." Faust has had high aspirations—much higher than those of most men—and he has striven with all the insight and strength at his command. He has seen into the secrets of the universe and of the soul, yet in action he has often erred. In the end, then, he too must harvest the consequences of his shortcomings and must experience that blindness which often accompanies lesser men throughout their entire lives.

> Sorge:
>
> . . . .
>
> Die Menschen sind im ganzen Leben blind,
> Nun, Fauste, werde du's am Ende!
>
> *Sie haucht ihn an.*
>
> Faust, *erblindet.*
>
> Die Nacht scheint tiefer tief hereinzudringen,
> Allein im Innern leuchtet helles Licht;
>
> (11497–500)

These first words of the blinded Faust embrace a cosmos. They speak both of the darkness and of the light—the archetypal polarity which underlies Goethe's *Farbenlehre*. We recall that for Goethe the colors are not simply contained in the "white" light but arise as "Taten des Lichts, Taten und Leiden"[1] as light encounters darkness. In Faust's words both realms appear as active. Not only does the light shine ("leuchtet") brightly within, but the darkness seems to penetrate ever deeper ("tiefer tief hereinzudringen"). Faust experiences both forces intensely. And in keeping with the metaphorical use of light and darkness throughout the poem both represent not only visual impressions but also moral qualities. It is therefore important that we ask just what this "inner light," of which Faust speaks, signifies.

The first clue is given in the following words, alluded to above:

> Was ich gedacht, ich eil' es zu vollbringen;
> Des Herren Wort, es gibt allein Gewicht.
> Vom Lager auf, ihr Knechte! Mann für Mann!
> Laßt glücklich schauen, was ich kühn ersann.
> Ergreift das Werkzeug, Schaufel rührt und Spaten!
> Das Abgesteckte muß sogleich geraten.
> Auf strenges Ordnen, raschen Fleiß
> Erfolgt der allerschönste Preis;
> Daß sich das größte Werk vollende,
> Genügt *ein* Geist für tausend Hände.
>
> (11501–10)

Faust is possessed by the megalomania of power. His visions of socially beneficial work have been perverted into the warped design of an anthill state with Faust its supreme guiding spirit. In view of his imminent death, there is a grotesque ambiance of unreality about this vision which Michelsen terms Faust's "Fiktion der Weltbeherrschung."[2] Michelsen points out correctly that it is Goethe's conviction that colors arise only through the interaction of light and darkness, and that in the present passage the two realms remain isolated and therefore unproductive.[3] They remain isolated because in his present state of mind Faust perceives the inner light purely egotistically. What lives in it can therefore not stream out into the world. Yet as we shall see, it was also Goethe's conviction that what lives as light within man is destined one day to ray forth and illuminate the world without. Thus another critic, Hartmann, speaks of the inner light as "zunächst das

[1] "Vorwort," *Zur Farbenlehre*, HA XIII, 315.

[2] "Fausts Blendung geschieht bei verschlossener Tür im Innern des Palastes, im Innenraum des sich isolierenden Individuums, das sich, mit Blindheit geschlagen, der Fiktion der Weltbeherrschung ergibt, in Wahrheit aber nur noch seinen letzten Gang 'ins enge Haus' (v. 11529) zu tun hat." Peter Michelsen, "Fausts Erblindung," *DVLG*, 36 (1962), 31.

[3] ". . . und wenn Faust im Innern ein helles Licht leuchtet, so ist das Entscheidende daran ja gerade, daß dieses Licht mit der es umgebenden Finsternis keine Ehe eingeht, daß kein buntes Kind gezeugt wird. Licht und Finsternis bleiben getrennt, unfruchtbar isoliert." *Ibid.*, p. 34.

Licht egozentrischer Illusionen."[4] These interpretations are entirely correct as far as they go. The inner light, as Faust perceives it *consciously*, is the light of illusion. Hartmann is aware that the image may contain further levels of meaning, for he qualifies his statement with the word "zunächst." In the same passage he goes on to say that it is a factor of Faust's present blindness that he denies his own immortal self ("das unsterbliche Menschen-Ich").

The Goethean term for the immortal self of man is the Aristotelian "entelechy." It is just this connection of the inner light with the entelechy which comes to expression in another critical view of the passage. Stöcklein notes that the attack of "Sorge" affects only Faust's physical organism but ricochets off the entelechy.[5] And Emrich refers to the immortal entelechy "die Goethe hier mythisch als 'inneres Licht' bezeichnet . . ."[6] He maintains that Faust's blindness overcomes death and that it directs his attention to the eternal creative force within: ". . . ihn auf die ewige Schöpferkraft des Innern—und etwas anderes ist nach Goethes Seelenlehre dies 'innere Licht' nicht—verweist."[7] For Emrich, then, the inner light may be interpreted *only* as the creative force within. Michelsen restricts his interpretation to that which gives itself up to the "fiction of world-rulership," that "light" in which live the dying Faust's last great illusions. Emrich limits his interpretation to the "creative force" of the entelechy which overcomes death.

The entelechy, for Goethe, is a being which manifests itself either strongly or weakly in proportion to what it has become: ". . . wir sind nicht auf gleiche Weise unsterblich, und um sich künftig als große Entelechie zu manifestieren, muß man auch eine sein."[8] If the inner light is to be identified, at least in part, with the entelechy, one must consider the forces which have formed that entelechy and have given it the radiance and power which it exhibits in Faust. It has grown in part simply through the inner drive, the will-power which characterizes Faust's unbounded striving. Yet Faust has not striven in a vacuum. The world around him has also contributed to his growth. Other beings with whom he has associated, both in the physical world (Wagner, Gretchen, the Emperor) and in the realms of spirit (the Mothers) have imparted forces to his soul which have had a profoundly formative effect and contributed directly to the growth of his entelechy. In this sense the image of the inner light encompasses the life experiences and especially the spiritual strength and love which have been acquired through

[4] "Das 'Licht' jedoch, das er nun stolz in sich zu finden meint, ist zunächst das Licht egozentrischer Illusionen. . . ." Otto Julius Hartmann, *Faust. Der moderne Mensch in der Begegnung mit dem Bösen* (Freiburg i. Br., 1957), p. 94.

[5] "Ihr Angriff erreicht aber nur die leiblich-vitale Sphäre; an der Entelechie prallt er ab." Paul Stöcklein, *Wege zum späten Goethe* (Hamburg, 1960), p. 150.

[6] Wilhelm Emrich, *Die Symbolik von Faust II* (Frankfurt a. M., 1964), p. 398.

[7] *Ibid.*, p. 397.

[8] To Eckermann, 1 September 1829. Ernst Beutler, ed., *Goethe, Gespräche mit Eckermann*, Artemis Ausgabe (Zürich, 1949), p. 371.

other people, notably Gretchen, and which will ray out into the light-filled world of "Bergschluchten" after the purely earthly, material qualities (the "Erdenrest," 11954) have been discarded.

The image of the "inner light," then, includes a number of levels of meaning, all of which are justified from their respective points of view. At the lowest level, as discussed by Michelsen and Hartmann, it refers to that which Faust experiences *consciously*—the world of private, illusory dreamings. On a higher level, as described by Emrich, it gives expression to the creative force of the entelechy, not "seen" consciously by Faust but experienced dimly in the striving itself. And we should like to suggest that on the highest level, of which Faust is here hardly aware in his conscious life, it refers to the *sources* of that force of the entelechy. This is the elevated sphere of spiritual ideas and love which has prompted Faust in his strivings, despite the fact that it is often lost sight of as he is deflected into the avenues of egotism and perversity. The image thus embodies not one meaning but several. It is not an allegory but a *symbol* in the Goethean sense of the word.[9]

The inner light as the source of clarity and spiritual love which fire the soul's aspirations and lead man on high is present in Faust as *seed*, obscured by the forces of darkness: egotism, lust, materialism. Only after death, in "Bergschluchten," will this seed quicken to new life, unfold its organs of perception and blossom forth, called to life by the light which is of its own nature and which is the etherial element in which the discarnate beings have their existence.

The opening scene of Part I bears the appropriate title "Nacht." Through his years of bookish study Faust has known the chill light of reason, has plumbed the depths of academic knowledge and honed his thinking to a razor edge in the "collegium logicum" of materialistic science. The result is a sense of imprisonment, frustration, despair—and finally the thought of suicide from which Faust is saved by music, memories of childhood and the forces of renewal borne to him in the Easter message. In his liaison with Mephisto Faust experiences three worlds which threaten to overcome the light of his nobler self: "Auerbachs Keller," the "Hexenküche" and the "Walpurgisnacht." In all three scenes, however, the spark of higher life within Faust, a life over which Mephisto has no final control, asserts itself. In "Auerbachs Keller" the students sink to the level of drunken bestiality. Faust says to Mephisto: "Ich hätte Lust, nun abzufahren" (2296). The "Hexenküche" is the world of unbridled sexuality. Faust succumbs in large measure to the lust incarnate of the beings which inhabit that world, yet he suffers a slight prick of conscience: "Mein Busen fängt mir an zu brennen!/ Entfernen wir uns

[9] "Die Symbolik verwandelt die Erscheinung in Idee, die Idee in ein Bild, und so, daß die Idee im Bild immer unendlich wirksam und unerreichbar bleibt und, selbst in allen Sprachen ausgesprochen, doch unaussprechlich bliebe.

Die Allegorie verwandelt die Erscheinung in einen Begriff, den Begriff in ein Bild, doch so, daß der Begriff im Bilde immer noch begrenzt und vollständig zu halten und zu haben und an demselben auszusprechen sei." *Maximen und Reflexionen*, nos. 749 and 750, HA XII, 470–71.

nur geschwind!" (2461–62). His clear thinking never abandons him entirely. In the face of the witch's grotesqueries he exclaims:

> Nein, sage mir, was soll das werden?
> Das tolle Zeug, die rasenden Gebärden,
> Der abgeschmackteste Betrug,
> Sind mir bekannt, verhaßt genug.
> (2532–35)

In both scenes it is a spark of the light of thinking, of reason, which dwells within Faust and struggles against the onslaught of the hosts of darkness. In the "Walpurgisnacht" it is more. Here Mephisto leads Faust not only into worlds of drunkenness and eroticism but to the portals of the very halls of Evil itself, of the palace of Mammon (3933) and the kingdom of Urian (3959). Here Faust sinks to the lowest level he has yet known. The force which brings him back to his senses is thus correspondingly powerful. It is not reason alone but the full awakening of conscience:

> Mephisto, siehst du dort
> Ein blasses, schönes Kind allein und ferne stehen?
> Sie schiebt sich langsam nur vom Ort,
> Sie scheint mit geschloßnen Füßen zu gehen.
> Ich muß bekennen, daß mir deucht,
> Daß sie dem guten Gretchen gleicht.
> (4183–88)

A prophetic vision of Gretchen's fate dawns in Faust's soul and unleashes the surge of remorse which fuels his attempts to persuade her to flee. From the point of view of certain modern psychological theories one may contend that it is the sense of guilt alone which moves Faust to action. To interpret the events thus narrowly, however, is to do violence to the organism of the poem. For in view of the "Gretchen"-scenes and of the final scene of Part II one must also take into account the outpouring of spiritual love which Gretchen has freely given to Faust and which she will continue to send forth to him from the spiritual world after her death. One must take this love into account in discussing Faust's vision in the "Walpurgisnacht" and the consequences of that vision if one seeks to interpret these passages with respect for Goethe's text. Gretchen's total surrender to Faust has brought her into disastrous conflict with the laws of society. Yet the love she has given him transcends the flames of passion. It is deeply spiritual. In Goethean terminology it is love "von Herzen" (3055, 3206). Faust's conscience awakens in the orgy of the "Walpurgisnacht," for the love which is Gretchen's great gift to him shines within his entelechy and in one of his darkest hours opens the inner eye to her impending passion and death.

When seen against the larger context of *Faust*, these events are themselves a tremendous prefiguration of Faust's two lines in "Mitternacht." For in the "Walpurgisnacht" the dark world of lewdness and evil envelops and penetrates

Faust from all sides: "Die Nacht scheint tiefer tief hereinzudringen." Yet just at this moment something stirs within him which is woven of the forces of Gretchen's love and which, as the power of conscience, literally casts light on the situation and shines into Faust's consciousness as a vision of Gretchen's destiny: "Allein im Innern leuchtet helles Licht."

Darkness and light: Faust's two lines are saturated with meaning. The meaning reveals itself on its various levels as one carefully examines the forces at work, not only in the immediate context but also in the larger; and always in the sense in which Goethe wished to have the world of light, darkness and color understood—not only outwardly ("sinnlich") but also inwardly, morally ("sittlich").

We have seen that in Faust's "inner light," when viewed symbolically, there live not only the conscious designs of his "grand illusion," nor alone the creative power of his entelechy, but both of these and in addition the forces of spiritual love which will unfold in the greater world of Light which he will soon enter. On these three successive levels we observe a process of increasing inwardness. Faust is fully conscious of the first, dimly conscious of the second and for the present virtually unaware of the third.

Goethe's great celebration of the power of the inner light is embodied in the figure of Ottilie in *Die Wahlverwandtschaften* (1809), whose genesis was contemporaneous with that of the *Farbenlehre* (ca. 1790 to 1810). Behind the figure stands the legendary Odilia (†720), patron saint of Alsace, who was born blind, gained the power of sight at her baptism, and later was famed for her charitable works. In his Strasbourg period the young Goethe lived in an area steeped in the saint's lore. Moreover, he found himself daily confronted with problems of the eye and vision, for his mentor, Herder, was plagued by a chronic eye ailment. In addition, the young Strasbourg friend Jung-Stilling, a rustic Pietist for whom Goethe expressed fond admiration, became at last a physician whose specialty was the removal of cataract. The story of this simple, God-fearing man's failure at an operation and the depths of despair and self-reproach into which the event plunged him, are movingly recorded in *Dichtung und Wahrheit.*[10] What is more, Goethe's conversations with Herder had led him to a new awareness of the fact that even the supreme sense-organ of man, the eye, can offend. It can become preoccupied with the sights of the outer world and "may well distract us from the pursuit of insight and inner sight."[11] Through his study of the Greeks Goethe the "Augenmensch" became aware of the need for the balanced development of all of man's faculties in order that the affective and cognitive powers establish themselves harmoniously in the body as a source of creative action.[12] For a time, there-

[10] Book 16, HA X, 87 ff.

[11] Elizabeth M. Wilkinson and L. A. Willoughby, "The Blind Man and the Poet," *German Studies Presented to Walter Horace Bruford* (London, 1962), p. 31.

[12] *Ibid.*, p. 38. This study is very helpful in that it demonstrates the *breadth* of experience which Goethe came to recognize as necessary to man's inner development. From this point of view the notion

fore, he became fascinated with the idea of the positive merits of blindness and even half wished to be blind.[13]

From earliest childhood Goethe possessed an extraordinary power to envision inwardly what he learned. The stories told him by his mother and particularly the world of the Old Testament lived vividly in his imagination. During the Frankfurt illness he exercised these faculties in a powerful new way through the study of the mystical, theosophical and alchemical works brought him by Susanna von Klettenberg. Mystical symbols and cosmic visions filled his consciousness and later found incorporation in the opening scenes of *Faust.* Through the events in Strasbourg the understanding of sight and of the role of the eye in man's inner development was deepened and balanced in the encounter with Herder. All of these experiences in Goethe's biography served gradually to prepare him to make the investigations which led to the later creation of what he himself considered to be his most significant work, the *Farbenlehre.*[14] In Weimar Goethe took the rigorously systematic discipline of his inner life into his own hands. He was then able to metamorphose his lifelong interest in the eye and the faculty of vision into a process of the precise observation and recording of color phenomena. Even in the heat of battle during the French campaign he went calmly about the business of observing and describing the optical phenomena at hand. Thus Goethe's early preoccupation with vision grew, expanded and clarified itself in his mature years. Working with his own observations as well as with the pertinent literature from the ancients to his contemporaries he evolved his *Farbenlehre*, a work which has remained highly controversial since its inception and which has begun to attract considerable interest in recent years. The *Wahlverwandtschaften*, as noted above, evolved at the same time as the color studies. Thus Goethe's statements on the eye and on the "inner light" in connection with Ottilie are the ripe fruit of a life-long development which culminated in the vast enterprise of the *Farbenlehre.* Two streams of activity in particular flow through Goethe's biography and find expression in that work. One is the painstaking observation of the outer phenomena of nature. The other is the inward, mystical interest kindled during the Frankfurt illness. The two merge in the epistemological stance which informs the *Farbenlehre* and they come to expression programmatically in the title of the famous section "Sinnlich-sittliche Wirkung der

of the growing "inner sight" (p. 31), or what we have called the inner light of the entelechy, is greatly expanded and deepened.

[13] *Ibid.*, p. 30.

[14] " 'Auf alles, was ich als Poet geleistet habe,' pflegte er wiederholt zu sagen, 'bilde ich mir gar nichts ein. Es haben treffliche Dichter mit mir gelebt, es lebten noch trefflichere vor mir, und es werden ihrer nach mir sein. Daß ich aber in meinem Jahrhundert in der schwierigen Wissenschaft der Farbenlehre der einzige bin, der das Rechte weiß, darauf tue ich mir etwas zugute, und ich habe daher ein Bewußtsein der Superiorität über viele.' " Conversation with Eckermann, 19 February 1829. *Gespräche mit Eckermann*, p. 328.

Farbe." It is against this background that the concept of the inner light expressed by Ottilie becomes clear. It emerges in a living way within Goethe's developing world view.

It is characteristic of Goethe's entire scientific posture that he is at pains not merely to think *about* the phenomena but to activate his thinking *within* them. "Das Höchste wäre: zu begreifen, daß alles Faktische schon Theorie ist. Die Bläue des Himmels offenbart uns das Grundgesetz der Chromatik. Man suche nur nichts hinter den Phänomenen: sie selbst sind die Lehre."[15] In the *Farbenlehre* Goethe therefore strives not merely to describe the color phenomena theoretically but to lead the reader into an experience of them, in order that in the experience they may themselves reveal their inherent "theory," the systematic laws of their appearance. This method of investigation proceeds from an inward stance. It presumes a systematic cultivation and refinement, even what one might term a purification of the cognitive faculties in order that when they are activated meditatively they will convey the objective content of the phenomena to the researcher just as they do when directed to the external world. The instruments of research which the orthodox scientist employs in his investigations (telescope, microscope, etc.) provide him with a check to any tendencies to draw conclusions which are muddied by elements of subjectivity. The need for such checks is so generally recognized that it is very difficult for those of us trained in modern science to make sense of Goethe's well-known assertion:

> Der Mensch an sich selbst, insofern er sich seiner gesunden Sinne bedient, ist der größte und genaueste physikalische Apparat, den es geben kann, und das ist eben das größte Unheil der neueren Physik, daß man die Experimente gleichsam vom Menschen abgesondert hat und bloß in dem, was künstliche Instrumente zeigen, die Natur erkennen, ja, was sie leisten kann, dadurch beschränken und beweisen will.[16]

The statement becomes clear as a plausible working hypothesis if one takes into account the one factor we have discussed: the presupposition that the scientist in the Goethean sense will take his own inner development into account as a prerequisite to his research. Through a self-directed inward schooling not only of his thinking but also of his feelings and volitional impulses the organs of cognition needed to pursue such a meditative science will be fashioned and will convey the facts of nature to the researcher inwardly with the same precision as do the finely constructed physical apparatus outwardly. The cornerstone of such a balanced inner training of the cognitive faculties is an honest *moral* striving. The importance of this factor for the appreciation of Goethe's suggested new mode of scientific inquiry is often overlooked, yet the entire undertaking is contingent upon it. Unless this factor, however strange it may seem to us, is taken into consideration

[15] *Maximen und Reflexionen*, no. 488, HA XII, 432.
[16] *Maximen und Reflexionen*, no. 664, HA XII, 458.

Goethe's discussion of the "sensory-moral effects of the colors" may be enjoyed as useful for art but can surely make no claim to being a science. Once this factor is taken into consideration, however, we can see that the inner development which Goethe himself undertook and which is implicit in his epistemological stance gives his entire undertaking a *method.* And a system of investigation which provides a method of inquiry may legitimately make claim to being a science. The method which underlies Goethe's science makes the most profound and rigorous demands on the investigator. What could be more difficult of implementation than the requirement that the researcher develop his faculties *morally* in order that he may unfold inward organs of perception that will enable him to deepen his understanding of nature's phenomena not merely quantitatively but also qualitatively and with the assurance that his observations are objective and may be verified by any other researcher who is willing to undergo the same inner discipline? Yet this is the high task which Goethe placed before the scientist. It is scarcely remarkable, then, that he has been ignored, perhaps even to some degree unjustly, through having been misunderstood. Yet to be misunderstood, says Emerson, is perhaps not entirely unfortunate. Some men must dare to answer only to their own best insights and thereby chart new waters for mankind, even at the risk of being misunderstood:

> A foolish consistency is the hobgoblin of little minds, adored by little statesmen and philosophers and divines. With consistency a great soul has simply nothing to do. He may as well concern himself with his shadow on the wall. Speak what you think now in hard words and to-morrow speak what to-morrow thinks in hard words again, though it contradict every thing you said to-day.—'Ah, so you shall be sure to be misunderstood.'—Is it so bad then to be misunderstood? Pythagoras was misunderstood, and Socrates, and Jesus, and Luther, and Copernicus, and Galileo, and Newton, and every pure and wise spirit that ever took flesh. To be great is to be misunderstood.[17]

In the *Wanderjahre* Goethe presents that figure who most strikingly embodies the power of inward vision, Makarie. So encompassing is her entelechy that she is able to soar at will into the vast extents of the solar system and investigate its nature:

> Makarie befindet sich zu unserm Sonnensystem in einem Verhältnis, welches man auszusprechen kaum wagen darf. Im Geiste, der Seele, der Einbildungskraft hegt sie, schaut sie es nicht nur, sondern sie macht gleichsam einen Teil desselben; sie sieht sich in jenen himmlischen Kreisen mit fortgezogen, aber auf eine ganz eigene Art; sie wandelt seit ihrer Kindheit um die Sonne, und zwar, wie nun entdeckt ist, in einer Spirale, sich immer mehr vom Mittelpunkt entfernend und nach den äußeren Regionen hinkreisend.[18]

[17] Ralph Waldo Emerson, "Self-Reliance," *Essays, First Series*, Centenary Edition (Boston and New York, 1903), II, 57–58.

[18] *Wilhelm Meisters Wanderjahre* III, 15; HA VIII, 449.

Moreover, she carries the light and activity of the whole within herself as well:

> Sie erinnert sich von klein auf ihr inneres Selbst als von leuchtendem Wesen durchdrungen, von einem Licht erhellt, welchem sogar das hellste Sonnenlicht nichts anhaben konnte. Oft sah sie zwei Sonnen, eine innere nämlich und eine außen am Himmel, zwei Monde, wovon der äußere in seiner Größe bei allen Phasen sich gleich blieb, der innere sich immer mehr und mehr verminderte.

This extraordinary woman possesses in a very high degree that power of in-sight, of inner vision which slumbers within the scientist and must be developed at first on a rudimentary level, through painful effort, in order that the colors, for instance, should be able to reveal their inner life. And it is therefore interesting that in the collection of aphorisms entitled "Aus Makariens Archiv" we find that Goethe has included a statement which is also highly pertinent to his view of the cognitive stance of the scientist, who must cultivate qualities of morality in order that his perceptions should be clear and objective: "Wo ich aufhören muß, sittlich zu sein, habe ich keine Gewalt mehr."[19]

As color scientist Goethe proceeded in the conviction that the power of inward seeing could be developed and applied step by step to the phenomena of the natural world. As poet he gave expression to the most striking manifestations of this power in such figures as Makarie and Ottilie. Makarie is able to live outside the limits of her earthly existence and brings wisdom-filled knowledge to those about her. She possesses in personal experience that encompassing transcendent vision of nature's cosmic harmonies for which Faust longs in the scene "Nacht." Ottilie is not so highly developed an entelechy as far as the sphere of knowledge is concerned. But she transcends the earthly world in the force of *love*, as does Gretchen, and is therefore of particular interest in connection with the theme of the inner light which Gretchen has helped to bring to birth in Faust. Just as in Goethe's science the cultivation of qualities of morality are an essential factor in the development of the light of cognition, so too do these moral forces awake and nourish the inner light which is borne by Gretchen and Ottilie. In the case of both women it is finally the force of renunciation which purifies their beings and elevates them to a high spiritual task. Through renunciation and penitence Gretchen becomes a servant of the Virgin in Glory and an educator of Faust. Through renunciation Ottilie extricates herself from a web of destiny in which she can no longer act as she has in the past. Thus she rises to the posthumous state of a legendary saint who possesses the power to heal.

Ottilie is the saint of the eye, the "Augenheiligin" par excellence. And it is in her diary that we find words which resound as a wondrous spiritual prophecy from the depths of Goethe's heart: "Man mag sich stellen, wie man will, und man denkt sich immer sehend. Ich glaube, der Mensch träumt nur, damit er nicht aufhöre zu sehen. Es könnte wohl sein, daß das innere Licht einmal aus uns

[19] HA VIII, 469.

herausträte, sodaß wir keines andern mehr bedürften."[20]

In our discussion of the *Farbenlehre* we noted that Goethe is anxious that the scientist not merely reflect on the phenomena but enter into them with his cognitive faculties in order to live consciously within them and let them reveal their essential nature. Similarly, we see in Ottilie's words an expression of that internalization of the specific sense of sight which enables that sense to reveal the inner nature of light—light which may then gradually shine forth, illuminating the world around. As such it is a power of insight which evolves within the soul and in its ability to reveal the secrets of the world is ultimately very much greater than the external light. Here we have an example of the manner in which Goethe's natural scientific thought and his poetic imagination illuminate and clarify one another, for they spring from the same world view. F. J. Stopp, who suggests that Goethe may have borrowed the term "inner light" from G. H. Schubert, the author of the *Ansichten von der Nachtseite der Naturwissenschaften*, characterizes this interiorization of the power of sight in his discussion of Ottilie:

> The power of sight, man's noblest sense, and the instrument by which, primarily, he explores the world and relates to his fellows, must be interiorized, so that from a function it becomes a state, from a mode of relation it becomes a source of energy, from a reflector a beacon. In relation to life and death, the central and most vital sphere with which we are here concerned, the whole thought is summed up in the concept of "das innere Licht."[21]

"A beacon"; this is precisely what Ottilie becomes. The strength to renounce which she finds within herself enables her to rise above her dilemma. For her renunciation is not passive withdrawal. It is activity, and hence a "source of energy." She must overcome her lower nature and in doing so she accomplishes a "Steigerung" of her love from the merely personal to the spiritual, to a love which can heal the sick. The concept of "Steigerung" is of course borrowed from Goethe's natural scientific writings. Through "Steigerung" the vegetative growth of the plant is refined and reborn as blossom. In the world of color the tension between the warm glow of yellow and the coolness of blue is resolved either through mixing (green) or through "Steigerung," or intensification, until it culminates in red. In an article entitled "The Significance of Goethe's Science," published in *The Goethe Year* (1949), Humphry Trevelyan describes the process:

> "Culmination" is a "zenith," a momentary touching of the highest, "ein augenblicklicher Höhepunkt" or—"ein höchster Augenblick"! Here we see how Goethe's poetry touches his science. And indeed what else should we expect? If the

[20] *Die Wahlverwandtschaften* II, 3; HA VI, 375.

The pertinence of these words to the problem of Faust's blindness was early recognized by scholarship. Witkowski mentions them in his notes. Georg Witkowski, ed., *Goethes Faust*, 10th ed. (Leiden, 1950), II, 396. In the more recent literature cf. also Emrich, *Die Symbolik von Faust II*, pp. 397–98.

[21] F. J. Stopp, "Ottilie and 'das innere Licht,' " *German Studies Presented to Walter Horace Bruford* (London, 1962), p. 121.

> pattern: "Polarität—Steigerung—Culmination" is God's creative formula it will be revealed not only in plants and colours but also in man's spiritual life. For Goethe in fact the ultimate purpose of each individual human being's life must be the achievement of "culmination," the supreme moment when all the warring dualities are reconciled and the erring human soul rises above itself to touch and to be, for a moment at least, pure spirit.[22]

Through this ability to achieve a spiritual "Steigerung" of her forces Ottilie's entelechy grows in power to such proportions that her "inner light" becomes a beacon and a source of strength to those who come after her. She frees herself from the earthly forces which have inhibited the full expression of her nature and she thereby realizes that transformation of which Goethe speaks in the "Geheimnisse": " 'Von der Gewalt, die alle Wesen bindet,/ Befreit der Mensch sich, der sich überwindet.' "[23]

Gretchen, too, renounces her earthly nature for the sake of the eternal when in the prison scene she accepts death rather than follow Faust and continue to live with a tormenting conscience. Yet her final words reach out to him, to the inner core of his self—his *name:* "Heinrich! Heinrich!" The words of the stage direction which precedes this call are "Stimme von innen, verhallend." On one level they refer to the physical location of the action on the stage. But they also prefigure Gretchen's relation to Faust in Part II. Her love now calls to him "from within," through the world of spirit, and at the end of Part II this love reveals itself in all its gentle radiance in a scene cast in this spiritual world itself. The voice "from within" then resounds in that inner world—now become visible on stage as the light-filled home of Faust's awakening—where all earthly shadows are overcome and the eternal entelechy, itself light, may unfold:

> Der früh Geliebte,
> Nicht mehr Getrübte,
> Er kommt zurück.
> (12073–75)

Gretchen's spiritual being, grown powerful through suffering, renunciation and penitence, is now truly a beacon to Faust, a beacon which guides him on his further journey. The angels have borne Faust's immortal parts on high: "*Engel schwebend in der höheren Atmosphäre, Faustens Unsterbliches tragend*" (SD 11934). In one of Goethe's manuscripts the line reads as follows: "*Chor der Engel, über dem Berggipfel, Faustens Entelechie heranbringend.*" The world in which Faust's entelechy shall unfold is a world of light—literally the world which is the home of the "inner light" of Ottilie. Gretchen's being attends the awakening of the immortal self of Faust in an atmosphere so luminous that the entelechy, newly arrived from the

[22] Humphry Trevelyan, "The Significance of Goethe's Science," *The Goethe Year*, Part 5 (London, 1949), p. 29.

[23] "Die Geheimnisse," HA II, 276.

"Trübe" and darkness of earth, is blinded by the spirituality of which its own nature is a created part:

> Sieh, wie er jedem Erdenbande
> Der alten Hülle sich entrafft
> Und aus ätherischem Gewande
> Hervortritt erste Jugendkraft.
> Vergönne mir, ihn zu belehren,
> Noch blendet ihn der neue Tag.
> (12088–93)

Ottilie, like Gretchen, has a quality of heavenly innocence to which Goethe refers variously throughout the *Wahlverwandtschaften*. She seems to Eduard "ein himmlisches Wesen."[24] Yet her love for him runs counter to the conventions of society and just as in the case of Faust and Gretchen the consequences of the situation find metaphorical expression in the form of a child which meets a tragic end by drowning. And in both cases a higher spiritual life is wrested from the tragedy through sacrifice. In the *Wahlverwandtschaften* this is powerfully prefigured in the motif of the frescoes with which the architect decorates the chapel. The faces of the angels show an increasing likeness to Ottilie, until one of them gives the impression that she is herself gazing from heaven down into the earthly world: "Genug, eins der letzten Gesichtchen glückte vollkommen, so daß es schien, als wenn Ottilie selbst aus den himmlischen Räumen heruntersähe."[25] This motif finds fulfillment in the last words of the novel when, after Eduard's death, he and Ottilie lie side by side in the crypt, gazed upon by the host of angelic faces which seem inwardly related ("verwandt") to the sleeping lovers: "So ruhen die Liebenden nebeneinander. Friede schwebt über ihrer Stätte, heitere, verwandte Engelsbilder schauen vom Gewölbe auf sie herab, und welch ein freundlicher Augenblick wird es sein, wenn sie dereinst wieder zusammen erwachen."[26] Ottilie's "inner light" appears here symbolically as a higher seeing. It has come forth metaphorically into the world and illuminates the scene as a "Schauen," the gaze of numberless angels' eyes. Ottilie and Eduard lie side by side under the angels' gaze; but Goethe does not reveal the further destinies of their entelechies beyond the portal of death. The end of the novel is clothed in the idiom of legend. Ottilie's soul releases powerful forces of healing into the world. Her being is connected with Eduard, yet we hear only that it "will be" a joyous moment when the two reawaken together. The *Wahlverwandtschaften* were completed in 1809, "Bergschluchten" approximately twenty-one years later, in 1830. The hint of an "Erwachen" of the entelechies at the end of the novel becomes "Ereignis" in the final scene of *Faust*. From the motif of death Goethe

[24] *Die Wahlverwandtschaften* I, 7; HA VI, 291.

[25] *Ibid.*, II, 3; p. 372.

[26] *Ibid.*, II, 18; p. 490.

wrests the force to dare to portray the complete unfolding of the entelechy in the very *world* of the "inner light" as the cosmic "stirb und werde" of Gretchen and Faust.

The "power of the entelechy," of which Emrich speaks, can become a beacon to other souls. It is in a constant state of evolution, nourished or retarded by all that life brings. We recall Goethe's characterization of the soul's need to further its own growth: "... und um sich künftig als große Entelechie zu manifestieren, muß man auch eine sein." Yet the potential for this growth lies dormant as seed within the soul just as in Goethe's view it is the spiritual light and colors *within* the eye that enable man to perceive their counterparts in the outside world. In reference to his own life Goethe gives us a striking example of this developmental law—an example taken from reflections on the genesis of *Faust.* Eckermann writes:

> Es ist aber, sagte ich, im ganzen Faust keine Zeile, die nicht von sorgfältiger Durchforschung der Welt und des Lebens unverkennbare Spuren trüge, und man wird keineswegs erinnert, als sei Ihnen das alles, ohne die reichste Erfahrung, nur so geschenkt worden.
>
> "Mag sein," antwortete Goethe, "allein hätte ich nicht die Welt durch Antizipation bereits in mir getragen, ich wäre mit sehenden Augen blind geblieben, und alle Erforschung und Erfahrung wäre nichts gewesen als ein ganz totes vergebliches Bemühen. Das Licht ist da, und die Farben umgeben uns; allein trügen wir kein Licht und keine Farben im eigenen Auge, so würden wir auch außer uns dergleichen nicht wahrnehmen."[27]

The passage is an autobiographical expansion of the neoplatonic monism which permeates Goethe's thought:

> Wär nicht das Auge sonnenhaft,
> Die Sonne könnt' es nie erblicken;
> Läg' nicht in uns des Gottes eigne Kraft,
> Wie könnt' uns Göttliches entzücken?[28]

This is the very essence of the epistemological mode of Goethe's natural science. The thought is developed in the introduction to the *Farbenlehre* in reference to the origin of the eye through the process of evolution: "Das Auge hat sein Dasein dem Licht zu danken. Aus gleichgültigen tierischen Hülfsorganen ruft sich das Licht ein Organ hervor, das seinesgleichen werde, und so bildet sich das Auge am Lichte fürs Licht, damit das innere Licht dem äußeren entgegentrete."[29] The last words, ". . . damit das innere Licht dem äußeren entgegentrete," illustrate a fundamental conviction underlying Goethe's science, and they do so in a form which echoes Ottilie's beautiful words describing the potential for spiritual perfection which rests within the entelechy of man: ". . . Es könnte wohl sein,

[27] *Gespräche mit Eckermann,* 26 February 1824, p. 98.

[28] HA I, 367.

[29] "Einleitung," *Zur Farbenlehre,* HA XIII, 323.

daß das innere Licht einmal aus uns heraustràte, sodaß wir keines andern mehr bedürften."

In these passages the same mode of thinking comes to expression on several levels. The light calls forth the human eye through the process of evolution in order that the inner light may emerge and meet the outer. So in the *Farbenlehre*. Ottilie speaks not of the sensory ("sinnlich") but of the moral ("sittlich") light which could one day come forth and form man's new environment. And in the passage from Eckermann Goethe uses the eye/light analogy to illustrate his view that the entelechy contains whole worlds within itself through "anticipation," worlds which may one day emerge and find new expression—in this case as art, as *Faust*. What, then, is that light which calls forth, nourishes and develops the entelechy of man? We have seen that in "Bergschluchten" Goethe has given his answer to this question. It is one of the deepest thoughts in the corpus of Goethe's poetry. The entelechy of Faust unfolds into the light, but this is light in the highest sense of the word "sittlich"—it is the light of wisdom and selfless love. It comes to expression in ever ascending levels of perfection through the beings, human and divine, whom Goethe portrays in the scene. "Bergschluchten" is set in the eternal world of spirit beyond the limits of time and space. This is why we have referred to it as the entelechy's *home*. For the entelechy, says Goethe, is a bit of eternity, "ein Stück Ewigkeit."[30] In any human being's biography the moral sunlight which awakes and revivifies the entelechy is love—the love of one soul for another. The entelechy is eternal and the selfless love which transcends passion and desire has its being in the eternal. This love lives and works through human beings, but it transcends the human level as well. The words "das ewig Weibliche" (12110) hint at its inexpressible essence. At this level it is divine Love—creative, healing, awakening. The above-quoted remarks of Goethe to Eckermann on the genesis of *Faust* through "Antizipation," with the comparison to the organ of sight in its relation to the light, are profoundly illuminated by the content of the final scene of the poem. Goethe bore the forces of love within his heart, as gifts of many souls whose lives were interwoven with his own. He was therefore not "mit sehenden Augen blind geblieben," but was able to pour the inner light of that love into his work. There it lives in the beings portrayed in the final scene of *Faust*. This is a tremendous "open secret" of the *Faust* poem: the entelechy of man bears the same relationship to divine Love which the eye of man bears to the light. The thought is drawn from that deep source within Goethe from which flow the intuitions of both his poetry and his science. It has often been observed that Goethe's work is at every turn an expression of his biography. His life and work are intimately related. This is perhaps the reason why in reading Goethe one has such a powerful impression of living in the *being* of its creator. And in the scene

[30] "Jede Entelechie nämlich ist ein Stück Ewigkeit, und die paar Jahre, die sie mit dem irdischen Körper verbunden ist, machen sie nicht alt." *Gespräche mit Eckermann*, 11 March 1828, p. 677.

"Bergschluchten" one can experience a heightening of this impression. The more deeply one studies Goethe's works, returning ever again to "Bergschluchten," the more one may experience in that scene a world of forces which live in the most intimate and holy sense at the center of Goethe's eternal individuality.

In the final version of his *Faust* with its culmination in the mysteries of spiritual Love Goethe had completed his testament to humanity. The times were confused and men were not ready to receive this bequest in the mood of reverence necessary for its appreciation. In Emerson's phrase, it would surely be misunderstood. And it was. Goethe was fully alert to the tenor of the times and he therefore left the manuscript for posthumous publication. On the seventeenth of March 1832, five days before his death, Goethe wrote to Wilhelm von Humboldt the last letter we have from his pen. It is inwardly fitting that in this letter Goethe should speak one last time about his *Faust*. The words are wrested from the loneliness of age and insight. They had to be written, but it took courage to write them:

> Ganz ohne Frage würd es mir unendliche Freude machen, meinen werten, durchaus dankbar anerkannten, weitverteilten Freunden auch bei Lebzeiten diese sehr ernsten Scherze zu widmen, mitzuteilen und ihre Erwiderung zu vernehmen. Der Tag aber ist wirklich so absurd und konfus, daß ich mich überzeuge meine redlichen, lange verfolgten Bemühungen um dieses seltsame Gebäu würden schlecht belohnt und an den Strand getrieben, wie ein Wrack in Trümmern daliegen und von dem Dünenschutt der Stunden zunächst überschüttet werden. Verwirrende Lehre zu verwirrenden Handel waltet über die Welt, und ich habe nichts angelegentlicher zu tun als dasjenige was an mir ist und geblieben ist wo möglich zu steigern und meine Eigentümlichkeiten zu kohobieren, wie Sie es, würdiger Freund, auf Ihrer Burg ja auch bewerkstelligen.[31]

Goethe was very seriously misunderstood. While the early lyrics and *Faust I* were celebrated, the spiritual message of his later works was all too often ignored. A century after Goethe's death the blindness of mankind had struck a new low-point. Moral darkness was enthroned in the heart of Europe and the attention of humanity was diverted from Goethe's Weimar to the altar of evil which men had built just ouside of the town: Buchenwald.

During the years following World War II mankind seemed to have awakened from a nightmare. All energies were directed toward the alleviation of suffering and the reconstruction of devastated lands. Before long the nightmare faded and a new prosperity absorbed men's attention. But it was in many respects a hollow, glittering prosperity and a profound sense of malaise lingered beneath the surface. Those who could look beyond external appearances stared into an abyss—an abyss peopled with all the questions which still had not been solved, indeed had hardly been faced. The legacy of these years is still with us today.

[31] *Goethes Briefe*, HA IV, 481.

Surrounded by prosperity and sensate enjoyments we feel a gnawing despair and helplessness within. Joy and sorrow are not fully felt. They can therefore no longer educate the soul, for somehow both merge into boredom, *ennui*. Many are well-fed while their brothers starve, and the well-fed are themselves the victims of a soul-spiritual starvation that hollows them out:

Sorge. Wen ich einmal mir besitze,
Dem ist alle Welt nichts nütze;
Ewiges Düstre steigt herunter,
Sonne geht nicht auf noch unter,
Bei vollkommnen äußern Sinnen
Wohnen Finsternisse drinnen,
Und er weiß von allen Schätzen
Sich nicht in Besitz zu setzen.
Glück und Unglück wird zur Grille,
Er verhungert in der Fülle;
Sei es Wonne, sei es Plage,
Schiebt er's zu dem andern Tage,
Ist der Zukunft nur gewärtig,
Und so wird er niemals fertig.
(11453–66)

Such starvation of soul and spirit takes its toll at last as it casts the frost of paralysis into the will:

Soll er gehen, soll er kommen?
Der Entschluß ist ihm genommen;
Auf gebahnten Weges Mitte
Wankt er tastend halbe Schritte.
(11471–74)

Even in the extremity of mental anguish there was always, for Goethe, one great source of restorative forces: sleep—the sleep of Egmont, the "Heilschlaf" of Orestes, and above all the sleep of Faust in "Anmutige Gegend." There Faust is renewed by spiritual beings who bathe him in the waters of forgetfulness, the dew of Lethe. Ariel sings to the elves:

Erst senkt sein Haupt aufs kühle Polster nieder,
Dann badet ihn im Tau aus Lethes Flut;
Gelenk sind bald die krampferstarrten Glieder,
Wenn er gestärkt dem Tag entgegenruht;
Vollbringt der Elfen schönste Pflicht,
Gebt ihn zurück dem heiligen Licht.
(4628–33)

Sleep is a forgetting. And Faust must needs forget the tragedy of Part I if that tragedy is not to paralyze him. The past will live on and will affect his actions, but its grip will relax. Sleep, for Goethe, allows man at regular intervals to plunge into the spiritual world and to rise from it refreshed. Without a proper rhythmical relation to sleep man is no longer spiritually and physically rejuvenated and thereby gradually forfeits his humanity:

> Sorge. . . .
> So ein unaufhaltsam Rollen,
> Schmerzlich Lassen, widrig Sollen,
> Bald Befreien, bald Erdrücken,
> Halber Schlaf und schlecht Erquicken
> Heftet ihn an seine Stelle
> Und bereitet ihn zur Hölle.
> (11481–86)

Without the restorative power of sleep man is defenseless. The full might of Care fetters him to the earth ("Heftet ihn an seine Stelle") and prepares him for the onslaught of the spirit of negation. At Faust's death Mephisto gloats over the termination of that struggle for freedom and self-determination for which he houses nothing but icy contempt. To the chorus' "Es ist vorbei" he retorts:

> Vorbei! ein dummes Wort.
> Warum vorbei?
> Vorbei und reines Nicht, vollkommnes Einerlei!
> Was soll uns denn das ew'ge Schaffen!
> Geschaffenes zu nichts hinwegzuraffen!
> "Da ist's vorbei!" Was ist daran zu lesen?
> Es ist so gut, als wär' es nicht gewesen,
> Und treibt sich doch im Kreis, als wenn es wäre.
> Ich liebte mir dafür das Ewig-Leere.
> (11595–603)

In our times of industrial technology these words have a peculiarly convincing, and therefore unsettling, ring. With the migration from a pre-urban agricultural society to life in the modern city man has increasingly lost his connection with the rhythms of nature—the alternation of light and darkness and the intimate communion with the natural processes of sprouting and withering in the course of the seasons. Instead he lives increasingly in communion with the machine, which knows no rhythms but the mechanical cycles built into it by human intellect. It is a commonplace of sensitive cultural analysis today that the effects of this revolution are scoring their impressive toll on man's spiritual-physical existence. The relationship of man to sleep, for instance, is disturbed on a grand scale. Confusion, anguish and doubt as to the ultimate purpose of existence have become fashionable topics of the day and the "unaufhaltsam Rollen" of what seems but senseless activity has gradually fostered a mood of boredom, of "vollkommnes Einerlei" which leaves men inwardly helpless in the face of life's challenges. The compelling logic of materialistic science has undercut the age-old religious traditions and established itself in their stead. Nietzsche's "God is dead" has risen to the status of a new theology. Especially since World War II the concepts of nothingness, the "reines Nicht," "das Ewig-Leere," *ennui*, anguish and nausea form the core of a stream of Existentialist thought which has captivated the imagination of many of the most alert and sensitive youth.

Such are the times in which we find ourselves. Inasmuch as they are prefigured in the passages quoted one may feel that *Faust* contains episodes peculiarly pertinent to our condition.

But "Bergschluchten?" Can one find any sound reasons for taking it seriously except as a literary curiosity? Is it not fundamentally a dated document of eighteenth-century optimism clothed in "Catholicized" imagery, overlaid with an application of Goethean notions of metamorphosis and impelled by that tedious Faustian "Streben"? What of the "entelechy"? Has our science found and described it? If, as it has been the hope of this essay to suggest, the "inner light" of which Faust speaks is on the deepest symbolical level an image for this being of man, as well as for the forces of wisdom and love which have fashioned and which nourish it, how are we to find access to it in a free, non-sectarian sense, in our times? Are there any voices within our present culture who describe such phenomena in a serious way?

The voice of the times speaks through men and women in many nations and in many ways. One will not find the great contributions to nineteenth-century realistic literature, for instance, confined to one region. It is an international impulse with eminent representatives in Germany, France, England, Russia, Scandinavia etc. In discussing the trends which are surfacing in our present culture we shall point to two of its most interesting representatives, one a celebrity in his own lifetime, the other less well known but by no means less significant. Both examples are drawn from one culture: France. The forces of which they speak, however, are at work in all nations and the two figures are chosen merely as particularly striking representatives of these forces.

The first voice is that of the most prominent representative of modern French Existentialist thought: Jean Paul Sartre. He is well known and need not be discussed in detail. Not alone through his philosophical treatises but perhaps most forcefully through his novels he has given articulate expression to the spiritual torment which it has now been the lot of more than one generation to inherit. The concepts of alienation, nothingness ("le néant"), anguish ("l'angoisse") and absurdity have found clear expression in Sartre's writings. Paul Roubiczek summarizes the consequences of this mode of thinking: "Thus it is no cause for surprise that Sartre lands himself in complete nihilism. He is forced to say: 'All existing beings are born for no reason, continue through weakness and die by accident . . . Man is a useless passion. It is meaningless that we are born; it is meaningless that we die.' "[32] The words are neither soothing to the ear nor particularly elevating in their sentiment. But they are spoken honestly. Their introduction here is in no sense intended as a criticism of Sartre. The thoughts which he articulates are disturbing but it is enormously important that they be formulated, in order that they may be directly confronted. They represent a point of view whose widespread popularity is influenced by the way of thinking of modern science and the social consequences to which that thinking has led. It is of very great importance to confront this point of view in a clear form and we are indebted to Sartre for having given it that form.

The second voice is that of Jacques Lusseyran, another highly gifted French intellectual and contemporary of Sartre. He was born in 1924 and died tragically, together with his American wife, in an automobile accident in France in the summer of 1972. In an accident at the age of eight he lost the sight of both eyes. For the rest of his life he remained totally blind. He completed his schooling and his university education and after the war became a professor of Romance languages in the United States.

After the German occupation the teenage Lusseyran organized and led a resistance movement of six hundred young men which later merged with the larger Défense de la France. He and his associates were finally betrayed to the Gestapo and were sent to Buchenwald. From an original shipment of two thousand he was one of thirty to survive. He tells the shattering and profoundly beautiful story of his life in *And There Was Light*.[33]

Some three months after the accident which blinded him the boy Jacques instinctively gave up straining to grasp the world in its outward forms as he had done while able to see. The result was a *new* seeing:

> Immediately, the substance of the universe drew together, redefined and peopled itself anew. I was aware of a radiance emanating from a place I knew nothing about, a place which might as well have been outside me as within. But radiance was there, or, to put it more precisely, light. It was a fact, for light was there.[34]

With this event a new world opened up within:

> I saw light and went on seeing it though I was blind.
>
> The amazing thing was that this was not magic for me at all, but reality. I could no more have denied it than people with eyes can deny that they see. I was not light myself, I knew that, but I bathed in it as an element which blindness had suddenly brought much closer. I could feel light rising, spreading, resting on objects, giving them form, then leaving them.

[32] Paul Roubiczek, *Existentialism, For and Against* (Cambridge, 1964), p. 125.

[33] Jacques Lusseyran, *And There Was Light*, trans. Elizabeth R. Cameron (Boston, 1963).

[34] *Ibid.*, pp. 16–17.

The old distinctions between brightly and less brightly illuminated objects vanished:

> ... I saw the whole world in light, existing through it and because of it.
>
> Colors, all the colors of the rainbow, also survived. For me, the child who loved to draw and paint, colors made a celebration so unexpected that I spent hours playing with them ...
>
> Light threw its color on things and people. My father and mother, the people I met or ran into in the street, all had their characteristic color which I had never seen before I went blind.[35]

Most impressive, perhaps, is the fact that this light developed into an intuitive guide to morality in thought, feeling and action. Anger, jealousy, impatience or unfriendliness brought darkness. Joy, serenity and good thoughts toward other people brought the reward of light: "Armed with such a tool, why should I need a moral code?"[36] We recall the aphorism from the *Wanderjahre:* "Wo ich aufhören muß, sittlich zu sein, habe ich keine Gewalt mehr." It is taken, as we noted, from the "archive" of Makarie, of whom it is said: "Sie erinnert sich von klein auf ihr inneres Selbst als von leuchtendem Wesen durchdrungen, von einem Licht erhellt, welchem sogar das hellste Sonnenlicht nichts anhaben konnte."[37]

The new world of colors carried on the inner light bore a precise relationship to the beings of the world without. This too is of particular interest, for it demonstrates that the new inward faculty of seeing was objectively related to the perceived world. Lusseyran describes a little child his own age named Nicole whom he met at the seashore. Through the way in which the light related to her being he began to receive instruction in what is meant by love. She radiated red and came into his life "like a great red star, or perhaps more like a ripe cherry." He writes:

> I thought her lovely, and her beauty was so gentle that I could no longer go home at night and sleep away from her, because part of my light left me when I did. To get it back I had to find her again. It was just as if she were bringing me light in her hands, her hair, her bare feet on the sand, and in the sound of her voice.
>
> How natural that people who are red should have red shadows. When she came to sit down by me between two pools of salt water under the warmth of the sun, I saw rosy reflections on the canvas of the awnings. The sea itself, the blue of the sea, took on a purple tone. I followed her by the red wake which trailed behind her wherever she went.
>
> Now, if people should say that red is the color of passion, I should answer quite simply that I found that out when I was only eight years old.

The little girl's redness colored the blue ocean purple and left a wake behind her

[35] *Ibid.*, pp. 17–18.

[36] *Ibid.*, p. 21.

[37] *Wilhelm Meisters Wanderjahre*, HA VIII, 449.

which Jacques could follow. The light which had dawned for the inner eye of his soul had begun to flow through the external world and to illuminate it. Here we have an exact description by a highly intelligent and balanced man of our times of that phenomenon which Ottilie had sensed would one day arise in man as a new cognitive faculty: "... Es könnte wohl sein, daß das innere Licht einmal aus uns heraustrate, sodaß wir keines andern mehr bedürften."

But Jacques Lusseyran was a man of the twentieth century. His light was called upon to shine as a beacon into the darkness of evil, despair and death. And there it shone the most brightly, in Buchenwald. He nearly died in Buchenwald, of an illness that lasted for weeks. His closest friend, Jean, whose last words, smuggled to Jacques on a scrap of paper in a prison camp in France were "I love you more than myself," died in the railroad car two hours before its arrival at Buchenwald. Lusseyran was told of the death of his friend the night before he fell sick, and his friend came to him and enabled him to survive the illness:

> The image of Jean never left me. Through all my illness it stayed with me constantly, watching over me. When, too weak to face the world outside, I was living entirely inside myself, his image was still there, my one remaining picture of the world without. For whole days and nights I had held Jean's hand in my thoughts, but in my mind it had shielded me more than his hand could have done in the flesh. How can I explain this strange phenomenon? All the longing for the life which Jean had not lived had flowed over into me, for, though I have put off saying the words, Jean was dead.[38]

After overcoming this nearly fatal illness the power to heal with the inner light grew ever stronger:

> I could try to show other people how to go about holding on to life. I could turn toward them the flow of light and joy which had grown so abundant in me. From that time on they stopped stealing my bread or my soup. It never happened again. Often my comrades would wake me up in the night and take me to comfort someone, sometimes a long way off in another block.
>
> Almost everyone forgot I was a student. I became "the blind Frenchman." For many, I was just "the man who didn't die." Hundreds of people confided in me . . .[39]

The situation in which Lusseyran here found himself represented the quintessence of what Goethe might have termed the moral ("sittlich") quality of darkness, the grim abyss of absurdity and nothingness which Sartre has so vividly described. The fact of Lusseyran's existence demonstrates that Goethe's deep commitment to the inner nature of light and color, a commitment which, taken abstractly, must appear irrelevantly mystical, flows from certain specific insights into the nature of man. In view of Lusseyran's life the experiences of inner vision embodied in

[38] Lusseyran, *And There Was Light*, p. 283.
[39] *Ibid.*, pp. 282–83.

Makarie and those described by Ottilie come vividly alive; and the light-filled world of "Bergschluchten" draws closer to us. Lusseyran's description of the way in which thoughts nourished by love rather than by anger let his light shine gives us a clearer appreciation of the deeper metaphorical import of that inner light which lives in Faust's entelechy. In it he bears the love of Gretchen and after his death that love will come to meet the entelechy "from without" and enable it to grow. Through the commentaries on man's state embodied in the worlds described by Sartre and Lusseyran one may draw a step closer to an understanding of what Goethe describes when he lets Care strike his representative of man with the fate of blindness which elicits from Faust the cry:

> Die Nacht scheint tiefer tief hereinzudringen,
> Allein im Innern leuchtet helles Licht.
>
> (11499–500)

At the heart of the problem which we have tried to treat from a number of points of view lies the mystery of the human entelechy. This concept, as Goethe uses it, may be studied from various standpoints. The present essay limits itself to one aspect—that of the metaphor of light as it is associated with the nature of the entelechy. We have seen that this light is woven not only of the wisdom gained through life experience but most importantly through the spiritual life of love—love both human and celestial. These facts will gradually become clearer as Goethe's scientific method is more deeply comprehended. We have suggested that Goethe's science will only begin to reveal its latent potential for development when it will be realized that its practice rests upon one cardinal condition: that the scientist mold *himself* into the instrument of observation by the gradual development of higher faculties of cognition through self-knowledge. And that the healthy acquisition of such self-knowledge is only possible through individual, freely undertaken moral development. When this is understood there will come a realization of what lies as unmined treasure in Goethe's *Farbenlehre*. Lusseyran's description of the objective relationship between his ability to find balance, serenity and loving thoughts, and the concomitant vividness of his inner perceptions will then be seen as a clear illustration of this cardinal condition of Goethe's method. One will then realize that Goethe also speaks as a *scientist* when he says in the *Wanderjahre* "Wo ich aufhören muß, sittlich zu sein, habe ich keine Gewalt mehr." One will appreciate in a deeper sense than is now generally the case the reasons why the *Wahlverwandtschaften* and the *Farbenlehre* evolved simultaneously in Goethe's biography. And above all one will discover that despite its shortcomings Goethe's vision of science is far from being the benighted fancy of a dilettante, for which it is still so widely taken. For its legitimacy will be seen to rest upon the proper appreciation of its method—a method which seems today to be "unscientific" because it requires that the scientist create and sustain within himself the instruments of inward investigation which may complement those which he constructs in the physical world for purposes of his external observations.

What Goethe attempted in his science was as daring in its time as was the deed of Copernicus in the Renaissance. Goethe virtually turns the epistemological basis of science inside-out. The very idea that one should speak of the "sinnlich-sittliche Wirkung der Farben" not merely as artistic but as *scientific* phenomena is astounding. But it is fully in keeping with the mode of cognition we have discussed. In his essay "Goethe's Farbenlehre," Michael Wilson takes the sum of the matter succinctly and correctly:

> Goethe's method is to search for the "unifying idea" behind all the different phenomena. Since he does not postulate that all visible effects are functions of matter or of material processes there is no difficulty in understanding that the same idea can express itself in the physical, physiological and moral spheres simultaneously. It is only the watertight compartments we have built between our various sciences which make such unification difficult.[40]

If indeed much in Goethe's *Farbenlehre* is in a deep sense true and its methodological foundation worthy of further elaboration and implementation it poses a tremendous question to those who feel a responsibility toward the future: will it be possible, following Goethe's path of development, to begin to unfold systematically that mode of awareness of the inner nature of the phenomena which began to manifest itself instinctively in Jacques Lusseyran through a blow of destiny? Will it be possible for a number of serious thinkers to develop such faculties in an ordered way, so that the healthy unfolding of inner "instruments" or organs of perception will result in the researchers' finding themselves in complete agreement as to the objective nature of the perceptions attained by this method? These are questions for the future. If they are one day answered in the affirmative the answers will necessarily be the result of objective experience which can be attained and communicated by any person who undertakes to create for him- or herself the conditions for its attainment.

Today we in the West often experience ourselves as in a state not unlike that in which Faust experiences his blindness. Assailed and paralyzed by Care we live on the brink of death. We sense the light within us, but turn instead to the light of the outward senses and experience the inner light only personally, as that of our often well-meant, yet grandly abstract and occasionally perverse designs for mankind. In the whole idea of the inner light Goethe saw much more. He saw the dawn of a new cognitive faculty for the future, as is demonstrated by the words of Ottilie. He gave his vision permanence in the *Farbenlehre*, in which he advanced his revolutionary scientific method. It is a method which he hoped would bridge the gulf between inner and outer, "subjective" and "objective"

[40] Michael Wilson, "Goethe's Farbenlehre," *The Goethe Year*, Part 5 (London, 1949), p. 35.

experience in an exact way. "Das schönste Glück des denkenden Menschen ist, das Erforschliche erforscht zu haben und das Unerforschliche ruhig zu verehren."[41] This statement sums up Goethe's view that in the presence of the primary phenomenon, the *Urphänomen*, one is at the border of what the mind can grasp. However, the statement does not assert, in a Kantian sense, that cognition comes to a halt at such a boundary. This point is decisive. In Goethe's words the cognitive faculties must transform their activities from intellectual investigation ("erforschen") to reverent contemplation ("verehren"). This is the step from "Sehen" to "Schauen," a religious communion with the spiritual forces which, for Goethe, are always at work *in*, not behind, the phenomena. And this is why Goethe is also able to make the following statement which, if taken merely intellectually, seems to contradict that quoted above: "Der Mensch muß bei dem Glauben verharren, daß das Unbegreifliche begreiflich sei; er würde sonst nicht forschen."[42]

The *Farbenlehre* is sleeping an enchanted "Dornröschenschlaf." It will come to life when thinkers arise who will proceed from a premise which must seem madness to many today—that nature is a creative Artist, the organism of the earth a "living raiment of the Divinity" ("der Gottheit lebendiges Kleid," 509). These are thoughts which man will comprehend deeply only as his science becomes inwardly moral. One hallmark of such a science will be its effort to bring to each phenomenon, to each being, only those concepts which are inwardly appropriate to its nature. Then a single mechanistic mode of cognition will no longer be applied to everything. The scientist will be careful, for instance, to distinguish between those concepts which he applies to the physical world and the more delicate concepts which he must apply to the life sciences if he is not to do violence to the biological phenomena. Such a scientist will be fully aware in the Goethean sense of the role which he, as observer, plays in the experiment. In the famous lecture "Die Goethesche und die Newtonsche Farbenlehre im Lichte der modernen Physik" the physicist Werner Heisenberg points to the fact that modern physics is not fully aware of this role:

> Während es ursprünglich das Ziel jeder Naturforschung war, die Natur möglichst so zu beschreiben, wie sie an sich, d.h. ohne unseren Eingriff und ohne unsere Beobachtung wäre, so erkennen wir jetzt, daß eben dieses Ziel unerreichbar ist. In der Atomphysik ist es in keiner Weise möglich, von den Veränderungen abzusehen, die jede Beobachtung an dem beobachteten Gegenstand hervorbringt.[43]

[41] *Maximen und Reflexionen*, no. 718, HA XII, 467.

[42] *Ibid.*, no. 298, p. 406.

[43] Werner Heisenberg, "Die Goethsche und die Newtonsche Farbenlehre im Lichte der modernen Physik," *Wandlungen in den Grundlagen der Naturwissenschaft*, 10th ed. (Stuttgart, 1973), pp. 72–73. The lecture was originally delivered on 5 May 1941 in the "Gesellschaft für kulturelle Zusammenarbeit" in Budapest.

Heisenberg then goes on to describe how the scientist, proceeding from this awareness of the effect of his activity upon the results of his inquiry, will seek the mode of cognition appropriate to each level of reality. In so doing, he will also recognize, as did Goethe, that the separation of reality into two spheres labelled "subjective" and "objective" is ultimately untenable:

> Wenn Goethe sagt, daß das, was der Physiker mit seinen Apparaten beobachtet, nicht mehr die Natur sei, so meint er ja wohl auch, daß es weitere und lebendigere Bereiche der Natur gebe, die eben dieser Methode der Naturwissenschaft nicht zugänglich seien. In der Tat werden wir gerne glauben, daß die Naturwissenschaft dort, wo sie sich nicht mehr der leblosen, sondern der belebten Materie zuwendet, immer vorsichtiger werden muß mit den Eingriffen, die sie zum Zwecke der Erkenntnis an der Natur vornimmt. Je weiter wir unseren Wunsch nach Erkenntnis auf die höheren, auch die geistigen Bereiche des Lebens richten, desto mehr werden wir uns mit einer nur aufnehmenden, betrachtenden Untersuchung begnügen müssen. Von diesem Standpunkt aus erschiene die Einteilung der Welt in einen subjektiven und einen objektiven Bereich als eine allzu große Vereinfachung der Wirklichkeit. Vielmehr könnten wir an eine Einteilung in viele ineinandergreifende Bereiche denken, die sich durch die Fragen, die wir an die Natur richten, und durch die Eingriffe, die wir bei ihrer Beobachtung zulassen, voneinander abschließen.[44]

In the future, then, the inwardly *moral* quality of science in the Goethean sense will come to expression through the scientist's acute awareness of the danger of distortion which inheres in his very presence as an investigator as well as through his efforts to deal with each level of reality in the cognitional mode appropriate to that level. When such a science has been evolved the material world will be dealt with in material terms and the world of life phenomena, such as the plants, with living concepts capable of metamorphosis. The beings endowed with the faculty of conscious inner perception (the older word is of course "ensouled" beings), the animals, will be treated with sympathy and respect for the suffering which is so often theirs to bear. And the human being will no longer be considered an animal whose faculties of self-consciousness are merely sublimated drives. A science in Goethe's sense will see in man's self-consciousness the workings of the unique human entelechy, whose capacity for moral intuition is a constant reminder to him to lift himself above the animals and earn for himself that crown of the spirit, "der Menschheit Krone" (1804), which consecrates each man as a species in himself:

> Edel sei der Mensch,
> Hilfreich und gut!
> Denn das allein
> Unterscheidet ihn
> Von allen Wesen,
> Die wir kennen.[45]

[44] *Ibid.*, p. 74.

[45] "Das Göttliche," HA I, 147.

Such a science will itself be not only "sinnlich" but also "sittlich." For as the entelechy of man develops and through "Steigerung" enhances its cognitive faculties it will find that the force which it must call upon to awake, to form and to guide them in a healthy way is love—love for the world and the beings, seen and unseen, which inhabit it.

The mystery of the human entelechy is one of the greatest which Goethe sought to comprehend. In the course of our discussion we noted that the entelechy of man is related to the forces of love as is the eye to those of the light. And in the highest sense the light is itself an expression of wisdom and love. Thus Goethe's extraordinary statement reported by Schopenhauer: "Was, sagte er mir einst, mit seinen Jupiteraugen mich anblickend, das Licht sollte nur da sein, insofern Sie es sehen? Nein, *Sie* wären nicht da, wenn das Licht *Sie* nicht sähe."[46] Who can say that he understands fully what Goethe is saying here? It is a vision of the Light as creator of the entelechy itself. The statement is sibylline. It is also deserving of our most intense meditative thinking. It speaks of the origin of man's being in a way strikingly parallel to the statement on the origin of the human eye: ". . . so bildet sich das Auge am Lichte fürs Licht damit das innere Licht dem äußeren entgegentrete." It is extremely difficult for us to enter into such thoughts today, for the whole tenor of our thinking has been formed in quite another way. We are trained to understand what the phenomena reveal to our outward senses and to view their inward essence as unknowable. Our culture itself is very much under the spell of the forces emanating from the old gray dame "Sorge," who chants:

> Bei vollkommnen äußern Sinnen
> Wohnen Finsternisse drinnen.
> (11457–58)

Our "inner light" is often mere illusion, dreams of grandeur and power such as those which flatter the Faustian ego.

Even in the night of our recent history's most terrible hours, however, other forces were at work, though scarcely noted by the world at large. The experiences of Jacques Lusseyran are but one instance of the workings of these forces. But they are an important instance, for they are an objective *fact* which should be placed side by side with the fact of the moral darkness which has such a powerful grip on modern man's imagination. Perhaps the darkness must grow very intense before we become sufficiently awake to perceive the more delicate facts which point to possible ways out of the prison which we have built around ourselves. Lusseyran lived through the hell of Buchenwald and expressed his gratitude for the years he subsequently spent in America by giving expression to two truths particularly close to his heart: "The first of these is that joy does not come from

[46] *Goethes Gespräche*, Artemis Ausgabe (Zürich, 1969), II, 937.

outside, for whatever happens to us it is within. The second truth is that light does not come to us from without. Light is in us, even if we have no eyes."[47] The strength that speaks out of these words flows from the fact that the man who speaks them passed through the severest trials. The words are consecrated in suffering and are therefore real.

"*You* would not be here if the light did not see *you*," Goethe admonished Schopenhauer. For Goethe the entelechy of man is created out of the Light of spirit. The entelechy is just that: pure spirit. It is therefore indestructible and it is not limited by the boundaries of birth and death or by the form of the physical body through which it expresses itself. It has its nature beyond the temporal world and works on actively "from eternity to eternity." Goethe likens it to the sun:

> "Wenn einer fünfundsiebzig Jahre alt ist," fuhr er darauf mit großer Heiterkeit fort, "kann es nicht fehlen, daß er mitunter an den Tod denke. Mich läßt dieser Gedanke in völliger Ruhe, denn ich habe die feste Überzeugung, daß unser Geist ein Wesen ist ganz unzerstörbarer Natur; es ist ein fortwirkendes von Ewigkeit zu Ewigkeit. Es ist der Sonne ähnlich, die bloß unsern irdischen Augen unterzugehen scheint, die aber eigentlich nie untergeht, sondern unaufhörlich fortleuchtet."[48]

". . . unaufhörlich fortleuchtet": how is one to come to know this spiritual being, the inner self of man, through similarly conscious insight? This is surely one of the deepest questions which Goethe's work raises for the future. Is it possible that when the inner light comes forth as Ottilie suggests that it will—comes forth, as the *Farbenlehre* says, to meet the light without, it will also greet the spiritual light which reveals the other man's being? If this were possible the deepest aspirations of Goethe's non-sectarian humanism would be realized through an elevation of consciousness—an elevation firmly anchored in both his poetical and his scientific vision. It would be a step into that sphere of which the chorus mysticus says: "Das Unzulängliche,/ Hier wird's Ereignis," into that sphere in which our communication with each other is transformed into spiritual communion. It is the lofty aspiration of all radiantly striving souls, and Emerson saw it and sang it as clearly as any: "By the same fire, vital, consecrating, celestial, which burns until it shall dissolve all things into the waves and surges of an ocean of light, we see and know each other, and what spirit each is of."[49]

[47] Lusseyran, *And There Was Light*, p. 312.
[48] *Gespräche mit Eckermann*, 2 May 1824, pp. 115–16.
[49] "The Over-Soul," *Essays, First Series*, p. 285.

Appendix

A Note on Goethe's Epistemology in Contrast to Kant

The epistemology underlying Goethe's scientific efforts is fundamentally non-Kantian. Goethe's position comes clearly into focus in the essay "Glückliches Ereignis." Here Goethe describes the famous encounter with Schiller to whom he refers expressly as "ein gebildeter Kantianer." He writes:

> Wir gelangten zu seinem Hause, das Gespräch lockte mich hinein; da trug ich die Metamorphose der Pflanzen lebhaft vor, und ließ, mit manchen charakteristischen Federstrichen, eine symbolische Pflanze vor seinen Augen entstehen. Er vernahm und schaute das alles mit großer Teilnahme, mit entschiedener Fassungskraft; als ich aber geendet, schüttelte er den Kopf und sagte: 'Das ist keine Erfahrung, das ist eine Idee.' Ich stutzte, verdrießlich einigermaßen: denn der Punkt, der uns trennte, war dadurch aufs strengste bezeichnet. Die Behauptung aus 'Anmut und Würde' fiel mir wieder ein, der alte Groll wollte sich regen, ich nahm mich aber zusammen und versetzte: 'Das kann mir sehr lieb sein, daß ich Ideen habe ohne es zu wissen, und sie sogar mit Augen sehe.'
>
> Schiller, der viel mehr Lebensklugheit und Lebensart hatte als ich, und mich auch wegen der Horen, die er herauszugeben im Begriff stand, mehr anzuziehen als abzustoßen gedachte, erwiderte darauf als ein gebildeter Kantianer; und als aus meinem hartnäckigen Realismus mancher Anlaß zu lebhaftem Widerspruch entstand, so ward viel gekämpft und dann Stillstand gemacht; keiner von beiden konnte sich für den Sieger halten, beide hielten sich für unüberwindlich.[1]

Goethe here clearly delineates the difference between his stance and Schiller's Kantian position. Schiller sees Goethe's "symbolic plant" *only* as idea, not as "Erfahrung." For Goethe the idea expresses itself objectively in the experienced world and is therefore itself a part of the "Erfahrung." Yet because of Goethe's expressed indebtedness to Kant this underlying non-Kantian stance is often misinterpreted. Thus for instance Chamberlain: "Goethe . . . erblickte diesen seinen zu einer Gestalt zurückgebildeten Gedanken dermaßen überzeugend leibhaftig, daß er die Urpflanze im Walde suchte und täglich zu finden hoffte—bis Schiller ihn über seinen Irrtum aufklärte."[2] Goethe, as we have seen from the

[1] "Glückliches Ereignis," HA X, 540–41.

[2] Houston Stewart Chamberlain, *Goethe* (München, 1912), p. 99.

quotation from "Glückliches Ereignis," was not "enlightened" by Schiller with regard to the "Urpflanze." On the contrary, their positions on this point remained separate.

Cassirer, too, fails to grasp the essence of Goethe's position in this regard. He argues that Goethe and Kant meet in their acknowledgment of limits to cognition: "According to Goethe, the greatest happiness of the thinker is to have inquired into what can be known and to revere in silence what cannot be known. Kant thought and felt likewise."[3] Cassirer reads Goethe's resignation as a Kantian dictum affirming the dogma that truth (the "Ding an sich") is by definition inaccessible to cognition. This is a basic misunderstanding of Goethe. Cassirer refers to Goethe's maxim: "Das schönste Glück des denkenden Menschen ist, das Erforschliche erforscht zu haben und das Unerforschliche ruhig zu verehren."[4] Goethe recognizes certain limits to the scientist's activities, but for him it is just in the contemplation of nature's activities *within* these limits that truth manifests itself directly to cognition. Kant set limits to knowledge in order to make room for faith. Goethe proceeds differently. For him scientific and religious truth are various manifestations of one larger Truth which reveals itself now to the intellect as "das Erforschliche" and now to higher organs of cognition as that which is worthy of reverence. Man's intellectual faculties take him as far as the archetypal phenomenon ("Urphänomen") before which he stands in awe. The "Urphänomen" stands at the "limits of cognition" and reveals that aspect of truth which cannot be grasped intellectually, but which can be understood through reverent contemplation. Thus in reply to Jacobi Goethe exclaims: " 'Die Natur verbirgt Gott!' Aber nicht jedem!"[5]

A correct and very penetrating description of Goethe's position in contrast to that of Kant will be found in Rudolf Steiner's commentary on Goethe's natural scientific studies in Kürschner's *Deutsche National-Literatur*. The following statement points to the nature of the difference:

> Von dem Grund der Dinge, von dem 'An sich' haben wir nach Kant keine Ahnung. Unser Wissen von den Dingen ist nur in Bezug auf uns da, ist nur für unsere Individualität gültig. Aus dieser Ansicht über die Welt konnte Goethe nicht viel gewinnen. Ihm blieb die Betrachtung der Dinge in Bezug auf uns immer die ganz untergeordnete, welche die Wirkung der Gegenstände auf unser Gefühl der Lust und Unlust betrifft; von der Wissenschaft fordert er mehr als bloß die Angabe, wie die Dinge in Bezug auf uns sind. S. unten den Aufsatz: 'der Versuch [als Vermittler von Objekt und Subjekt']. . . wo die Aufgabe des Forschers bestimmt wird: er soll den Maßstab zur Erkenntnis, die Data zur Beurteilung nicht aus sich, sondern aus dem Kreis der Dinge nehmen, die er beobachtet. Mit diesem einzigen Satz ist der tiefe Gegensatz Kantischer und Goethescher Denkweise gekennzeichnet. Während

[3] Ernst Cassirer, *Rousseau Kant Goethe* (Princeton, N. J., 1973), p. 80.

[4] *Maximen und Reflexionen*, no. 718, HA XII, 467.

[5] *Ibid.*, no. 3, 365.

> bei Kant alles Urteilen über die Dinge nur ein Produkt aus Subjekt *und* Objekt ist und nur ein Wissen darüber liefert, wie das Subjekt das Objekt anschaut, geht das Subjekt bei Goethe selbstlos in dem Objekte auf und entnimmt die Data zur Beurteilung aus dem Kreis der Dinge.[6]

Another excellent study which delineates the distinctions between the Kantian and Goethean epistemologies will be found in Weinhandl, *Die Metaphysik Goethes.*[7] Weinhandl, as well as Steiner, is clear as to the non-Kantian epistemology underlying Goethe's science and therefore does not fall into the common error illustrated by the quotation from Chamberlain, which supposes Goethe to have considered the "Urpflanze" to be a "real," physical plant.[8] Weinhandl also points out that the very title of Goethe's essay "Anschauende Urteilskraft" reveals the fundamental difference between Goethe's position and that of Kant.[9]

[6] Rudolf Steiner, ed., *Naturwissenschaftliche Schriften* (Berlin and Stuttgart, 1883), II, lix; in *Goethes Werke*, part 34; *Deutsche National-Literatur*, ed. Joseph Kürschner, vol. 115.

[7] Ferdinand Weinhandl, *Die Metaphysik Goethes* (Berlin, 1932), Book II, Ch. I, "Goethe und Kant," pp. 136–72.

[8] Cf. Weinhandl's discussion of the "Urpflanze." *Ibid.*, Book I, Ch. IV, pp. 43–49.

[9] *Ibid.*, p. 166.

Bibliography

This bibliography includes all sources quoted in the text as well as a number of other works which were of particular interest in connection with the preparation of these essays.

Atkins, Stuart. "A Reconsideration of Some Unappreciated Aspects of the Prologues and Early Scenes in Goethe's 'Faust'," *MLR*, 47 (1952), 362–73. Also the subsequent exchange with D. J. Enright, under "Miscellaneous Notes," *MLR*, 48 (1953), 189–94.

Barfield, Owen. *Romanticism Comes of Age*. New and aug. ed., Middletown, Connecticut: Wesleyan University Press, 1967.

———. *Saving the Appearances*. London: Faber and Faber, 1957.

Berger, Alfred Freiherr von. *Goethes Faust und die Grenzen des Naturerkennens*. Wider "Goethe und kein Ende" von Emil Du Bois-Reymond. Wien: C. Gerold's Sohn, 1883.

Beutler, Ernst. *Essays um Goethe*. Bremen: C. Schünemann, 1962.

Binder, Alwin. *Das Vorspiel auf dem Theater. Poetologische und geschichtsphilosophische Aspekte in Goethes Faust-Vorspiel*. Bonn: Bouvier, 1969.

Brieger, Peter H., ed. *The Trinity College Apocalypse*. London: Eugrammia Press, 1967.

Carlyle, Thomas. *The Works*. Centenary Edition. New York: Scribners, 1897.

Cassirer, Ernst. *Rousseau, Kant, Goethe*. Trans. from the German by James Guttman, *et al.* Princeton, N. J.: Princeton University Press, 1973.

Chamberlain, Houston Stewart. *Goethe*. München: F. Bruckmann, 1912.

Chomsky, Noam. "The Case against B. F. Skinner." *The New York Review of Books*, 17, no. 11 (1971), 18–24.

Danckert, Werner. *Goethe. Der mythische Urgrund seiner Weltschau*. Berlin: de Gruyter, 1951.

Diener, Gottfried. *Fausts Weg zu Helena; Urphänomen und Archetypus*. Stuttgart: E. Klett, 1961.

Du Bois-Reymond, Emil. *Goethe und kein Ende.* Rede bei Antritt des Rectorats der koenigl. Friedrich-Wilhelms-Universität zu Berlin, am 15. October 1882. Leipzig: Veit & Comp., 1883.

———. *Über die Grenzen des Naturerkennens, Die sieben Welträthsel.* Zwei Vorträge. Leipzig: Veit & Comp., 1884.

Eliot, T. S. *On Poetry and Poets.* London: Faber and Faber, 1957.

Emerson, Ralph Waldo. *The Complete Works.* Centenary Edition, ed. Edward Waldo Emerson. 12 vols. Boston & New York: Houghton Mifflin, 1903–04.

Emrich, Wilhelm. *Die Symbolik von Faust II.* 3rd ed. Frankfurt a. M. & Bonn: Athenäum, 1964.

Friedenthal, Richard. *Goethe—sein Leben und seine Zeit.* München: R. Piper & Co., 1963.

Friedrich, Theodor & Scheithauer, Lothar J. *Kommentar zu Goethes Faust.* Stuttgart: Reclam, 1968.

Goethe, Johann Wolfgang. *Gedenkausgabe der Werke* (Artemis Ausgabe), ed. Ernst Beutler. 24 vols. Zürich: Artemis, 1948–60.

———. *Gespräche mit Eckermann.* Artemis Ausgabe, ed. Ernst Beutler. Zürich: Artemis, 1949.

———. *Goethes Briefe.* Hamburger Ausgabe, ed. Karl Robert Mandelkow & Bodo Morawe. 4 vols. Hamburg: Christian Wegner, 1962–67.

———. *Goethes Faust.* Ed. Georg Witkowski. 2 vols., 10th ed., Leiden: Brill, 1950.

———. *Goethes Gespräche.* Artemis Ausgabe, ed. Wolfgang Herwig. 4 vols. Zürich: Artemis, 1965–.

———. *Goethes Werke. Deutsche National-Literatur,* ed. Joseph Kürschner. 36 parts, vols. 82–117. Berlin & Stuttgart: W. Spemann, 1882–1897.

———. *Goethes Werke.* Hamburger Ausgabe, ed. Erich Trunz. 14 vols. Hamburg: Christian Wegner, 1960–62.

———. *Goethes Werke.* Weimarer Ausgabe. 143 vols. Weimar: H. Böhlau, 1887–1919.

Gray, Ronald D. *Goethe the Alchemist.* Cambridge: Cambridge University Press, 1952.

Grützmacher, Richard H. *Die Religionen in der Anschauung Goethes.* Baden-Baden: P. Keppler, 1950.

Hartmann, Otto Julius. *Faust. Der moderne Mensch in der Begegnung mit dem Bösen.* Freiburg i. Br.: Novalis-Verlag, 1957.

Heisenberg, Werner. *Wandlungen in den Grundlagen der Naturwissenschaft.* 10th ed. Stuttgart: S. Hirzel, 1973.

Heitler, Walter. "Die Naturwissenschaft Goethes. Eine Gegenüberstellung Goethescher und modern-exakter Naturwissenschaft." *Der Berliner Germanistentag 1968*, ed. Karl Heinz Borck & Rudolf Henss. Heidelberg: C. Winter, 1970, pp. 13–23. Also published in Walter Heitler, *Naturphilosophische Streifzüge.* Braunschweig: Vieweg, 1970, pp. 66–76.

Hertz, Gottfried Wilhelm. *Goethes Naturphilosophie im Faust.* Berlin: E. S. Mittler und Sohn, 1913.

Hiebel, Friedrich. *Goethe. Die Erhöhung des Menschen.* Bern & München: Francke, 1961.

Hughes, Robert. *Heaven and Hell in Western Art.* New York: Stein & Day, 1968.

Jantz, Harold. *Goethe's Faust as a Renaissance Man.* Princeton: Princeton University Press, 1951.

———. "Patterns and Structures in *Faust:* A Preliminary Inquiry." *MLN*, 83 (1968), no. 3, 359–89.

Kindermann, Heinz. *Das Goethebild des 20. Jahrhunderts.* 2nd ed. Darmstadt: Wissenschaftliche Buchgesellschaft, 1966.

Koch, Franz. *Goethe und Plotin.* Leipzig: J. J. Weber, 1925.

Korff, H. A. *Geist der Goethezeit.* 7th ed. 5 vols. Leipzig: Koehler & Amelang, 1964.

Kraft, Werner. "Goethes Türmerlied." *The Goethe Year*, Part 5. London: Maxson and Co., 1949, pp. 52–56.

Lehrs, Ernst. *Man or Matter.* 2nd ed. New York: Harper & Bros., 1958.

Lohmeyer, Dorothea. *Faust und die Welt.* Potsdam: Akademische Verlagsgesellschaft Athenaion, 1940.

Lusseyran, Jacques. *And There Was Light.* Trans. from the French by Elizabeth R. Cameron. Boston & Toronto: Little, Brown, 1963.

Magnus, Rudolf. *Goethe als Naturforscher.* Leipzig: J. A. Barth, 1906.

Martens, Wolfgang. "Goethes Gedicht 'Bei Betrachtung von Schillers Schädel,' motivgeschichtlich gesehen." *JDSG*, 12 (1968), 275–95.

Matthaei, Rupprecht. "Die Farbenlehre im 'Faust.' " *Goethe*, 10 (1947), 59–148.

May, Kurt. *Faust II. Teil, In der Sprachform gedeutet*. München: Hanser, 1962.

Meyer, Rudolf. *Goethe der Heide und der Christ*. 2nd ed. Stuttgart: Urachhaus, 1965.

Michelsen, Peter. "Fausts Erblindung." *DVLG*, 36 (1962), 26–35.

Moé, Emile A. van, ed. *L'Apocalypse de Saint Sever*. Paris: Les Editions de Cluny, 1943.

Möbus, Gerhard. *Die Christus-Frage in Goethes Leben und Werk*. Osnabrück: A. Fromm, 1964.

Murry, John Middleton. *Heaven and Earth*. London: J. Cape, 1938.

Mystifizinsky, Deutobold Symbolizetti Allegoriowitsch, pseud. of Friedrich Theodor Vischer. *Faust. Der Tragödie Dritter Theil*. Tübingen: H. Laupp, 1886.

Obenauer, Karl Justus. *Goethe in seinem Verhältnis zur Religion*. Jena: E. Diederichs, 1921.

Ostwald, Wilhelm. *Goethe, Schopenhauer und die Farbenlehre*. Leipzig: Unesma, 1918.

Politzer, Heinz. "Vom Baum der Erkenntnis und der Sünde der Wissenschaft: Zur Vegetationssymbolik in Goethes *Faust*." *JDSG*, 9 (1965), 367.

Raphael, Alice. *Goethe and the Philosophers' Stone*. London: Routledge and Kegan Paul, 1965.

Richter, Gottfried. *Faust. Ein christliches Mysterium*. Stuttgart: Urachhaus, 1973.

Roubiczek, Paul. *Existentialism, For and Against*. Cambridge: Cambridge University Press, 1964.

Schaeder, Grete. *Gott und Welt*. Hameln: F. Seifert, 1947.

Schiller, Friedrich. *Sämtliche Werke*. 5 vols. München & Leipzig: Hanser, 1958.

Schmidt, Peter. *Goethes Farbensymbolik*. Berlin: Erich Schmidt Verlag, 1965.

Seidlin, Oskar. "Ist das 'Vorspiel auf dem Theater' ein Vorspiel zum 'Faust'?" *Von Goethe zu Thomas Mann*. Göttingen: Vandenhoeck & Ruprecht, 1963, pp. 56–64.

Shelley, Percy Bysshe. *Shelley's Literary and Philosophical Criticism*. Ed. John Shawcross. London: H. Frowde, 1909.

Skinner, B. F. "A Lecture on 'Having' a Poem." *Cumulative Record. A Selection of Papers*. 3rd ed. New York: Appleton Century-Crofts, 1972. Also published in *Saturday Review*, 55/29 (15 July 1972), 32–35.

Spranger, Eduard. *Goethe. Seine geistige Welt.* Tübingen: Rainer Wunderlich Verlag Hermann Leins, 1967.

Staiger, Emil. *Die Kunst der Interpretation*. Zürich: Atlantis, 1955.

Steiner, Rudolf. *Geisteswissenschaftliche Erläuterungen zu Goethes Faust*. 3rd ed. 2 vols. Dornach: Verlag der Rudolf Steiner-Nachlaßverwaltung, 1967.

———. ed. *Goethes naturwissenschaftliche Schriften*. Vol. 115 of *Deutsche National-Literatur*, ed. Joseph Kürschner. Berlin and Stuttgart: Union Deutsche Verlagsgesellschaft, 1883.

———. *Goethes Weltanschauung*. 3rd ed. Berlin: Philosophisch-anthroposophischer Verlag, 1918.

———. *Grundlinien einer Erkenntnistheorie der goetheschen Weltanschauung*. 6th ed. Dornach: Verlag der Rudolf Steiner-Nachlaßversaltung, 1960.

Stöcklein, Paul. *Wege zum späten Goethe*. 2nd ed. Hamburg: Marion von Schröder Verlag, 1960.

Stopp, F. J. "Ottilie and 'das innere Licht.' " *German Studies Presented to Walter Horace Bruford*. London: Harrap, 1962, pp. 117–22.

Storz, Gerhard. *Goethe-Vigilien*. Stuttgart: Klett, 1953.

Trendelenburg, Adolf. *Zu Goethes Faust*. Berlin & Leipzig: de Gruyter, 1919.

Trevelyan, Humphry. "The Significance of Goethe's Science." *The Goethe Year*, Part 5. London: Maxson and Co., 1949, pp. 26–32.

Viëtor, Karl. *Goethe: Dichtung, Wissenschaft, Weltbild*. Bern: Francke, 1949.

———. "Goethes Gedicht auf Schillers Schädel." *PMLA*, 59 (1944), 1156–72.

Wachsmuth, Andreas B. "Goethes Farbenlehre und ihre Bedeutung für seine Dichtung und Weltanschauung." *Goethe*, 21 (1959), 70–93.

———. "Goethes naturwissenschaftliches Denken im Spiegel seiner Dichtungen seit 1790." *Geist und Zeit*, no. 5 (1959), 32–52.

Wahr, Frederick B. *Emerson and Goethe*. Ann Arbor, Michigan: George Wahr, 1915.

Weinhandl, Ferdinand. *Die Metaphysik Goethes*. Berlin: Athenäum-Verlag, 1932.

Wells, George A. "Goethe's Qualitative Optics." *Journal of the History of Ideas*, 32 (1971), 617–26.

———. "Goethe's Scientific Method and Aims in the Light of His Studies in Physical Optics." *PEGS*, 38 (1968), 69–113.

White, Leslie A. *The Science of Culture*. New York: Noonday, Farrar, Straus and Giroux, 1949. 3rd printing 1971.

Wilder, Thornton. "Goethe and World Literature." *Perspectives U. S. A.*, no. 1 (1952), 131–40.

Wilkinson, Elizabeth M. & Willoughby, Leonard A. *Goethe: Poet and Thinker*. New York: Barnes & Noble, 1962.

———. "The Blind Man and the Poet." *German Studies Presented to Walter Horace Bruford*. London: Harrap, 1962, pp. 29–57.

Willoughby, Leonard A. "The Image of the 'Wanderer' and the 'Hut' in Goethe's Poetry." *ÉG*, 6 (1951), 207–19.

Wilson, Michael. "Goethe's Farbenlehre." *The Goethe Year*, Part 5. London: Maxson and Co., 1949, pp. 32–35.

UNIVERSITY OF NORTH CAROLINA
STUDIES IN THE GERMANIC LANGUAGES
AND LITERATURES

45. Phillip H. Rhein. THE URGE TO LIVE. A Comparative Study of Franz Kafka's *Der Prozess* and Albert Camus' *L'Etranger*. 2nd printing, 1966. Pp. xii, 124. Cloth $6.00.
50. Randolph J. Klawiter. STEFAN ZWEIG. A BIBLIOGRAPHY. 1965. Pp. xxxviii, 191. Cloth $7.50.
51. John T. Krumpelmann. SOUTHERN SCHOLARS IN GOETHE'S GERMANY. 1965. Pp. xii, 200. Cloth $7.50.
52. Mariana Scott. THE HELIAND. Translated into English from the Old Saxon. 1966. Pp. x, 206. Cloth $7.50.
53. A. E. Zucker. GENERAL DE KALB, LAFAYETTE'S MENTOR. Illustrated. 1966. Pp. x, 252. Cloth $7.50.
54. R. M. Longyear. SCHILLER AND MUSIC. 1966. Pp. x, 202. Cloth $7.50.
55. Clifford A. Bernd. THEODOR STORM'S CRAFT OF FICTION. The Torment of a Narrator. 2nd aug. ed. 1966. Pp. xvi, 141. Cloth $6.00.
56. Richard H. Allen. AN ANNOTATED ARTHUR SCHNITZLER BIBLIOGRAPHY. 1966. Pp. xiv, 151. Cloth $6.00.
57. Edwin H. Zeydel, Percy Matenko, Bertha M. Masche, eds. LETTERS TO AND FROM LUDWIG TIECK AND HIS CIRCLE. 1967. Pp. xxiv, 395. Cloth $12.50.
58. STUDIES IN HISTORICAL LINGUISTICS. FESTSCHRIFT FOR GEORGE S. LANE. Eighteen Essays. 1967. Pp. xx, 241. Cloth $7.50.
59. Wesley Thomas and Barbara G. Seagrave. THE SONGS OF THE MINNESINGER, PRINCE WIZLAW OF RÜGEN. Illustrated. 1967. Pp. x, 157. Cloth $6.00.
60. J. W. Thomas. MEDIEVAL GERMAN LYRIC VERSE. In English Translation. 1968. Pp. x, 252. Cloth $7.50.
61. Thomas W. Best. THE HUMANIST ULRICH VON HUTTEN. A Reappraisal of His Humor. 1969. Pp. x, 105. Cloth $6.00.
62. Lieselotte E. Kurth. DIE ZWEITE WIRKLICHKEIT. Studien zum Roman des achtzehnten Jahrhunderts. 1969. Pp. x. 273. Cloth $8.00
63. J. W. Thomas. ULRICH VON LIECHTENSTEIN'S *SERVICE OF LADIES*. 1969. Pp. x, 229. Cloth $8.00.
64. Charlotte Craig. CHRISTOPH MARTIN WIELAND AS THE ORIGINATOR OF THE MODERN TRAVESTY IN GERMAN LITERATURE. 1970. Pp. xii, 147. Cloth $7.00.
65. Wolfgang W. Moelleken. LIEBE UND EHE. LEHRGEDICHTE VON DEM STRICKER. 1970. Pp. xxxviii, 72. Cloth $6.50.
66. Alan P. Cottrell. WILHELM MÜLLER'S LYRICAL SONG-CYCLES. Interpretation and Texts. 1970. Pp. x, 172. Cloth $7.00.
67. Siegfried Mews, ed. STUDIES IN GERMAN LITERATURE OF THE NINETEENTH AND TWENTIETH CENTURIES. FESTSCHRIFT FOR FREDERIC E. COENEN. Foreword by Werner P. Friederich. 1970. 2nd ed. 1972. Pp. xx, 251. Cloth $9.75.
68. John Neubauer. BIFOCAL VISION. NOVALIS' PHILOSOPHY OF NATURE AND DISEASE. 1971. Pp. x, 196. Cloth $7.75.
69. Victor Anthony Rudowski. LESSING'S *AESTHETICA IN NUCE*. An Analysis of the May 26, 1769, Letter to Nicolai. 1971. Pp. xii, 146. Cloth $6.70.
70. Donald F. Nelson. PORTRAIT OF THE ARTIST AS HERMES. A Study of Myth and Psychology in Thomas Mann's *Felix Krull*. 1971. Pp. xvi, 160. $6.75.
71. Murray A. and Marian L. Cowie, eds. THE WORKS OF PETER SCHOTT (1460–1490). Volume II: Commentary. Pp. xxix, 534. Paper $13.00. (See also volume 41.)
72. Christine Oertel Sjögren. THE MARBLE STATUE AS IDEA: COLLECTED ESSAYS ON ADALBERT STIFTER'S *DER NACHSOMMER*. 1972. Pp. xiv, 121. Cloth $7.00.
73. Donald G. Daviau and Jorun B. Johns, eds. THE CORRESPONDENCE OF ARTHUR SCHNITZLER AND RAOUL AUERNHEIMER WITH RAOUL AUERNHEIMER'S APHORISMS. 1972. Pp. xii, 161. Cloth $7.50.
74. A. Margaret Arent Madelung. THE LAXDOELA SAGA: ITS STRUCTURAL PATTERNS: 1972. Pp. xiv, 261. Cloth $9.25.

For other volumes in the "Studies" see page ii and following pages.

Send orders to: (U.S. and Canada)
The University of North Carolina Press, P.O. Box 2288
Chapel Hill, N.C. 27514
(All other countries) Feffer and Simons, Inc., 31 Union Square, New York, N.Y. 10003

UNIVERSITY OF NORTH CAROLINA STUDIES IN THE GERMANIC LANGUAGES AND LITERATURES

1. Herbert W. Reichert. THE BASIC CONCEPTS IN THE PHILOSOPHY OF GOTTFRIED KELLER. 1949. Reprint.
2. Olga Marx and Ernst Morwitz. THE WORKS OF STEFAN GEORGE. Rendered into English. 1949. Reprint. (See volume 78.)
3. Paul H. Curts. HEROD AND MARIAMNE. A Tragedy in Five Acts by Friedrich Hebbel. Translated into English Verse. 1950. Reprint.
4. Frederic E. Coenen. FRANZ GRILLPARZER'S PORTRAITURE OF MEN. 1951. Reprint.
5. Edwin H. Zeydel and B. Q. Morgan. THE PARZIVAL OF WOLFRAM VON ESCHENBACH. Translated into English Verse, with Introductions, Notes, and Connecting Summaries. 1951, 1956, 1960. Reprint.
6. James C. O'Flaherty. UNITY AND LANGUAGE: A STUDY IN THE PHILOSOPHY OF JOHANN GEORG HAMANN. 1952. Reprint.
7. Sten G. Flygt. FRIEDRICH HEBBEL'S CONCEPTION OF MOVEMENT IN THE ABSOLUTE AND IN HISTORY. 1952. Reprint.
8. Richard Kuehnemund. ARMINIUS OR THE RISE OF A NATIONAL SYMBOL. (From Hutten to Grabbe.) 1953. Reprint.
9. Lawrence S. Thompson. WILHELM WAIBLINGER IN ITALY. 1953. Reprint.
10. Frederick Hiebel. NOVALIS, GERMAN POET–EUROPEAN THINKER–CHRISTIAN MYSTIC. 2nd rev. ed. 1959. Reprint.
11. Walter Silz. REALISM AND REALITY: STUDIES IN THE GERMAN NOVELLE OF POETIC REALISM. 4th Printing. 1965. Pp. xiv, 168. Cloth $6.00.
12. Percy Matenko. LUDWIG TIECK AND AMERICA. 1954. Reprint.
13. Wilhelm Dilthey. THE ESSENCE OF PHILOSOPHY. Rendered into English by Stephen A. Emery and William T. Emery. 1954, 1961. Reprint.
14. Edwin H. Zeydel and B. Q. Morgan. GREGORIUS. A Medieval Oedipus Legend by Hartmann von Aue. Translated in Rhyming Couplets with Introduction and Notes. 1955. Reprint.
15. Alfred G. Steer, Jr. GOETHE'S SOCIAL PHILOSOPHY AS REVEALED IN *CAMPAGNE IN FRANKREICH* AND *BELAGERUNG VON MAINZ*. With three full-page illustrations. 1955. Reprint.
16. Edwin H. Zeydel. GOETHE THE LYRIST. 100 Poems in New Translations facing the Original Texts. With a Biographical Introduction and an Appendix on Musical Settings. 2nd rev. ed., 1965. Reprint.
17. Hermann J. Weigand. THREE CHAPTERS ON COURTLY LOVE IN ARTHURIAN FRANCE AND GERMANY. 1956. Reprint.
18. George Fenwick Jones. WITTENWILER'S "RING" AND THE ANONYMOUS SCOTS POEM "COLKELBIE SOW." Two Comic-Didactic Works from the Fifteenth Century. Translated into English. With five illustrations. 1956. Reprint.
19. George C. Schoolfield. THE FIGURE OF THE MUSICIAN IN GERMAN LITERATURE. 1956. Reprint.
20. Edwin H. Zeydel. POEMS OF GOETHE. A Sequel to GOETHE THE LYRIST. New Translations facing the Originals. With an Introduction and a List of Musical Settings. 1957. Reprint.
21. Joseph Mileck. HERMANN HESSE AND HIS CRITICS. The Criticism and Bibliography of Half a Century. 1958. Reprint.
22. Ernest N. Kirrmann. DEATH AND THE PLOWMAN or THE BOHEMIAN PLOWMAN. A Disputatious and Consolatory Dialogue about Death from the Year 1400. Translated from the Modern German Version of Alois Bernt. 1958. Reprint.
23. Edwin H. Zeydel. RUODLIEB, THE EARLIEST COURTLY NOVEL (after 1050). Introduction, Text, Translation, Commentary, and Textual Notes. With seven illustrations. 1959, 1963. Reprint.
24. John T. Krumpelmann. THE MAIDEN OF ORLEANS. A Romantic Tragedy in Five Acts by Friedrich Schiller. Translated into English in the Verse Forms of the Original German. 1959. Reprint. (See volume 37.)
25. George Fenwick Jones. HONOR IN GERMAN LITERATURE. 1959. Reprint.
26. MIDDLE AGES–REFORMATION–VOLKSKUNDE: FESTSCHRIFT FOR JOHN G. KUNSTMANN. Twenty Essays. 1959. Reprint.
27. Martin Dyck. NOVALIS AND MATHEMATICS. 1960. Reprint.

For other volumes in the "Studies" see preceding and following pages and p. ii.

UNIVERSITY OF NORTH CAROLINA
STUDIES IN THE GERMANIC LANGUAGES
AND LITERATURES

28. Claude Hill and Ralph Ley. THE DRAMA OF GERMAN EXPRESSIONISM. A German-English Bibliography. 1960. Reprint.
29. George C. Schoolfield. THE GERMAN LYRIC OF THE BAROQUE IN ENGLISH TRANSLATION. 1961. Reprint.
30. John Fitzell. THE HERMIT IN GERMAN LITERATURE. (From Lessing to Eichendorff). 1961. Reprint.
31. Heinrich von Kleist. THE BROKEN PITCHER. A Comedy. Translated into English Verse by B. Q. Morgan. 1961. Reprint.
32. Robert W. Linker. MUSIC OF THE MINNESINGERS AND EARLY MEISTERSINGERS. 1962. Reprint.
33. Christian Reuter. SCHELMUFFSKY. Translated into English by Wayne Wonderley. 1962. Reprint.
34. Werner A. Mueller. THE NIBELUNGENLIED TODAY. 1962. Reprint.
35. Frank C. Richardson. KLEIST IN FRANCE. 1962. Reprint.
36. KÖNIG ROTHER. Translated into English Verse by Robert Lichtenstein. With an Introduction. 1962. Reprint.
37. John T. Krumpelmann. THE MAIDEN OF ORLEANS. A Romantic Tragedy in Five Acts by Friedrich Schiller. Translated into English in the Verse Forms of the Original German. 2nd rev. ed. 1962. Reprint.
38. Rudolf Hagelstange. BALLAD OF THE BURIED LIFE. Translated into English by Herman Salinger. With an Introduction by Charles W. Hoffman. 1962. Reprint.
39. Frederick R. Love. YOUNG NIETZSCHE AND THE WAGNERIAN EXPERIENCE. 1963. Reprint.
40. William H. McClain. BETWEEN REAL AND IDEAL. The Course of Otto Ludwig's Development as a Narrative Writer. 1963. Reprint.
41. Murray A. and Marian L. Cowie, eds. THE WORKS OF PETER SCHOTT (1460–1490). Volume I: Introduction and Text. 1963. Reprint. (See also volume 71.)
42. Herbert W. Reichert and Herman Salinger, eds. STUDIES IN ARTHUR SCHNITZLER. Centennial commemorative volume. Introduction and 8 Essays. 1963. Reprint.
43. Clifford A. Bernd. THEODOR STORM'S CRAFT OF FICTION. The Torment of a Narrator. 1963. (See volume 55).
44. J. W. Thomas. GERMAN VERSE FROM THE 12TH TO THE 20TH CENTURY IN ENGLISH TRANSLATION. 1963. Reprint.
46. Edwin H. Zeydel. ECBASIS CUIUSDAM CAPTIVI. ESCAPE OF A CERTAIN CAPTIVE. An Eleventh-Century Latin Beast Epic. Introduction, Text, Translation, Commentary, and an Appendix. 1964. Reprint.
47. E. Allen McCormick. THEODOR STORM'S NOVELLEN. Essays on Literary Technique. 1964. Reprint.
48. C. N. Stavrou. WHITMAN AND NIETZSCHE. A Comparative Study of Their Thought. 1964. Reprint.
49. Hermann J. Weigand. THE MAGIC MOUNTAIN. A Study of Thomas Mann's Novel *Der Zauberberg*. 1964. Reprint.

For other volumes in the "Studies" see preceding pages and p. ii.